# AROUND THE WORLD IN NEW YORK

# AROUND THE WORLD IN NEW YORK

BY

KONRAD BERCOVICI

*Illustrated by*

NORMAN BORCHARDT

THE CENTURY CO.
NEW YORK & LONDON

Copyright, 1924, by
THE CENTURY CO.

Printed in U. S. A.

TO MY NAOMI

AGAIN—AND AGAIN,
WITH WHOM THIS BOOK HAS
FIRST BEEN PLANNED

28982

## AN ACKNOWLEDGMENT

I want to express my thanks and gratitude to my friend and secretary, Mr. Edmond Brown, who has been of enormous assistance to me in the gathering of the material for this book.

KONRAD BERCOVICI.

New York, March 1, 1924.

# CONTENTS

# AROUND THE WORLD
# IN NEW YORK

# AROUND THE WORLD IN NEW YORK

## CHAPTER I

### NEW YORK

NEW YORK! A fold that has multiplied one hundred and twenty times the original size in a hundred years. A fold that has increased itself not from within, of its own kind, but from without, from people of all nations, coming from all directions, black men from Africa, yellow men from Asia, Slavs from Russia, Celts, Teutons, Gauls, Romans, Iberians; people from the yellow sand deserts of Syria, people from the green and snow-clad mountains of Switzerland, Lowland people, Highland people, the worst and the best of every race, of every nation. The strongest and the weakest, the most virtuous and the most vicious. Running away from the home of their crimes, others running to where they could practise the virtues, serve God in their own fashion, interpret the "word" according to their own lights. Hating one another, loving one another, agreeing and disagreeing in a hundred different languages, a hundred different dialects, a hundred different religions. Crowding one another, and fusing against their wills slowly with one another, without ever becoming a compact whole. The weakest, like base metals, melting first, while the strong, like gold, only becoming tarnished from the heat that had melted the others.

New York! A huge big sieve, into which all was thrown to be sieved, until each falls according to its own size and its own weight, gravitating toward where it belongs, then again resifted and resorted to where one may again fit better with the others.

New York! A city requiring sixty thousand bushels of wheat to feed it one day. Several thousand head of cattle are hardly sufficient to feed it one meal. New York! Which requires forty thousand people to amuse its population in theaters where are seated over a million people nightly. The city toward which lead a thousand roads, by water and by rail, above ground and underground, by numerous criss-crossing roads. The whole city one of steady wayfarers who spend their days in toil, and throbbing from one place to another. New York, not a city, but a world. With suburbs as distant as Chicago and San Francisco depending on it; feeding, decrying, denouncing, yet depending on it, nevertheless. New York, an oasis, a well in the desert, toward which stretch all the heads of all the continents, like thirsty camels in a desert for water; subjected, crushed by an all-potent, invisible power; by a vortex which rules and attracts by its own terrific and terrifying motions in all directions. New York, swirling with undercurrents that rise to be surface currents, and vortices encompassing a hundred other vortices, crunching, crying, crushing, yelling, overpowering all that is within its reach; and its reach is as wide and as far as its fame has spread.

Like a phenix, it has risen a hundred times from its ashes. Like Lazarus it has risen from the dead, after pestilence has succeeded pestilence; a hundred times ruled by mobs, and ruled and overruled by greater mobs that crushed the preceding ones. London and Paris and Rome were world cities when New York was a village; world cities when New York had fifty thousand inhabitants, when New York was a village in the wilderness of a new continent, surrounded by covetous enemies with tomahawks and blunderbusses, and within ear-shot of the cry of the wolf and the lugubrious plaint of the coyote at night. The Old World had experienced all the arts, all the sciences, when New York was still burning witches, Catholic priests were tortured on the wheel in the open squares and executed by lighting the fire under the *auto da fe,* negroes suspected of insurrection; when Peter Stuyvesant ruled that the Jews were an encumbrance of the earth and were therefore not to be permitted to live within the city, lest greater evil befall it. The nineteenth century knocked at the gates of time when the celebrated Doctors' Mob, upon a report that a number of dead bodies had been dug up by the medical students from the Potter's Field and the Negro Burial Grounds, stormed the New York Hospital and destroyed and burnt all that was within, until jail was the only safe place for the doctors of the city. Neither Clinton, Hamilton, nor Jay could argue the angry crowd away from the jails. They wanted to storm them to capture the doctors. To disperse them the militia had to fire on them. That same crowd later attacked fiercely the house of Sir John, the British minister, mistaking the name on the sign to mean "Surgeon," and never for many months afterward asking the advice of physicians, even when the pestilence had broken out.

New York, with its hundreds of theaters, the first of which was mobbed and destroyed by the people because of an unpleasant remark about the insurrectionists made by one of the actors; and the second one again destroyed because of a mob opposing Macready, the English actor, and favoring Foster, their own. And to-day New York, the city of thousands of physicians, of thousands of theaters; of hundreds of Catholic churches and Hebrew synagogues.

One could still put his fingers on houses which were built when Canal Street was a miniature sea in the heart of the city, with food for anglers; when about its unwalled low shores, crowded by merry picnickers in their freshly laundered, colored Dutch garb, sheep and goats pastured leisurely. The Negro Burial Ground on Washington Square was so far away from the heart of the city that there was no expectation that it might ever grow beyond that. And to-day the square is hardly more than the first vertebra of the spine of the city.

While Napoleon was bringing pyramids from Egypt the plow was still broken on the forest stumps where Twenty-second Street now is. Beyond that was the wilderness, inhabited by wild Indians, infested by wolves. Beyond that was the land of the Gnomes and impossible fears. There still are among the living men who remember the Debtors' Prison in City Hall, where the imprisoned used to hang out their old shoes at the window to solicit alms of passers-by. Ah! These New York prisons. One can study the development of the city through the increase of their numbers and size. There was the Brideweil Prison, built by the English on the site where the Liberty Pole once was. They used to come every morning to the jail and call out, "Rebels, turn out your dead!" So sure were they that among the many hundreds imprisoned, where there was hardly room for one tenth that many, would be enough dead during the night to fill the cart ready to haul them to the trench in which they were thrown. The Bridewell Prison, the stones of which, when the jail was torn down, were incorporated into the building which is now the Tombs, the grim Tombs where between its sections once stood the public hanging-place. And there were the Sugar-Houses, compared to which the cells of the Inquisition of Spain were luxurious palaces; for it was a dear buy, the liberty from the English, which the Dutch burghers of the city paid.

And yet the site of the Liberty Pole, around which all aspirations of liberty and independence centered, was never paid for, though it was bought by the city from the descendants of Jacob Spear, who owned it.

New York, built in a hundred styles in that many years. With low windows by the Dutch and high windows by the French, and the cottage-like porches of the English. Smacking here of Italian, there of Greek, raising buildings of Moresque fineness, with laces of stone and elegant arches, and constructing homes and public places as squat and heavy as cannon cupolas on board war-ships. New York! Where only yesterday, because of a superstition against marble, no working-man could be found to put up the marble front of the first American museum, until one had to be released from Sing Sing Prison on the promise that he would perform the work. And how many marble fronts flatten the light now, while there still live men who remember such superstition, such prejudice!

What a city of mobs it was! When they did not like the treaty proposed by the English, then warring with the French, Alexander Hamilton was dragged bodily through the streets and the treaty burned on the commons. When they did not like what Rivington's newspaper contained they wrecked the printing-shop of the paper. When they did not like something or other in the theater they destroyed the theater. What they did not agree with was destroyed. They who had bought liberty so dearly repressed all liberty of the others.

New York, from the Battery to Canal Street, is history; from Canal Street upward, it is real estate. Respect for religion was not raising higher than land values. One can still point out the place at Madison Street near Pearl, Pearl Street which was the first street of the city, one could still point out the place where was the first free school, with Clinton as president of the school movement. There are still girders and stones of the landing of the first ferry between Brooklyn and New York, when Brooklyn was Breukelen, at Peck Slip; in the days when Tompkins Place was a salt meadow, and the celebrated singer Malibran sang at the opera in the Park Theater.

I have met men who still remember Twenty-third Street and thereabouts to the Hudson River as a farm place, where they used to pasture their goats on the free meadows; men who remembered when Potter's Field was in Washington Square, when Twenty-first Street was Love Lane, and when Broadway ended at Astor Place. Who would ever have dreamt then of the potentiality of New York? Less than a hundred years ago financiers could not get backing to clear up the land around Canal Street; nobody expected the city to expand that far, when at Chambers Street and Broadway the Negro Burial Grounds were far and away, on the exact site where the marble Stewart Building was later erected. It was only in 1820 that burials were prohibited below Canal Street, in a fantastic expectation of a greater development of the city from some office-building visionaries.

And Wall Street, the Exchange, now the most powerful exchange in the world, toward which all the gold of the world gravitates, the exchange that conducts the finances of the world, which makes and unmakes wars thousands of miles from its cold, gray stone buildings; Wall Street, whose tentacles reach to the remotest corners of the earth. It originated in the Tontine Coffee-House early in the nineteenth century, by the will of a handful of merchants when the London and Paris bourses and the Berlin and Rome bourses were tremendous contending powers. Who can, after seeing New York and feeling the throb of its pulse, think of more gigantic enterprises, more complicated machineries, under which labor and hiss, live and die, a million other machines? For whosoever becomes part of the city is swirled into its wheels and becomes added power. Who can even dare conceive of the future? When rows of twenty-story buildings grow up in places where only yesterday were rocks; wand-risen castles and palaces, before even the wooden shanties which formerly stood there had had time to disappear; before the hares and groundhogs had had time to distance themselves and burrow their habitations elsewhere; from whence they shall again be driven away by the noise and crunching vibration of the sharp drill boring into the rocks. It is this febrility of incessant building and growing, of continual hammering and boring, the soaring and burrowing, the speeding and stretching, that gives the city its feverish pulse. The ring of trains, incoming and departing, carrying away and bringing in in one hour more people than houses a large town. Hundreds of boats, headed toward the shore, waiting their turn to be moored, with the flags of all nations unfurled. People of all nations travel thousands of miles for the privilege of knocking at our doors, hoping, if chance be with them, to gain admittance. Like lava flowing down from the top of a volcano, the unending stream of running people in the morning from the outlying districts and suburbs. Like the return of the tide, the unending flow of the people at evening after the day's labor has been done. They gush forth from a hundred streets at once, running, in one compact mass that overcrowds the underground and overhead rail-running conveyances, and fills the boats that cross the rivers, to the north and south and east of the city, into trains winding like illumined snakes; into hundreds of ferry-boats like giant glow-worms, snaking, twirling their way, hooting, yelling, screeching, calling to one another, lest they crowd one the other too closely for the safety of the sardine-packed crowd on their decks.

And at night, New York's streets that are overcrowded in the day are like streets of a dead city at night. Streets deserted in the day whirl with people at night. The Long Island coast, the Jersey coast, miles deep on both sides of the Hudson River—fifty, sixty miles in length—are the bedrooms of New York. A million pillars of light, blinking, like a huge, giant hive in which every cell is lit. Shadows run to and fro, as behind a curtain, a giant lit curtain that had suddenly been drawn like an apron over the city. And within that hive greater life yet than in the day. Streets that had been so densely populated until nightfall one had to wedge his way through are completely deserted when the day is over. And others where there had been no traffic are now as overwhelmed as the first had been in the morning. For millions of pleasure-seeking people come in daily into the city from the remotest corner of the continent. Like bees they swarm, each for his mouthful of honey to carry back to where he came from; or like wasps they have come only to sting and to carry back their own sting and bitterness with them.

Sixteen twenty-five—the year the first white child, Sarah Rapaelje, was born in what is now New York, the year the first stockade was erected by the servants of the Dutch West Indies Company, almost the year in which Peter Minuit purchased Manhattan Island of its Indian owners for about twenty-four dollars' worth of baubles.

Where are the beams of the house in which Sarah was born? What is there left of Minuit's home? It was not a city these first settlers had come to build; it was a bazaar —a bazaar at the gateway of a new world; a cluster of houses around a stockade in the low marshes eastward from the Battery, hugging the shore of the East River, close to the wharf; near to the boats that brought them and were ready to take back the hundred or so of bow-legged, blue-eyed children of Netherlands polders, where they should again erect dikes to save their homes and fields from the ravages of the North Sea.

And now, after three hundred years, New York is still a bazaar. The spirit of the first settlers still hovers over Manhattan Island. But a bazaar the like of which three hundred years of dreams could not have fancied more fantastically.

If bridges and towers were not of steel and stone but of moonlight and sunbeams, what magic wand would have called to life more superb ones in such profusion in such a short time? And as fantastically as they rise they also disappear, to make place for other baubles of millions of tons of iron and of stone that span rivers and kiss the skies, better dreamed out and more daring than the ones before.

More than two million souls live on the sites of the six "Boweries," the farms the Dutch settlers had parceled out for themselves on the meadows along the shore of the East River. On the "Maagde Paatje," rechristened Maiden Lane by the English, where young maidens spread the wash to dry on the greensward of the hill, stand huge buildings, in which the daily trade is greater than the total wealth of the Netherlands in those days.

Over the "Kolch," the fresh-water pond, runs Canal Street and Broadway; and instead of the light boat with lovers on the shimmering waters, electric cars pursue the selfsame path on steel rails extending the whole of the island and crossing over a bridge to another part of the world—terra incognita then to the whites; where the wolves lived next to the tents of the red men.

Of Captain Kidd's house, on what is now Liberty Street, there is not a trace left. But who can pass the street, night or daytime, without visualizing the swaggering pirate lurking from some dark corner? Why, it was only yesterday when, because of him, Arabian gold was current coin in New York. His home was a warehouse stored with rare fabrics of Teheran and Samarkand, brought by pirate ships to be sold to the wives of merchants homing around Battery Place and Bowling Green.

Some old homes still possess Persian rugs bought from Captain Kidd—Persian rugs and carpets, bizarre bric-à-brac, silks and cashmeres from India and brocades and robes woven for Eastern queens. For the women of those days, still musing that they might be on the shorter passage to India, styled such robes in an anticipating spirit.

Man's strivings, man's creative impulse, has had nowhere opportunity as in New York. Below all the different characters and temperaments which gravitate from all sides toward New York, another current, though seemingly giving way, rises above everything. A city, in which mob rule in its most violent forms has existed for decades, evolved to be one of the cities, speaking of the largest ones, in which mob rule is the least influential. A city in which the beginnings of education were so adversely received, where the early city fathers fought against anything like a public school, arguing that the only place for a free school was in the almshouse, the children of the poor to be continually at elbow's-length of the destitute who had fallen into the almshouse, it has now the vastest network of free schools in existence. A city where the first college, Columbia College, with its low beginnings in Park Place, was the most scorned institution of learning when the Sorbonne in Paris flourished, and the institutions of learning of England were at their height, New York to-day spends more for learning than either of these countries do, buying learning in unheard-of quantity. A city where the doctors had to fight mob rule, as shown previously, has to-day the most sought-after schools of medicine in existence. A city in which the preaching of the gospel in any other language but Low Dutch was forbidden, where the first sermon in English was preached at the end of the eighteenth century, listens now to sermons being preached in thirty different languages. A city where the Catholics and the Jews were equally persecuted, those denominations are to-day the greatest powers in the city. Between two intolerant powers, the early intolerance of the Dutch and the later Puritan intolerance of the Anglo-Saxons, one fighting the other, one excluding the other, a hundred others have sprung up and by their sheer numbers compelled the most intolerant burg into the most tolerant city. The early Dutch hated anything that was not Dutch. The early English hated anything that was not English. And yet in spite of these two hatreds people of different religions and different conceptions clustered between the rivers that encompassed the city.

New York, like no other city, offers the best study of

the nations of the world, samples of each being centered in different sections within easy reach of one another. You can go into the Spanish quarter and forget easily you are in an Anglo-Saxon country. You will be in vaulted, Alhambresque Spain while you are there; listening to songs with guitar accompaniments and feeding on food flavored with condiments imported from Spain. More than that, you can be in different provinces of Spain; for the people of these different provinces, on coming here, gather and form folds of their own, until the Spanish district forms in itself a copy of Spain. The people of each province live in the same proximity to one another as they do in their own country. And not only do they live in the same neighborhood, but they lead the same lives, sing their own songs, and speak their own tongue, which is jealously guarded by the older ones in fear lest the younger ones might lose it and thereby lose their identity as Spaniards of a certain province.

You can go into the French district, and live in France while you are there, with Parisians clustering by themselves nearer to where there is light and gaiety, and the Normans further away on the side streets, withdrawing within themselves as northern people are wont to do. The Bretons, frugal and sober, keep to themselves. The southern Frenchmen from Marseilles and Orleans and Tours gather in their own cafés and restaurants to discuss and talk about their gardens at home across the waters, and to sing their own songs, their own provincial love-songs. You will hear talk of Verlaine and Mallarmé and Anatole France among the Parisians, and talk of Mistral among the

Provençals; and you will, if you know, recognize the Parisian woman as she steps within the door of a café or a restaurant.

If you go further, into the Italian colonies, for there are many in the city, you will see the streets of Naples, the sidewalks littered with fruit- and vegetable-stands of all kinds; and the gay Neapolitan call of the fishermen on Mulberry Street is the same gay call of the fishmonger of the Neapolitan Strada. If you walk through Little Italy at night you will hear voices floating through open windows, singing to the accompaniment of guitars the songs of Genoa and Naples, of Rome and Triest, and never for a moment think that you are elsewhere than in a southern Italian city. And there is the same antagonism between the northern Italian and the southern one. There is the big, bellowing Calabrian who detests his smaller-sized brother from Sicily, and the Roman-born who has contempt for both of them. The Milanese and Tuscanese consider themselves so far above the other Italians they disdain living in their neighborhood, and have their own quarters elsewhere. Political intrigues, camorras and secret societies, jealousies and hatreds that frequently break out in most violent forms, are agitating the Italians here as abroad. And yet! what light-heartedness! What magnificent forgetfulness of all worries when night has come!

There is the Russian district, with moody Slavs worrying themselves, torturing themselves about this and that and the other eternal question. Big, heavy-boned, broad-shouldered, sunken-eyed Slavs with a mixture of Tartar blood, colorful in their barbaric emotions, powerful in their inert solidarity, more daring because less flighty, more influential because of their resolute steadiness. It was among them here that the overthow of Russia's old régime was planned. And living close to them their gay and lighter cousins, the Czechs and the Croatians and the Slovenes, dancing to lighter tunes and singing lighter songs, ready to sacrifice all their worldly goods to an ideal, carrying their patriotism further than any other nation, further even than the Poles, their immediate neighbors in the city; the Poles who even in the most adverse circumstances, even in bondage and slavery, still persisted in the belief of being the aristocracy of all nations. "In Poland," they say, "only noblemen are born."

And what is one to say about the Hungarian quarter? Where the children of Attila have kept their own tongue so pure that not a single Anglo-Saxon word has penetrated their speech. You can see them daily. Their homes, in crowded tenement quarters, still retain that individuality which is their own. The color schemes of their decorations and the manner of arranging their furniture and the relation between the older and the younger element, and their quick reactions, stamp them as a kind apart in this maelstrom. The gay Pusta children, cousins of the Turk, who have never been absorbed by any nation and have never succeeded in absorbing any other one, are what they were and will remain so. Watch their lives in their own district, Little Budapest, near the shore of the East River, with gay cafés and sad violin music made by Gipsies of their own country come to amuse them.

Further below them is the Rumanian quarter, a race of

men considering themselves superior to all others of the Balkan states because they are the descendants of the old Romans, Trajan's soldiers, who conquered the Dacs of Decebal more than fifteen centuries ago, proud of their tongue because it is still the nearest to Latin of any language; they have their own poets here, their own musicians, uninfluenced by the life and the jazz about them, as if they still lived in Bucharest, which in Europe is known as Little Paris. Their own Gipsies live among them, despised and loved by them; hard-working peasants vainly trying to adapt themselves to a different life, disliking the Hungarians, suspecting the Russians, neighbors at home across the Carpathians and the Pruth, neighbors here across a dividing sidewalk.

The great German population of the city, divided and subdivided when there is peace on the other side, is united when its integrity is attacked or endangered. Slow, careful artisans; slow, careful merchants, with the same *Gemütlichkeit* as at home, still reading their home papers to their wives and children, still leaning back in their soft, comfortable chairs, in their immaculately clean homes. Neighborhoods may change and switch about them, but they remain where they have once settled. Other peoples may constantly rise and go elsewhere, seeking other quarters, as Bedouins raise their worsted tents in search of better pasture. The Germans remain where they have been, where they are, only expanding slowly but surely as their population increases further and further. The Drang nach Osten, the Urge Eastward, is also the urge of the German population here.

And there are Danish and Finnish, and Norwegian and Serbians, and Slovak and Swedish quarters, each one with its own life, guarding jealously its national characteristics. There is the Syrian district with one principal street and several side streets, one of the oldest streets in the city, with the houses built a hundred years ago. The

houses are falling upon themselves, crumbling stone by stone. The rear houses, to which the sun never reaches, swarm with people who live as crowded as they did in the city of Damascus, singing and quarreling in the old Arabic which we have always thought of as a dead language.

And the Chinese quarters, with the picturesque signs and pagoda-style houses, the red-brick walls of streets pasted with announcements and signs and newspapers, on yellow- and green-tinted paper, in that curiously decorative hieroglyphic script in which the laws of Confucius and Lao-tsze are printed.

The Greeks live in close quarters in proximity with peoples near which they live at home, as if New York were a reproduction of some old Levantine city, Alexandria or Saloniki, with a dash of Stamboul on Madison Street, a block from Washington's first home in this city.

There are over a million and a half Jews in New York. Jews of different nationalities. There are petty quarrels among them, with all the characteristics of all the nations with which they have formerly lived, voluntarily living in Ghettos, though there is no constraint upon them.

And there is the great negro district, where, under the outward tendency to acquire the characteristics of the people they are living with, there is an undercurrent of self-affirmation, of a desire for culture all their own, cultivating qualities inherent in them. There are streets where the white man is as unwelcome in their midst as the colored man was unwelcome, and still is, among white people.

A map of Europe superposed upon the map of New York would prove that the different foreign sections of the city live in the same proximity to one another as in Europe: the Spanish near the French, the French near the Germans, the Germans near the Austrians, the Russians and the Rumanians near the Hungarians, and the Greeks behind the Italians. People of western Europe live in the western side of the city. People of eastern Europe live in the eastern side of the city. Northerners live in the northern part of the city and southerners in the southern part. Those who have lived on the other side near the sea or a river have the tendency here to live as near the sea or the river as possible. The English, islanders, living on the other side of the Hudson as if the river were the channel that separates them from the rest of Europe.

A reformation of the same grouping takes place every time the city expands. If the Italians move further up Harlem, the Greeks follow them, the Spaniards join them, with the French always lagging behind and the Germans expanding eastward. And yet these people hate one another as only neighbors can hate one another. It is not love that attracts them to where the others are. Hatred proves a more potent element of attraction than love. Is there another city in the world with fifty-two newspapers published in twenty-two different foreign languages? Is there another city where one can travel from one country into another in less time than it takes to think of doing so? Is there another city that so holds the imagination of the entire world, toward which every head is stretched, toward which so many things gravitate? Over the whole continent, this side of the ocean, the verdict of New York is waited on everything that is being done, whether in industry or art, in politics or religion. New York is the arbiter. What New York accepts is accepted. What New York dislikes is disliked. If New York has put its approval on a book, or a play, or a painting; that book, that play, that painting is accepted. If New York has put its approval upon a musician, or an actor, or a preacher, he is accepted by the rest of the continent. A baseball player, a prizefighter, a reformer, whether it be in Argentina, or Chile, or San Francisco, or Chicago, waits for the approval of New York before he feels that he has been accepted. How many dashed hopes! And even the people on the other side of the continent, though reluctantly, also come to ask the approval of New York.

There is no other city where you can listen in one and the same night to a play played in Russian by the best Russian players, or one played in German by the best German players, or one played in French by the best French players; to Shakspere's "Hamlet" in English, and Shakspere's "Hamlet" played in Armenian, by Armenian players specially come from Tiflis. In the quaint old Chinese theater, where the landscape and settings are indicated by a sign on the wall, the heroine, after having been shot to death in the play, rises after a few seconds in full view of the spectators, before the curtain is down, and disappears behind the wings, but comes back for her cap, which lies on the floor and which she has forgotten to pick up.

There are Jewish theaters playing tragedies and comedies written this and the other side of the ocean, and Hebrew players, playing in the old language of the prophets. There are Spanish theaters, Arabic, Scandinavian, and Dutch, each one playing in its own language, each one competing not only for the favor of its own people but for the favor of others. At the Italian theater here, play the best Italian actors, in a city with more Italians than Rome. Greek dancers compete with Swedish ballets on Broadway. A dozen languages playing in one night in one city, twenty halls in which music of all the civilizations is being performed at one time, by artists come from the ends of the earth to compete and court approval.

From all this mass there is a slow filtering, drop by drop, into a different civilization, giving of its best as it has given of its worst. Carbon distilling itself into diamonds.

As through hundreds of centuries atoms of carbon form the purest diamond through crystallization, so does now, under our very eyes, take place the crystallization of the spiritual forces all these people have brought here; a crystallization which has no counterpart anywhere in the world, or anywhere in history. All that has been brought here, whether it has immediately taken root or not, remains here, blown hither and thither at first until it takes root, until it finds its particular soil to grow into. Physically, New York has not yet reached its limit of expansion. Eastward and westward and southward it is limited only by the rivers, which are being spanned; and there is height, height, space conquered by human ingenuity.

Spiritually also the city's growth has only begun, though already such a tremendous power in the world. Not another Rome, not another Alexandria, not another Paris, not another London, but an aggregate of which there is no counterpart anywhere. A giant that may break only of its own weight, of its own strength.

City of a thousand schools and a hundred jails. City of a thousand churches and a thousand market-places. City of steel and stone. City of all virtues and all vices. City of magnanimous charity and cruel indifference. City where toil kills as many as joy destroys. City of restlessness, crushing what it has elevated, speeding on rumbling. Thundering madly along, healing, devastating. New York. I am a fragment of one of its million whirling wheels. . . .

## CHAPTER II

### THE SYRIAN QUARTERS

TO one just come from the Occident, from somewhere in New York, a descent upon the Syrian quarters is like a dream travel. It is as if some undreamed-of means of transportation had suddenly been realized, and we could at will, in a few minutes, land across the seas into some remote, outlying district of Damascus; Damascus, referred to by the Syrians of the desert as the Paradise on Earth; Damascus, the city that has remained as ancient as it was two thousand years ago.

Take the Sixth Avenue Elevated at Forty-second Street, or wherever you happen to be, and in a few minutes you are in Rector Street; walk a block westward to Washington Street and you are in Syria.

The street in itself, cut a hundred years ago, is in the same condition as it was at the beginning of the last century, with here and there a wide marble front of a modern-looking banking-house that enhances the poverty of the adjoining brick dwellings. Squalid, dark hallways lead into still more squalid rear houses where the sun never penetrates. The cobblestoned inner courts are disputed by cats and dogs conquering them in turn. Looked at from the opening of a hallway, the courts and rear houses are not welcome perspective. Both sides of the street are lined with stores, in the windows of which are retailed all kinds

of Oriental wares; long amber-piped narghiles, the smoking paraphernalia of the Orientals; heavy, bulging, mandolin-like musical instruments; and in transparent jars roots and dried fruits of all kinds that grow one knows not where and are put to one knows not what use.

Every second store is a coffee-house or a restaurant, duplicates of such as are in existence in the Orient, somewhere around Constantinople or Smyrna, Saloniki or Damascus itself. And in those dimly lighted coffee-houses, around rough pine tables, sit swarthy men drawing the cool smoke from the aromatic *titun* that burns slowly in the brass container over the large jar filled with rose-scented water through which the smoke passes before it is drawn by the smoker. Small coffee-shells, into which the mud-thick coffee is being continually poured, are being served all around by the large, majestic, dark-brown owner of the *khava,* whose bare feet are incased in pointed, heelless slippers, *babouches,* dragged *flippity, flippity, flop* as he walks around. In some of the cafés large negroid women, Syrians from the inner desert, with nostrils pierced where the ring has once been, placidly watch the guests, nodding seriously from time to time to an acquaintance, smiling but rarely; yet so languid are their movements one feels they are as remote from the actual place of existence as if their being here were nothing but a dream within a dream. How have they come here, and why?

A little further down the street, toward Battery Place, are the small banking-houses, so dear and necessary to the Levantines for the exchange of money; the *zarafs* of the Orient, bankers, letter-writers, advisers, partners, financial agents, and heads of everything that is being done in that district. It takes two generations to forget to translate everything one gets or gives in the moneys of one's own country. In the larger and more pretentious stores are exhibited profusions of Oriental laces, those delicately wrought needleworks of which there is no counterpart elsewhere; showers of rugs, rugs from Persia and Turkestan, rugs from Turkey and Syria, rugs on which five generations have worked, and rugs which have been turned out by a mill somewhere in the neighborhood to fool the ignorant who does not know the difference between the real thing and imitation, and comes to pick up bargains. Swarthy, tall, well-dressed men, mostly Armenians, stand idly fingering these priceless things, their faces responding voluptuously to the feel of some genuine article between their fingers, or screwing up disdainfully when an imitation is shown to them. The signs in the windows, though a few of them are in English, are mostly in that beautifully decorative Arabic script which looks more like a lace design than a conveyor of sound. Women, thin-boned and oval-faced, olive brown, with long, Semitic noses and fleshy chins, with large black eyes, almond-shaped eyes, under heavy eyebrows, and lustrous hair hanging profusely about their shoulders, walk quietly and somewhat stealthily along the walls. The older ones are not yet accustomed to the Occidental ways, as if they still belonged to the harem, to the secluded part of the house where the women's quarters usually are in the house of the Syrian at home, even if he be a Christian. Their feet, in high-heeled slippers, amble insecurely on the smooth sidewalk, their soles instinctively searching for the cobblestones of the Damascus streets under them, over which they have trod in soft *babouches* or in their bare feet. Their demure and quiet garb hangs loosely on them as if they were manikins upon which misfit clothing had been thrown. Even when gowned perfectly, the silver ear-rings dangling from their necks, or the way in which they wear their bracelet on the wrist, or the carmined finger-nails would betray them wherever they should be for what they are, Syrians from somewhere in Damascus or the Lebanon Hills.

The men wear their trousers upon their slightly bowed

legs as they have worn their wide, homespun *shalvaris*. The stiff derby hat or the soft Stetson always stands on the top of their large, egg-shaped heads; somewhat in the manner they have worn their fezzes, or as they still wear their fezzes in the intimacy of their own homes.

That is but a description of the main street of the Syrian quarters. If one were to speak of the side streets, going to Greenwich Street, Morris and Rector Streets, and Carlisle Street, where because of the very formation of the street houses lean on one another as if they were ready to crumble down and fall, with crooked stairways going this way and that, dark in the daytime and ill lit at night, narrow side streets with broken pavements and neglected, sloping sidewalks, and the low lights of the stores and the coffee-houses about them, where most of the Syrian families in that district live, one would still better realize how Oriental the Syrian quarter is.

How people do transform the quarter they live in to suit their national temperament and habits! These houses had all originally been occupied by good Dutch burghers a hundred years ago. It is not only age that has told on the houses, but also a different attitude of the inhabitants toward them. The Dutch looked upon these places as homes, as permanent habitations for themselves and the future generations. The Syrian quite unconsciously considers every abode as a temporary housing-tent. Successively these houses have been occupied by many nations. It was an Irish district not very long ago. Some Irish families of longshoremen still live there. Then the Italians followed, and were joined by a number of French families. Greeks, Armenians, always the late comers, and other Levantine folk from maritime ports, who settled upon their arrival here as near the Battery as possible—near the sea, to preserve a semblance of their habitats at home. Within these walls one occasionally sees traces of the different nationalities that have passed through. There is in one a wide wooden mantelpiece, Dutch as Dutch can be, made of the red pine which was so abundant near New York when these houses were built. In another house I have seen birds molded on the ceiling by some Italian inhabitant who passed on. A few French verses are carved with a knife on the door-sill of another house. From under the successive paints that have been applied on the walls protrudes the Gothic inscription of "God Save the King," painted in black letters.

There are some three thousand souls living in that cramped little space, within sight of the Liberty Statue, and deafened by the continual roar and sound and clang of the boats that pass on the river and the bay. But even those born here, the youngsters, although going to the schools of the neighborhood, are as easily distinguishable from the rest of the population two blocks away as if they had never lived and should never live in such proximity.

There are two red-brick churches, one the St. George and the other the St. Joseph, belonging to the Ecclesia Maronita Catholica. Within these churches at all hours devotees can be found kneeling and prostrating themselves, very much in Moslem manner, before the candy-white decorative altars. The decorations and pictures and images, of the crudest kind, and in the loudest color, make one think of the beginnings of Christianity some two thousand years ago, when the Copts buried their prayer-houses deep in the ground.

One day, walking down Washington Street, a man of unusual appearance attracted my attention. Short and compactly built, he strode down the street with a majestic stride. His bare head was covered with a mass of loosely hanging, long black hair. The upper part of his body molded in a military khaki tunic much too narrow for him. From the too-short sleeves two beautiful, delicate hands hung out at least six inches above the wrist. When I had caught up with him his beautiful ascetic brown face, illumined by two big black eyes, impressed itself upon me as that of a prophet. Although he must have been aware I had remained standing at a distance to watch him pass by me, he paid no attention to the stranger and looked steadily ahead above my head, until he disappeared into one of the hallways in the middle of the block.

I went up to my friend, the editor of "Al Hoda," the Syrian newspaper published here in the Arabic script, and asked him who the man was. He hesitated for a few minutes; then he dismissed my query with one remark:

"A religious ascetic."

"What more do you know about him?" I asked.

"A philosopher of some sort," the editor answered, "one of those dissatisfied men."

"And from where does he come and what is he doing?"

But my friend refrained from giving any further information about the man, dismissing the matter again by saying:

"Oh, I don't know, and nobody knows much about him. He has just arrived. He works in the office of some paper, sweeping out or something like that."

I obtained the same answer from several other Syrian friends of mine of whom I inquired. A few days later I met the same prophetic-looking ascetic again. This time I accosted him. He brushed past me after having looked at me severely with his condoning eyes, as if he had said, "How dare you disturb me, poor sinner!"

Still I persisted. I greeted him in English, walking after him, trying to catch up with him. He entered his hallway and disappeared without noticing me.

That evening I heard him harangue a few young men who had just stepped out from one of the pool-rooms with which that district had been Americanized. I did not understand what he said, but I watched the effect of his cool stream of words upon his unwilling and rebellious listeners. In a few minutes their arrogant gaze had changed from derision to humility. They lowered their eyes as they listened to what he said. Soon they closed in nearer to better absorb his words, oblivious to what was going on on the other side of the street, oblivious to the heavy trucks that were rumbling in the middle of the road, oblivious to the loud calls of their pals from the open windows everywhere. As he spoke the man seemed to grow in stature until they all looked much smaller than he did; because their knees sagged, their heads bowed. They were still standing that way after he had left them. When I asked one of this group who that man was, one of the young men answered, "A saint."

In a few months because of lack of business that pool-room had disappeared from the street. I have never since asked again who this man was, but I see him frequently and greet him humbly as I pass him down the street. Thus I am certain the early apostles lived in the slums of Alexandria, Jerusalem, and Damascus, talking to the people on the streets, changing, reforming, not by ax and fire but by word of mouth, by appeals to the soul of man. One can better understand Paul and Peter after a visit to the Syrian quarters of New York.

The editor of "Al Hoda" took me down for dinner to one of the restaurants in the district. The low pine tables standing one close to the other in a row, three rows one after the other, all covered with colored table-cloths, were set with heavy porcelain. The owner, a thick-set man in shirt-sleeves and clean white apron, stood at the inner end of the long hall, welcoming the guests as they arrived by nodding to them or calling their names. A young Syrian poet was asked to sit at our table. The menu was printed in Arabic, and as if were in Arabia the dinner was started with a cup of sour milk, *yoghurt,* the sour milk, the *leban* offered to the traveler at a tent of the deserts of Syria. Little pieces of lamb's meat, fried on a spit, were served on wooden plates, and the flat, round, soft biscuits, little leavened and little salted, tasted as if they had been baked in the red-hot sand, or a small mud oven, such as is in every household of Arabia, and not in a modern oven.

While we were dining various people came in, and each seated himself at his respective place. At that restaurant the same clients came night after night for their dinner. During the meal I gained the acquaintance of another man, Mr. Narian, who spoke French fluently. He had been educated in the French schools of the Orient. When my editor friend and the poet departed I remained talking with Mr. Narian. A tall, scholarly man, he was sounding me as to my sympathies about the situation in the Orient. He thought the Arabs had received the short end of the bargain in the Balfour declaration about Palestine, that the Jews had been unduly favored.

"Would you like to have coffee with me in my room?" he asked me later on in the evening.

Upon my willing acquiescence we mounted two rickety flights of stairs to a top room. When the door of that room opened I was in one of the most luxurious Oriental chambers I have ever seen. The walls were fist thick, covered with priceless tapestries. The low, rug-spread divans all around the room, the pieces of silk thrown haphazard here and there, the different sets of narghiles, the hand-beaten copper pots, the ornamental brassware, competed with the numberless incrusted and inlaid firearms and swords which lay in profusion everywhere. We lit our amber-stemmed pipes, sitting on our heels, Moslem fashion, each waiting for the other to begin conversation. I remembered the breach of etiquette of admiring too greatly anything in an Oriental house; because the host feels obliged to offer as a gift what one admires very much, he resents too high praise of the thing he must then give you.

A few minutes later another gentleman, looking more or less of the same caliber and class as Mr. Narian, entered the room without knocking. That visitor was followed by another, and another, and another, until there were eight in the room. After every one's pipe had been lit and the coffee was ready, the conversation started in French. But it slipped immediately into Arabic, leaving me out of its understanding. Only from the few words which were later related to me I discovered that I had unwittingly been present at a meeting at which the policy of the Arabians in Palestine who were opposing the English and Jewish plans there had been settled. The gentlemen were the heads of the Arabian patriotic movement, which later caused so much trouble in Palestine.

Feeling myself an intruder, I bowed myself out, back to the rickety stairs and into the street. The political attitude of the Arabians in Syria was being settled on the third floor of a house on a street in New York!

Maluf the jeweler, the one who beats out with his small hammer on his little anvil, held between his knees, the most intricate legends on small silverings; Maluf, as dry and parched as a mummy, with dancing eyes and grinning face, whose fingers are so immeasurably long and thin, and so, brittle, one wonders they do not break like glass; Maluf, from whom I have repeatedly bought rings, asked me whether I should like to accompany him where there was a dance. He had not seen me in many moons and wanted to celebrate. I did not refuse.

He led the way to an upper floor of a house, where coffee was served to a dozen people. They looked to be freshly landed, most of them. Some still wore red-brown fezzes and homespun shirts. Two stout, negroid-looking women, dressed very lightly, for it was quite warm, slowly turned their heads when we came in and greeted Maluf with grins and low laughter. They sipped, from a tall glass, a reddish drink. Their long hair was woolly and curly. Their eyes, small and deep-set under penciled brows, were moving rapidly like scared mice. Their noses were flat, and their lips were full. They looked like sisters, twins.

"Who are they?" I asked Maluf.

"The dancers," he replied, his tongue smacking over his lips as he looked at them.

Then he rose from his seat and went over to them. A few minutes later he returned to my table and said:

"They will dance. I have asked them to dance. I have told them you were one of ours. They will dance. They will dance."

From underneath the table one of the women pulled out an instrument which was a cross between a mandolin and a guitar, and began to pluck its strings. And then, with eyes fixed on me, the other woman stood up and began to move slowly. Her feet remained in one place. Only her body moved and swayed; at first slowly and languorously; than, as the music became faster and faster, she brought her arms and hands and fingers into the dance. The swaying movement went from hips to breast and from breast to neck and from neck to head. She turned slowly on her heels, in a thousand different contortions, her eyes dilating themselves more and more, dancing as much as the body danced, compelling every fiber in her to respond a hundred times to every twang of the guitar. And then when she had reached the heights she suddenly took the guitar from the other woman, sat down, and motioned to her to take up the dance from where she had left it. Beginning in as rapid movement as the other had ceased, and rising to greater voluptuous motions, she gradually descended all the range of her emotions until she finished the dance in exactly the same slow tempo the other one had started with. It was a perfect cycle. A perfect story told in motions.

I looked around. Maluf's eyes were half closed. He had completely relaxed. I looked at the other visitors. They were all dreamy, as if under the power of some narcotic, and I realized then better than ever what the dance of the Orient really is. Not a licentious and lascivious form of movement, but the song of the limbs and the body, through which all the emotions can be expressed. I later asked Maluf what the two women had danced. It was "Going Away and Coming Home" they had danced, he told me. It meant perhaps a good deal more than Maluf had expressed, but I was satisfied with that.

Malupa is fifteen, and maybe she is sixteen. Her mother, for she is fatherless, keeps a little fruit-stand on the street. Malupa is very much about. Once at evening she asked me to buy her an ice-cream. I gave her a ten-cent piece. When she had come out from the candy store she asked me for fifty cents. Would I not give her that amount? When I refused, Malupa looked at me scornfully, declaring that I was no sport. A few days later Malupa spoke to me again. She offered herself. She knew a place where nobody would disturb us, she said.

"Malupa, don't you go to school?" I asked.

"What are you bothered about?" she answered.

I tried to talk to her, but she sulkily answered, "You are not a sport."

A few days ago I met Malupa again. She wore better clothes than I have ever seen on her. This time she told me she had a room all to herself, unbeknown to her mother, where she received her guests. Would I not come up?

"And what do you do with the money?" I asked Malupa.

"I am saving it, so as to buy myself a hat and French slippers and a silken dress, like the American girls have. It costs money to be an American."

"And what if your mother finds you out, Malupa? She will kill you!"

"No, she won't do much," Malupa assured me, although a tremor passed through her slender frame.

"How do you know?"

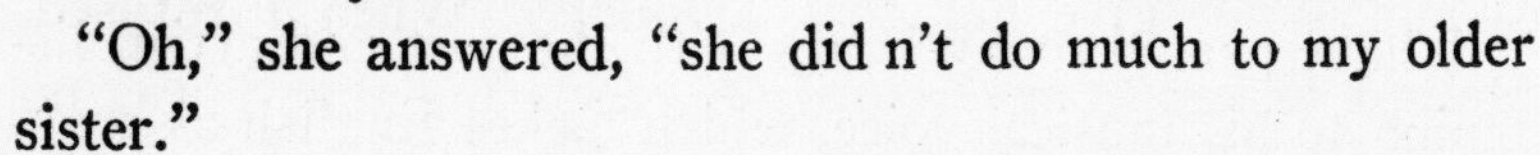

"Oh," she answered, "she did n't do much to my older sister."

That day a young Syrian girl committed suicide because her lover had been killed by another man who loved her.

There are two daily papers printed in Arabic in the city. The better situated Syrians, the wealthier ones, have long since moved away from Washington Street and its immediate neighborhood, and are now living in Brooklyn, in the Bensonhurst district and on the Park Slope. The youngsters there, most of them born here, for the Syrian colony is forty years old, seldom speak their own language among themselves, using it only when they address their parents. But the English they use has quaint turns and is phrased like Arabic. The two daily papers combined have a circulation of about a thousand a day.

Another publication, "Al Fanoon" "The Arts," is edited by Khalil Gibran, whose beautiful book, "The Madman," written in English, was a literary sensation when it appeared a few years ago. "Al Fanoon" also prints drawings by Khalil Gibran. It would be impudent to praise Khalil Gibran as an artist. His works have a quality so much their own one can neither compare nor classify them. They are as subtle and pervading as the rarest perfumes; religious, Oriental perfumes. The colors are so delicately shaded, they are but suggestions of hues. And yet it is vigorous of its own vigor and strong of its own strength. Occasionally "Al Fanoon" also prints articles in English. No other magazine in the country is so beautifully got up as this one.

I have passed many hours with the poet and artist, listening to his musical voice, which makes English as sonorous as if it were Italian, as he read me his poems. Faultlessly attired, Khalil Gibran looks more like a cultured Frenchman than a Syrian. But at home, in his large studio on Tenth Street, discussing with me the Orient, he instinctively bends his knees under him as he sits down on the divan to sip the thick coffee, the preparation of which is his particular pride, when he makes his guests feel at home. Everything Occidental is forgotten on entering his room and facing him. Instantly all feeling of hurry is banished. The day seems to be longer; the hours seem to be slower; even the rumbling below, in the street, the noise coming through the heavily shuttered windows, seems to be more

distant than it actually is. And listening to him I have always felt as though he were a brother to that other man I had met and whom his listeners had called a saint.

The wheels of the city are reaching for the youth of the Syrian district. Here and there young girls have already been dragged into shops to help turn out the hundreds of thousands of pairs of trousers which New York provides for the rest of the world. Many of the homely arts which the Syrians have practised in New York until a few years ago have slowly been abandoned for more remunerative work in factories and sweat-shops; whence they bring home that brand of Americanism so distasteful to the older generation. Maluf has gone back home. Another silversmith has taken his place. But this new man, much younger than Maluf, is turning out things much faster and less beautiful, and instead of selling them singly to such as love beautiful things, he sells them dozenwise to wholesalers who retail them as antiques and rare wares on Fifth Avenue. The dancing-place has recently been closed by prohibition agents. Less nasal song is being heard; plaints in old Arabic. The hoarse phonograph grinds out jazz tunes and rags. But after the youngsters have had their share of fun the older Syrians put on records on which songs of their own people have been matriced.

Among my many friends in the Syrian district there are few I like better than I do Parkyan, the rug dealer. Parkyan is a man of about fifty. His forefathers have been merchants. One day he showed me a beautiful rug he had just received, which had been made of wool of natural colors; from brown-wooled sheep, silver gray, black, reddish and yellow sheep, such as are bred on the plains of Turkestan. It was a magnificent piece of work, and I admired it greatly. He told me the story of that rug; for every rug has a story.

From time to time Americans come down to Parkyan's store to price and buy rugs. One day while I was there a large automobile slowed up in front of it. An elderly man, accompanied by a lady, evidently his wife, entered and demanded to see Oriental rugs. Parkyan showed them the rug he had so highly praised to me, asking for it a hundred dollars, which seemed to me a most ridiculously low sum. Certain the man would buy the rug; I regretted my backwardness in asking what the price was. The man looked at it, then passed it up with the remark that it was not worth half the amount. He offered fifty dollars for it; and turning around to his wife, he said:

"Do you think, dearest, it would do for the hall?"

The lady hesitated. "I don't know."

Parkyan rolled the rug away and said: "No, it won't do. But I 'll show you something much better."

I breathed easier. I wanted that rug.

Then Parkyan produced from his shelves a number of other rugs considerably inferior to the first one, for which he asked five and six hundred dollars apiece. Evidently the gentleman had been told the Orientals generally ask twice as much as the value of the merchandise; for when he had finally picked out three of the rugs shown to him he offered exactly half of the sum asked. Before a half-hour was over Parkyan had sold him a thousand dollars' worth, and the automobile carrying the precious rugs had departed. I waited until Parkyan had rearranged his shelves, singsonging softly to himself.

"If it is a hundred dollars you are asking for that rug I want to buy it, Parkyan."

"I have not offered it to you," he replied, turning around very much taken aback.

"I cannot see that my money is different from the other man's," I answered.

And then Parkyan explained.

"This rug is my test-stone. With it I test a new customer's knowledge of rugs. If he passes that up after I ask him a hundred dollars, which is not one tenth its value, I know that he does not know rugs. I then offer him anything and am sure to close a favorable deal. Do you understand now?" I understood.

This happened two years ago. The other day Parkyan showed me that he still had the rug.

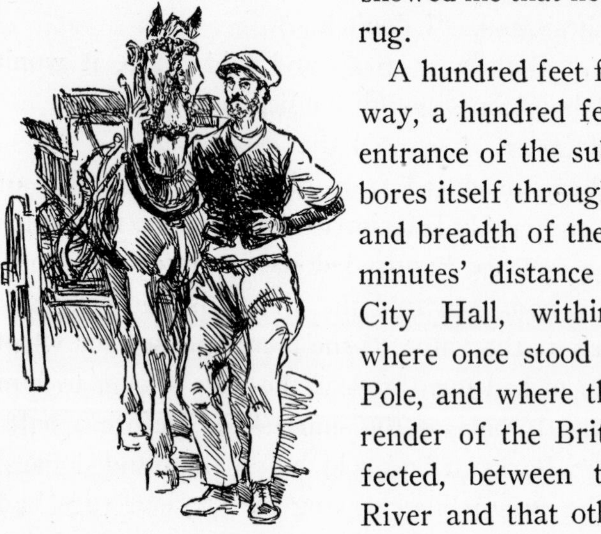

A hundred feet from Broadway, a hundred feet from the entrance of the subway which bores itself through the length and breadth of the city, a few minutes' distance only from City Hall, within sight of where once stood the Liberty Pole, and where the final surrender of the British was effected, between the Hudson River and that other river of steel, the elevated, that flows up town, there is a separate little world, a world that lives its own life. Hundreds of these people have never gone out of their district and do not know much about the life that surges about them. People from a different world, Christians with Moslem habits, still feeling that they are the Nasrani of the deserts of Syria, the Kellas and settlements of Arabia, and the lowlands of Palestine, although they are so far away from them now. Kavas and bazaars and dancing houses, *zarafs* and their own Arabic newspapers, living pell-mell and crowded in tottering old brick houses, a people of a different seed, of an older civilization that has ever been reluctant to the new, distilling a certain pigment into the dull grayness of our modern lives.

Through the open doors one can see the long wax candles flickering in curved rows right and left of the altar in the church. Through open windows floats the melancholy chant intoned by a nasal voice. And the calls in Arabic of the mothers to their children romping on the street mingle with the jazz screechings from another home and the Homeric curses of the truck-drivers on their way to the wharves. An old Arab sits peacefully on the threshold and grinds coffee in a brass pestle. Within the store his daughter is ringing a cash-register. Suddenly the scene is enlivened by a quarrel of neighbors across the street. Heads appear over window-sills. Turbaned heads, fezzed heads, grave, smiling tolerantly, with Oriental indifference, to women's doings. A large steamer from the Orient has moored to a near-by pier and is discharging its merchandise. In the stillness of the air hover the pleasant flavors of dates and figs, of dry raisins and cinnamon-cane, and citrons and lemons. . . . Windows are shut down, and in groups the men and women stand in the middle of the street and breathe in the perfumed greetings from home.

# CHAPTER III

## GREECE

FROM Syria to Greece is not a very long journey. It can be made overland or by sea. The route I took was the land route, although the sea route is just as fascinating, and perhaps even shorter. You can take a motor-boat at the Battery, and when the rollers raised by the large steamers have settled, you slip through, wave a hand to the government ferry to Ellis Island, from which people of a hundred nations call to you in a Babel of tongues, avoid the numerous barges towed up and down the Hudson, or coming from the East River for some longer trip, carrying on their decks railroad-cars, and after you have adroitly and safely negotiated the currents formed by the merging of the East River with the Hudson, it is but a choice at which pier you should land on South Street, capricious South Street that follows the contour of the shore. There is the old Market Slip which looks out from the water, or the Catharine Slip with its broad piazza and dejected, rat-infested, windowless old dwellings that have been transformed into warehouses, or you could land at old Peck Slip, the most picturesque of all the wharves in the city, where the boats that came from Brooklyn when it was yet Breukelen were towed back and forth, to give the farmers from across the river a chance to market their wares.

But it is more convenient to travel the land route. One gets a whiff of the western civilization that lies between Syria and Greece. You hurry through West Broadway. If it is daytime you will have to work your way between the trucks and street-cars and automobiles; with a passing glimpse at Trinity Church, with a smile perhaps to one of the beautiful young ladies eating her lunch in the cemetery of the church, or keeping a tryst on the benches between old tombstones. But if the time be after sundown, that part of Broadway is as deserted as if evacuated because of a disease or before the bombardment of some enemy. The impossible gray architecture of the Post-office is to the right; the Woolworth Building is to the left. Its gilded façade and the tall, slender colonnades which hold this tremendous structure give one fear that it might suddenly break somewhere, bulge and break, so slender and crisp in its elegance, so slender in its strength which carries it so high above the ground, as if it were a magnified structure of a vase by Benvenuto Cellini.

You may take a rest, if you are tired, in City Hall Park, the park which was the cradle of the Revolution and on which once reveled the Manhattan Indians; the fierce and ferocious offshoot of the Lenni-Lenape nation. All the temporary failures of the world seem to congregate there, occupying benches and looking bewilderedly about them. The ones coarsened to their condition, collarless, sleep peacefully on; while the younger ones who had come to see the big city, from Oshkosh and Oklahoma, from Darmstadt or the Volga, from Turkestan or Orleans, the youngsters still trying to preserve decent appearance for a possible job on the morrow, are continually awakened by the piercing hooting and shrieking of the boats on the rivers near-by—when they are not rapped on the heels by the policeman's club. City Hall faces you with its clock and the broad stairs that seem to lead nowhere.

On the other side of the open space is Park Row, from which angles away Nassau Street. Narrow, crowded, hurried, perspiring Nassau Street, broadened out toward its mouth, where numerous street fakers and peddlers hawk their wares. Watch out! If you look like a prosperous provincial a man in overalls will approach you with an offer of a gold watch which he has just found; a precious gold watch he is willing to sell for only ten dollars. He follows your steps, walks by your side, and shows you his find in his cupped palms. And if you are anxious for bargains, perhaps to make the expenses of your trip, the watch will soon be yours. But you may soon discover, when you anxiously look a little later at it, that the gold watch is a heavy brass onion, costing probably a dollar and a half, and worth a good deal less. Diamond rings and ear-rings, furs and cigarette-cases and other things, are sold that way by a special class of the underworld. It were also better to hurry on when a sailor-looking man is offering you a bottle of this or that or the other liquor that he has just carried off the boat. You will be lucky if it is only tea.

Pass rapidly under the arch of the bridge that extends from the Municipal Building to Brooklyn Bridge, near the Pulitzer Building which at the time of its erection was the tallest in the city, and is now dwarfed by buildings three times its height, pass on and you emerge to where you get

a glimpse of the East River, and you are in a dark street, lined with pawn-shops and hardware shops on both sides, with dingy restaurants where saloons have been, and sulphur-smelling hotels, and drunkards decrepit and broken down, leering with shifty, watery eyes at you from every hallway, accosting you with demands for a cup of coffee and a cruller. The pullers-in of the second-hand stores cry their wares in your face, barring your way to the middle of the street. A Gipsy woman wants to tell your fortune. Half a dozen boys offer you papers. A Chinaman looks at you.

Forget that you are in New York. This is the lower part of a Levantine port. Cross one of the right-hand streets into Pearl Street. Walk up to the corner of Canal Street, after passing Fraunce's Tavern where Washington was received by his friends, and you are at the old Jewish Cemetery, which, according to the tablet on the arched door inside, beyond the huge iron fence, was inaugurated in 1656, and had been fortified during the Revolution. The cemetery is between an old wooden shanty inhabited by a Greek cobbler and an Italian grocery store on the corner. The gray and brown tombstones lean pitifully on one another as if looking for support in the last agony of their lives. Long lines of wash flutter diagonally across the burial-grounds. Colored aprons and children's dresses and underwear filled with the wind will make you think of what life is; a momentary inflation of a flexible shell and then deflation again. Thus the traveler has improved his mind by humbling himself.

Look up! Between Henry and Oliver Streets stands the massive square structure of the old Mariners Temple, which had originally been the Baptist Meeting-house in 1795. This part of Oliver Street, in rows of old red-brick houses, is still inhabited by old Dutch families, who so much resent the foreign invasion about them that their children, if any, are seldom seen on the street. There are some wonderfully beautiful doors and copings in these old houses. The street is remarkably clean . . . but without any animation. The Greek and Italian children in the neighborhood call it Old Man's Street.

I say Greece, but I should perhaps say a Greek city;

perhaps only a reproduction of the Greek quarters in Stamboul. Stamboul on the Hudson! For though the down-town Greek section is in many respects the principal one, there are several other Greek quarters, the importance of the Madison Street district being chiefly in the fact that the Greeks living there and on the side streets leading toward the East River wharves are here with their families, while the other Greek quarters up town, between Twenty-seventh and Thirty-sixth Streets and Sixth Avenue, are only merchants' quarters. Their families are living in Greece, and their children are brought up there until they have reached the working age, when they are imported here to work, if "Patera" has not returned to Corfu or Candia a millionaire meanwhile. For whatever one may say of the Greek he is a very calculating and economical animal. It is cheaper to raise a family in Greece, where American dollars are translated into drachmas and lephtas. One can live there a month on what it would take to live here two days. The growing family is being visited every other year or so. It is absentee fatherhood with a vengeance.

One is struck on Madison Street by the innumerable coffee-houses. The windows are curtainless and the swarthy men inside play cards as furiously, as passionately, as if their lives depended on the turn of the next card. There are numerous small banking-houses, combined with barber-shop and tobacco-dealing facilities. The banker, between more important business, is keeping his fingers supple rolling cigarettes in the window of his establishment. On the street men drag their *babouches* slowly.

The hurry, the noise and bustle do not affect them. They are accustomed to it from childhood. Born somewhere near other wharves, on the Ægean or the Ionian Seas, life there is at as rapid a tempo as here. Not because of individual hurry, but because of the simultaneous multitude of movements in different directions.

Madison Street, from Pearl Street to Market Street, is the main street of the principal Greek section of New York. At Market Street it ends, after thinning out at the fringe like a border town, where the Italians and the Jews are disputing for supremacy, with the Italians in the better strategic position. The boundary line at Market Street is marked by the Maternity Center. On the steps, after school hours, the older children wait for the doors to open so they can see their mothers within, and their new little brothers and sisters. It is an Italian Maternity Center. One might as well concede that, but the ground is still disputed. Close by the Maternity Center, in one building, is a Spanish barber in the basement, an Italian political association on the ground floor, and a Jewish congregation on the floor above that.

The streets branching out from Madison Street and Cherry Street, from Pearl Street on, are all occupied by Greek families. Only on the fringe toward South Street, which is the shore-line of the East River, are living Spanish families. They are mostly recent settlers, who cannot pay the high rents of the Spanish district further up town. They are wedging in in the continual displacement of group populations in the city. One can easily see the difference between the two peoples, not only in the signs on the

Spanish store windows, but also in the bits of color that appear, and the red and green curtains with which the doors of the grocery stores are hung. The Spaniard loves to live behind curtains, the Greek in a show-case.

There are but few Greek stores. They are further up town. The first thing a Greek business man does when looking for a location is to ascertain there are not many Greeks living in the neighborhood. It is indeed a very difficult matter for one Greek to sell to another and make profit on the transaction.

The old houses are probably the most decrepit in the city. The rear houses especially seem unfit for human habitation, with their peeling walls and rickety stairs, and none of the modern accommodations. Even the comfort-rooms are down-stairs, as well as the water. Many of the oldest houses have no gas and are using kerosene lamps. It is only chance, and because the people living there have lived in similar conditions across the water, that fires do not occur more frequently in that district. Should anything happen, whether it begins on Cherry Street, the first house under the bridge, which is a wooden shack, or begins at the other end near Catharine Slip, the whole section might go up in flames ere the fleetest firemen could apply their hose to it. In such a holocaust I have no doubt many people would perish, for there is a great scarcity of fire-escapes or other means of saving oneself from such a catastrophe. It is interesting to note that according to official figures the density of population on the lower East Side is three times greater than the densest London quarters.

From Catharine Slip, from the corner of South Street,

where the San Catharine Mission is, or from the mission-house at the corner of James Slip, standing under the sign over the barred windows, "You must be born again," one can see the spans of three bridges, Brooklyn, Manhattan, and Williamsburg, from the same point. I know of no more magnificent sight at night when the bridges are lit; or early, on a misty morning with the gray buildings across the river rising like giant shadows into the dusky light above. It is worth while staying up late; worth while getting up early.

Most of the Greeks living in this neighborhood are not only dark but also extremely pale. The air is thick. The houses are so close to one another, the rooms so small, so dark, dank, and lifeless, that only the celebrated "lung blocks" owned by one of our wealthiest churches can compete in darkness. The morning starts around three o'clock, when the rumbling trucks to and from the wharves begin to pass through the narrow streets, the wheels entangling themselves in one another, the drivers cursing, the horses neighing, the automobiles roaring, and above all rises the shrill, hollow siren call from the incoming and departing steamers. The day ends at midnight. Sleep is impossible.

On Cherry Street the Spaniards, the ones lately arrived, have wedged in. This also is disputed territory. The Spaniards envy the *better* homes of the Greeks, not daring even to think of the luxurious homes of the Italians in the neighborhood. One side of the street is inhabited by Greeks, the other by Spaniards pressing further down. The windows of the few Greek stores are pasted with announcements of incoming and departing boats. The windows of the Spanish barbers in the neighborhood carry big show-cards advertising the Spanish Players performing at the Daly Theater.

At 24 Cherry Street there is an open-vaulted portico, which ends in a large square place, margined by the high brick walls of adjoining factories. The cobblestones of the pavement are in figured patterns, squares, circles, triangles, of the most beautiful and perfect design. At night, when the children of the neighborhood play in that walled in square, it is as if Victor Hugo's Cour de Miracles had suddenly materialized. Evidently the place has once been a fortification of some kind. In daytime it is now an open-air stable.

Through the district, to the squat Presbyterian Church at Henry and Market Streets, there are beautiful old doors and fine window openings, with bits of fine masonry work. What pity that such beauty is lost in the decrepitude surrounding it!

This Greek district has not been Greek for very long. The Greeks formerly occupied the Syrian section, and have been pressed out from there. Of twenty children below sixteen years, I have only found one that was born in this country. It is only very recently that some of the Greeks have called their families here. The rest of them are still transitory, waiting until they have made a sufficiency to return. Compared with other people, the Greeks have the smallest native-born population in this city. There is not a single public library in the district, not one park or public playground, except Jackson Park, further down beyond the Greek section, and not one public bath.

These are not the descendants of the old Greeks, not the descendants of Plato, Socrates, Euripides, or Demosthenes, but just Levantines, mixtures of a hundred races, that have come to be called Greeks. But here and there, among the men, women, or children, there looms up a beautiful face, as though carved in bronzen marble, the paleness of which is accented by the shock of black hair, like a black onyx crown on a golden figure. Here and there, while the children dance to the music of the organ-grinders, to some old jazz or rag tune, one sees beautiful limbs that move about more gracefully than any. There is my little friend Perisa, the daughter of a barber in the neighborhood. I hope no Broadway manager ever puts his eyes on her, to curb and destroy the rhythm with which she was born. To see Perisa dance in the mud-puddles formed by the depressions in the pavement of the street, to see Perisa walk down the sidewalk, to watch Perisa toss her head, is great enough a delight for living near wherever she lives, so as to see her frequently enough.

On Water Street is the store of Yanaides. It is in that part of Water Street which is inhabited by Jews. Yanaides is one of the oldest Greek inhabitants of that district. I went to see him, desiring information from him about several things of which I was inquiring. I talked to him in English. He did not understand me. His Greek was rusty. But he spoke a perfect Yiddish. This was the language he had learned in this country. As his store is open seven days a week, and he is very stout and heavy, Yanaides has never been above Pearl Street and never further than Second Street. The rest of New York he will see, as he told me, through the windows of the hearse when they carry him on his way to the cemetery. He has heard of the existence of a Broadway. He reads in the Yiddish papers of things that go on in other parts of the

city. His family, whatever there is of it, is still living in Greece, because, as he says, "It is too expensive to keep them here."

"Every day it becomes more expensive," he complained. "Things for which I pay wholesale here five dollars, my family can get there retail for one tenth that price."

"But then why live if you do not expect even to return home with your riches?" I asked Yanaides.

He shrugged his shoulders enigmatically, as if he would say: "I myself do not know. But I merely go on."

"You must like the Jews very much to prefer living among them?" I asked.

"Like them! I? I hate them! They are spendthrifts!"

Some years ago I met in one of the coffee-houses a young Greek poet who had come to this country with the firm desire to uplift his people. He was a young and handsome chap, and his wife, equally handsome, had a beautiful voice. The couple used to go from coffee-house to coffee-house, where Greeks assembled, and recite and sing their songs, after which they used to sell the mimeographed ditties. They lived in a little garret on Roosevelt Street, where I visited them frequently. The poet was a scholar, a reformer, and a nationalist. He cursed America for what it had done to the Greek. It had debased him through gold. The influence showed itself even in Greece, where all the youth dreamt of America and the flow of dollars. Greece was being transformed into a country of women. "Nurseries for America!" he exclaimed often.

I found the young couple one day in a very dejected mood. They were making no headway. Their work made but little impression on the people. They were poor, hungry, starved. They were being mocked and derided. The couple had some admirers in the neighborhood, notably a Greek wholesale grocer, who proposed to them that the poet and his wife should give themselves over to business for a few years. He would let them manage one of his stores on Nineteenth Street below Avenue A, which is also a Greek quarter in miniature, after which they might retire on the profits made and saved, and produce poetry without depending on it for bread and butter. They were tempted to accept.

I saw my friend the poet a few years after that, greasy and stout and sloppy, and his wife heavy from not moving about enough, for she was standing the whole day behind a cash-register, and I talked to them. They were still of the same mind. Another year and they would withdraw from business to return to poetry and uplift work.

I saw them again the other day, back on Roosevelt Street, my poet considerably thinner than when I had last seen him, with patches of gray hair on his temples, and his wife haggard and worn out. They were again at it, singing their poetry in the neighborhood coffee-houses.

"What has happened?" I asked my friend.

"Well," he answered, "after I had withdrawn from business with enough money and a comfortable home, I could not write poetry. It had all evaporated with the smell of oil and cheese and kerosene. I had a nervous breakdown. The doctor advised travel. And so we traveled until we finished our last dollar. Then we came to live here again, and I am writing poetry as good as when I left it off. And from all the years of business all that is left to me is this." And he showed me his gray hair.

There is another man I know and love. Cresoveloni is his name. He is a Greek philosopher, living on I do not know what, dressed in the garb of philosophers of two thousand years ago, speaking beautifully French and English, and he holds forth about his theories of life to the truck-drivers and chauffeurs waiting their turn to line up at one of the wharves. I have seen many a truck-driver listening earnestly and sincerely to Cresoveloni's theories about Plato, whom he accuses of all the ills of the world; because he had corrupted the philosophy of Socrates, and rationalized paganism out of existence. "Business, hurry, bee work, all caused by Plato's philosophy."

At other times the philosopher, sitting on one of the brownstone steps, between two garbage-cans overflowing with the litter of the street, the streets of the district being so very seldom really cleaned, is teaching the children Greek. He makes them recite after him the Philippics of Demosthenes. School fashion, the children repeat after him, "Pedi che vechia Athena," "Children of old Athens," while bonfires made by the Italian boys across the street crackle and spit sparks, and old mattresses and broken-down furniture are thrown with loud huzzas on the fire. Above the hissing of the flames around, Cresoveloni's voice, accompanied by the twenty or more voices of the children, rises in one of the old Greek chants.

It is people like my poet friend and Cresoveloni the philosopher who will eventually do something, or are already doing, to bring relief to the crushed and displaced souls in that neighborhood. Not the settlement workers who come to them bearing precious gifts in charity. They do not understand and do not appreciate the struggle of these people. It is not physical only. The factory-fashion Americanizers who hold forth for a few minutes on the corner of the street, before election, telling them what a great man this and that and the other politician is, will also have no influence on them. And not even the public schools in the neighborhood, grinding out Americans in the same fashion as sausages, all in the same casing though from different kinds of meats. Not from any of these agencies will relief ever come, relief or understanding or help in the assimilation process. Their own poet and their own philosopher speak to them in a language they understand, in a manner they understand, appeal to them with an appeal that comes from the same source as their own; appealing to them to be better Greeks first, that they may become better Americans. It is a crime that people should be permitted to live in such homes as they do. It is a blotch on civilization that there should be owners who receive rent, profits from such kennels. Razing these houses to the ground would be good Americanization work. Otherwise we merely desire multiplying peanut-venders, shoe-shiners, petty merchants, waiters, consumptives, insane, and degenerates.

It is remarkable that commercially in this city the Greeks have competed only with the Italians. The two nations are competitors in every port of Europe. In the last ten years the Greeks have practically appropriated the whole shoe-shine trade of the city, indeed of the country. Wherever there was an Italian is now a Greek. It is not because the Italians have gone on to more remunerative occupations, but because of the better padrone system, the hiring of cheaper labor by the Greeks, that one man was able to buy off ten, twenty, thirty, or more shoe-shine stands. They import young boys from Greece, and deduct the cost of the ship ticket from the next-to-nothing salary. Yet, living economically, these youngsters save enough to open their own shoe-shine parlors or stands, and import themselves one or more laborers, whom they in turn exploit as mercilessly as they have been exploited.

The fruit-stand business of the city has passed from the hands of the Italians into the hands of Greeks. It is true that in this particular trade the Greeks excel the Italians because of the numerous fruits in their own country, which they know how to preserve and keep beautiful and fresh. The Italian is neither as economical nor as hard-working as the Greek. At first the Greeks opened competitive stands with the Italians, underselling them. Having accomplished that, having driven them out, the Greeks returned to the original prices and soon bettered them. There is no competition among Greeks. Chains of stands and stores are owned by one individual in a section of the city.

The ice-cream parlors, and the small quick-lunch rooms all over the city, and in practically every other big city of the United States, are in the hands of Greeks, and have been taken away from the Italians who were running them until a few years ago. They are run according to an Old-World system, by *gerie* or share partnerships, on a ten-per-cent-of-profit basis. It is the system most in vogue with the Greek business men here. A share of the profits instead of salary stimulates business.

An example of this competition between the Greeks and Italians can be seen on Ninth Avenue and Thirty-sixth Street, where the Greek business men are trying to squeeze the Italian business men out of the street. Already the Greek stores are more numerous. They compete by im-

porting the same products as the Italians, only they import from Greece at a smaller cost, and are therefore able to undersell the Italians in their own stronghold. The Italian woman buys where it is cheaper. The Greeks also have a much more attractive way of displaying their wares. Greeks are born advertisers. They know how to arrange the wares in an attractive manner. They are also more adroit because of greater experience in foreign countries. You will seldom find Italian stores away from the Italian districts. But Greeks avoid their own districts. Their people are too economical. The Italians spend their earnings in food and clothing. There is no profit in selling to one's own people, who know the exact value of the thing they buy. There is not a block in the city that has not a Greek store of some sort in its neighborhood.

There are two Greek newspapers in the city, the "Atlantis" and the "National Herald," both of them published up town. There are also several magazines but very few book-stores, for illiteracy among the Greeks is very great. A young Greek who had been shining my shoes for several years once asked me if I could read his language. I told him that my knowledge of it was very rusty. Whereupon he insisted that he speak Greek to me every time I came in. A few months later, while he was alone with me in the store, he begged me to read him a letter he had received from his family. Remarking that the postmark of the letter was six months old, I asked:

"Why, have n't you had that letter read to you before?"

"No," he answered me. "There is not a single man in whom I have confidence to read that letter. I expect important news from my family."

It turned out to be a communication written for his mother by the public letter-writer of Piræus, the port near his birthplace, in which she told him that their goat had given birth to a kid.

"By golly," he remarked in English, "they must be milking that kid now already."

"It may be a buck," I told him.

"No, no, it is a milch goat. Otherwise mother would not write. It costs more to write a letter than a he-goat is worth. She would have killed him for food."

With a little practice one can find out by the odor in what part of the city he is. The odors that rise from kitchens and restaurants are like signs in windows. The Greek odor is one of olive-oil, cooked tomatoes, and garlic. These three things seem to be the main foundation of their cooking. The Greeks have also a different method of brewing their finely ground coffee, the odor of which is much stronger than the odor of the coffee ground in any other Oriental district. There are not half as many desserts as there are, for instance, in the Syrian restaurants. Food is considered a necessity, not a luxury. One gets along with as little as one can, the Greeks being as frugal as the Arabs or the Spaniards.

All the years of my association with Greeks here, Greeks in all the walks of life, I have never seen any drinking among them. Here and there a man would nip from a little bottle of *rachiu.* Though the Greek liquors have the best name in Europe, they are very little drunk in their native country. They are made for sale, not for home use.

I do not believe there are a hundred manual workers, in factories or shops, among the Greeks in this city, although there are some thirty thousand living here. Still, wherever the Greek may have his business place, whether it is a peanut stand at Bronx Park, a florist shop in Washington Park or on Fifth Avenue, or a restaurant on Broadway, at the close of his business he will go among his own people. And when I say among his own people, I do not mean merely among the people of Greece. For there are streets occupied by Greeks whose home originally was in Alexandria, Egypt, and other streets of Greeks whose home was in Cairo. The Greeks of old Stamboul, descendants of the Fanariots, the fathers of many of whom have under duress accepted the religion of the Moslem, live separately from the others. The Greeks from Corfu crowd in one part, and the Greeks from Athens in another part of the district. Really the Greek quarter is another repetition of factional Greece, which though to us known as an entity is only so geographically; while, racially, it is composed of people as different from one another as any other people might be.

So far the Greeks have contributed nothing to the spiritual life of the country. They take no interest in the political life of the country, either. New York is to them a transitory station on the way to . . . nowhere.

# CHAPTER IV

## ON THE EAST SIDE

ONE can go to the territory where a particular nationality has settled, and, traveling and inquiring, living there with them, listening to their dreams and aspirations, analyzing their past, one can make some approach to the truth of their being. But there are as many different Jews as there are nationalities in this world. Chinese Jews, Abyssinian Jews, Moroccan Jews, Turkish Jews, Spanish Jews, Russian Jews, Rumanian Jews, German Jews, English Jews; in short, Jews from everywhere. And each variety of them is in itself a special group, with some of the customs its people have acquired from those with whom they have lived, above their own, which in the process of adaptation to those countries have changed so they are not nearly as like one another as the world supposes them to be. There is a vast difference of character, modus of life, and behavior between the German Jews and the Russian Jews, and still vaster difference between the English and the Russian. And though the Rumanian Jews are neighbors with the Russians and Austrians and the Hungarians in their homeland, separated by a river on the one side, by an arbitrary frontier line on another, and a mountain chain on the third, the difference exists nevertheless. The Jews of one nation are friendly or unfriendly with the Jews of a neighboring nation according to the friendliness or unfriendliness of the nation with which they live. It is true that in a great calamity, which endangers all the Jews as a race, they all come together and act in concerted manner, but in the every-day life there is anything but similarity, anything but friendliness, between Jews of different nationality. The dispute as to whether the Jews are a race or a nation is still raging among the Jews themselves. I dare not hold an opinion on the subject.

One would like to think of the Jewish quarter in New York, the East Side especially, as if it were Palestine. The Jews have independence and freedom as if they were in their ancestral homeland. They elect judges, senators, congressmen, assemblymen. They practically have their own industrial world, their own institutions, their own hospitals, own charities, own libraries; they have their own political factions and newspapers and magazines.

Yet one cannot help upon first going into the East Side, say from the lower end of it, from as far down as Monroe Street or Cherry Street, beyond which the Italians by slow infiltration have formed one of their quarters, one cannot help noting that that part of the East Side is really a vast Russian territory. One hears on the streets a good deal more Russian talk than Yiddish, and even the Yiddish the people speak is much more corrupted with Russian words than it is with English or any other language.

Briefly sketched, the history of the Jews in America is as follows: A ship loaded a number of Sephardic Jews, some three hundred years ago in New York, when New

York was yet New Amsterdam. They had fled the Torquemadas of Spain and gone first to Brazil, where the Portuguese then reigned. And as Brazil was not over-friendly to them, those who escaped the *auto da fe* embarked again, seeking a more hospitable shore, in the hope that the Dutch living there might be more tolerant, as tolerant as Holland had been to the Spanish Jew refugees. However, fate was again unkind. Peter Stuyvesant was then the head of the city, and he was unfriendly to all non-Dutch people, and still more so to Jews. He argued in council they should not be allowed to remain here, for they were "the scum of the earth."

But the Jews weathered the first storm, worked hard, and prospered. Fearing to antagonize the rest of the population, they built their huts a little westward, eastward, and northward of the other settlers. Humble, hard-working, and saving, they prospered and multiplied and were in time, as the attitude of the burghers toward them changed, looked upon with more favorable eyes than at first. The first cemetery they erected on Oliver Street was frequently defiled by the neighbors and was the cause of much dispute, although it was farther away from the town than any other cemetery. It was practically at the foot of a hill which rose then in that neighborhood, and as near the marshes which were formed by the Kolk, the sweet-water pond which is now Canal Street, and water seeped frequently into the graves. It is because of that that the cemetery was built on an elevation, the ground being probably raised artificially so as to keep it above the seeping waters.

Later on, when the English replaced the Dutch and the city spread westward, the Jews followed the tide. There is another cemetery, the Portuguese-Jewish cemetery, at Eleventh Street and Sixth Avenue, back of a pastry-shop, which shows that. But though the English had treated them fairly, most of the Jews were Rebels and warred for independence. They thought that their haven of refuge should be an independent nation, and the wealthy merchant Haym Salomon put all his fortune at the disposal of Washington. There were probably a good many other merchants who had contributed to the Salomon fund, although such a thing is not recorded anywhere.

With the first large German immigration, with the forty-eighters of Germany, there came a number of German Jews, a very cultured element at first, among them the lamented Professor Jacobi. In their wake followed a merchant element from the same country, who, having for many decades previously been trading with the Dutch and English, were better suited to do business with these people then living here, and laid the foundation of the later great fortunes made here by the German Jews, first, so to say, freeing themselves of many imports with which they had burdened themselves. Clerks of the great merchant stores, dealers from Leipsic and Munich soon afterward, after coming here, saw the great opportunity awaiting founders of a clothing industry in this country.

Humbly following the German Jews, mostly merchants, there arrived great masses of Russian Jews, mostly working-men, tailors and weavers from the great Russian centers. The German Jews put them to tailoring work in the factories and shops; the trade was sectionalized. The sewing-machine had meanwhile made its appearance, and with its help the great factories employing hundreds and thousands of men were beginning to turn out clothing for the whole country. Raw material was still imported from England and Germany, but soon after that even this was remedied, and the great worsted factories and cotton-mills were established here.

Attracted by the reports of fabulous wealth and the tremendous earnings of working-men, and because of the persecution in Russia and in Galicia, waves of Jews, comparable only to the great exodus spoken of in the Bible, left Europe to come to work here in the factories established by the German Jews.

Russian and Galician Jews, who had lived on a much lower standard at home than the German Jews, saved considerably from their meager wages. In the first flush of ambition they worked so hard that hundreds, nay, thousands, of them perished of the white plague from overwork, bad housing, and underfeeding, in the attempt to accumulate enough wealth to establish themselves in business—sweat-shops in which the newly arrived immigrants were exploited by people from their own villages, importation of cheap labor, child labor, sixteen-hour work-days under the most impossible conditions, in rickety dark shops, which were shops only in the daytime—for at night the owner and his family slept in these windowless houses—with, as a general rule, no sanitary conveniences. These people slaved and slaved, until the ones who had risen to the top superseded the German manufacturers, underbid them, undersold them, because they managed their labor much more cheaply than the Germans, because they knew how to exploit it better; and in a decade the whole industry passed from the hands of the German into the hands of the Russian Jews.

Parallel with the clothing industry, the women's dress industry, the underwear and shirt industry, followed suit.

The Sephardic Jews who had first come here were overwhelmed by the first numbers of the German Jews, with whom, because of their character, they were unable to compete. The Sephardic Jew is too contemplative and Oriental. The German Jews on arriving here had come with their intellectual leaders. They had been as a matter of fact already so thoroughly assimilated in Germany that they were much more German than Jewish, and although the German population here was not over-friendly to them they were content and satisfied with whatever culture they had brought with them. Heine, Goethe, Schiller, Grillparzer, and the rest of the German romanticists and poets were their intellectual fare, next only to the rather perfunctory religious exercises in their temples.

It so happened that at the same time with the Russian Jews' immigration, there also happened a great political exodus. Those were the days of the nihilists in Russia, in which the young Jews had played a very important rôle. Escaped from Siberia, escaped from other places of exile, from the mines of Saghalin and the mines of Kamchatka, Russian Jewish university students, sometimes more Russian than Jewish, and at other times more Jewish than

Russian, thronged here, mostly because their relatives and parents had preceded them, and sometimes because there was no other place to go. London and Paris had meanwhile become like midway stations on the way to Mecca.

On the one hand the Russian Jewish merchants built up a tremendous industry, and on the other hand from their own midst those who had formerly languished in the prisons of the czar for the betterment of the Russian

muzhik now began to fight with the same energy against the sweat-shop exploiters here. It was they who organized the big trades-unions. It is they who are the foundation of the big socialist movement in this city. Strike succeeded strike; and strikes were not the polite affairs they are to-day. It was a question of life and death. A good many of these intellectual leaders, fiery, idealistic, passed over into the movements of other industries in which people of other than their own nationality were engaged.

In this striving and battle they established their own culture, a revolutionary culture in Yiddish. The English language had meanwhile remained more or less of a mystery to them. One could address his own people only in their own language. And as a good many of these Russian Jewish students had never known Yiddish, they set about and learned it in order to be able to help their people. Most of the editors of the Yiddish newspapers—and some of them are still conducting these newspapers—learned Yiddish in this country, because it was expedient, because it was immediately necessary. The Russian Jews' philosophy is expediency. It was only in their intimacy that they pursued the culture of their own language, which was Russian. It is owing to them that Russian literature, Russian music, and Russian art had such a tremendous impetus in this country.

To-day there are five newspapers printed in Yiddish, several Russian newspapers edited by Jews, several magazines, a dozen Yiddish theaters in Greater New York (which Yiddish theaters are the source of all the Yiddish theaters of the country); there has sprung up a whole Yiddish literature in America which at its best can hold its head with any literature in the world. The East Side is the cradle of all this culture.

If you care to go from Greece to the Jewish down-town quarter, the matter is a very easy one. Walk back to the elevated and continue your way up to Grand Street, after passing at your right the magnificent entrance to the Manhattan Bridge. Perhaps the best time to go there would be toward evening, when the thousands upon thousands of people arriving from all directions stream homeward in a hurry. Seeing Manhattan Bridge with its magnificent wide plaza, at the entrance, you might think it a good deal too beautiful for the innumerable trucks that pass over it in such a disdainful and careless way, with no regard, with no sentiment for its pillars and porticos that rise so elegantly and eloquently from the flat, large base, turning semicircularly around it.

There is great temptation to turn into Canal Street because of the whirling color about you, the whirling color and noise and bustle, and that imitation of Broadway on the right- and left-hand side of the street, caused by the stores and jewelry shops, and big electric signs everywhere. But we shall come back here soon. Do not stop, for there might be some religious procession at your left hand from the Italian quarter just passing the other side of the street, with children holding big lighted wax candles in their hands and some ikon under a baldaquin of red silk carried by little girls holding on to white poles.

Just walk on until you reach Grand Street under the elevated railway overhead. Then turn to the right. You are now exactly on the spot which was once the summit of a hill from which the early settlers used to espy the country about them when they were warring with the Indians. From here one could have seen the whole island with the undulating valleys and hills about it, and the little gurgling streams that covered network-like the Manhattan Island. Streams and outlets, fresh-water and salt-water ponds, with the largest one, the Kolk, right at the foot of the hill. There are tomahawks and stone axes still being found every time foundations are dug in this neighborhood. It must have been a good battle-ground for the Manhattan Indians, for they were anything but a peaceful tribe. Much of this spirit, multiplied a thousandfold, seizes any one as soon as he enters Manhattan. It is something hovering in the air, contagious, compelling.

We are now on Jewish Main Street. Both sides are lined with push-carts which groan with wares of all kinds. Although there are stores, large stores, selling the selfsame wares inside, which are also exposed in the windows, the push-cart trade is brisker than the indoor one. You will see expensive furs and jewels and art objects, fine laces, antiques, pell-mell with holy prayer-shawls, rugs, neckties, perfumes, and needles and thread, one near the other, one on top of the other, in a continual riot of color; thrown pell-mell as if some ship had suddenly been emptied in haste after it had gone on the rocks. There seems to be no order. The push-cart venders call out their wares in a Babel of tongues, in the singsong of the Talmud and the wailing of the prayer of the Day of Atonement. Bearded men and mustached men, blond men and high-cheekboned men, with their wives, stout and thick, and their daughters, bob-haired and trim, stand behind the glare of the burning white light of the acetylene lamps, yelling, talking, calling, and singing while dealing and bargaining with the customers pressing around them. One is carried along by the wave of humanity pressing homeward and from all sides. If one wants to buy something at a push-cart one holds on to it as if firm ground in an attempt to get to the shore had suddenly been struck.

A little further is the old Grand Street Theater, now a moving-picture and vaudeville house, which had once been

too far up town for the Jews to go to and which is now too far down town. Walk on further down. The tide lets up, for the home-comers diverge into the side streets, and you have more leisure to look at the expensive and beautiful things in the windows of the stores. If you think you can pick up bargains there you may be mistaken, for Grand Street is as expensive as Fifth Avenue and Broadway. But you may find better workmanship. Grand Street knows, for those who buy the expensive dresses and gowns have only yesterday been the ones who have made them in sweat-shops and factories. Jewish women dress and jewel above their means.

You come, on crossing the street, upon several book-stores, the finest one kept by Mr. Maisel, where you may find things you cannot find in any other book-store. A little further down is the Neighborhood Playhouse, founded and built by the Lewisohn sisters. There may be a bill on of which you have not read in the theatrical advertisements in the papers. But you will after inquiry find out that it may be so only because it is much too highbrow for Broadway. You will feel a different atmosphere on entering the theater. The very sight of Joe Davidson's engraved tablets in the vestibule will compel you to know you are at a theater that is different. Ibsen, Björnson, Hamsun, O'Neill, the best and the newest in the drama of every land has at some time or other been played there by non-professional actors picked and trained from the neighborhood—actors very often superior to some of the most highly praised talent on the professional stage. The incidental music is a delight to hear, and if there is anything at all to be said against it, it is that the place is all too well patronized by the people from up town, by the wealthy patrons and friends of the place, instead of being visited by the people of the neighborhood. The East Side is educating the rest of the city to better theatrical fare.

Turn again to your right and hurry through any of the streets without much looking to the right or the left, until you reach East Broadway, at the corner of Division Street. There is a little coffee-house there which from the outside looks in no way different from any other coffee-house in the neighborhood. It requires no particular audacity to go in and inspect it from the inside. Strangers are welcome. I have been there so frequently that the third table from the window has grooves in the marble top from the frequent resting of my elbows. Nowhere else am I as comfortable.

Each patron of the place has his favorite table, to which he comes to sit at fixed hours. The first one belongs to Abram Raisin, the Yiddish poet. Gray-haired, dark-faced, slender, his black eyes look at one piercingly, penetratingly, then cover themselves with a misty film; transported as suddenly to another world as if he were in complete solitude. He is undoubtedly at present the greatest living Jewish poet. His songs, set to music, are sung by all the millions of people speaking Yiddish.

Although in his fifties, he is young and alert. The entrance of a fair lady attracts his attention, and, leaving his admirers at a table in the midst of a conversation, he would approach her and inquire and cover her with a thousand delicate flatteries.

The younger poets show him their manuscripts; what they have done or are doing is first shown to him, and Raisin reads everything before it has gone to print. He offers his praise as frankly as he censures, pointing out defects, arguing, teaching, as if the coffee-house were some college and he the professor.

The table next to Raisin belongs to David Pinski, the dramatist, whose works have been translated into English. Pinski is the very opposite of Raisin. He is shy and reticent, seldom speaking in praise or blame in public. Though he has been here a matter of some thirty years, he will pick his English carefully when he wants to say something.

Sholem Ash, the other playwright, and one of the very finest *prosateurs* in Yiddish, wanders from one table to the other, laughing and talking with Raisin, but very serious in his conversation with Pinski. Boisterous Sholem Ash, always just returned from some long travel in Europe, will have something to say, and he will say it thunderously; for even in his individual conversation he talks as if he were addressing an audience.

There are many other notables who come to that café. It is the center of all Jewish culture in America. The place was once owned by a lover of literature and the theater. It is now run on a more businesslike basis; but tea or coffee is five cents a cup, and the rest of the food, though good, is equally reasonable in price.

One day on going to my table I found it occupied. I exchanged glances with the waiter. The face of the intruder, a middle-aged man of the cast and build of a Russian peasant, was so stern and forbidding that Henry, the waiter, did not dare to ask him to give up his place. I saw he could not bring himself to do it.

For the first time in years I tried to drink my tea at another table. But the tea was not half as good; the chair was too high; the place was too noisy. The peasant-looking man was staring vacantly at the white marble top, while his tea was cooling.

Then the telephone-bell rang and the waiter called out: "Matteo Bensman! Mr. Matteo Bensman!"

The man's face lit up suddenly. "Bensman," he said; "I am Bensman." And he went to the telephone booth.

Bensman! In Paris my music teacher had spoken to me about a great composer of that name. Could it be that the great Bensman was sitting there unknown to any of the patrons? Why had no paper in town reported his arrival?

When Bensman returned to finish his tea I was sitting opposite his place.

"Mr. Bensman?" I inquired.

"Yes," he answered, still standing up.

"I know you by reputation."

"So!" he exclaimed, and sat down, placing his elbows in the grooves I had made in the marble top. My grooves! And then we talked about many things. He had just arrived from abroad, about a month before, and was encountering difficulty establishing contact with the powers in the musical world of our city.

In 1905 Bensman had won the Verdi prize with his oratorio. His "Opera Nova" was produced there with great success. His violin concerto was played by every great European master in the principal cities of the Old World.

His "Palestine," a symphony with ballet, was performed forty times in one year.

But here the great maestro was neglected, as Wagner had been neglected, as Mascagni had been driven to desperation. And he was sitting at my table and complaining bitterly.

"And what have you done to come into contact with conductors?" I asked. "Have you written to them?"

"I? I? Why should I do anything? They should know I am here. It 's to their interest." Childlike, he sulked and pouted.

"They should know. They should come to look for me, no matter where I am. They should come here to look for me. I am the maestro. I am the creator; they are only the middlemen between the creator and the public."

And so the great Bensman was waiting for Gatti-Casazza, Bodanzky, or Damrosch in that little restaurant where he deepened the grooves I had made with my elbows on the table.

And they did not come quickly enough. Matteo Bensman starved. He died the night they gave a first performance of his symphony at Carnegie Hall.

Around the corner from the café is the office of the "New Truth," edited by L. E. Miller. Mr. Miller himself is one of the first intellectuals who came here in the wake of the great immigration of thirty years ago. Though a university student, his first occupation in this country was that of a shirt-sleeve maker. Short, well built, with piercing black eyes and a florid face, of which the wide brow is the most prominent part, he laughed, telling me the story:

"A German Jew taught me shirt-sleeve making. Satisfied after my third or fourth day of work, he called the other people of the shop to see how well I had put in a sleeve and said, 'The time will come when this young man here will be able to make a whole shirt.' "

Miller is most certainly the best and wittiest and sharpest editorial writer of the Yiddish press, which has since the very beginning, when he was its father, multiplied like the proverbial sand of the sea and stars of heaven. An essay of his, printed in "The Century Magazine," called "A Nation of Hamlets," is a masterful study of the Russian people. The past can be understood and the future deduced.

Further down the street is the office of "Forward," the socialist paper, of which Abram Cahan is the editor. To-day those who have founded the paper and been its first readers while working in sweat-shops and factories have become themselves the owners of shops and factories. A good many of them are very wealthy landowners, living up town, kings of industry, but they still read the socialist paper. It 's a habit. They could themselves when necessary talk as much against exploitation as if they themselves were still working-men. Yet they are the bitterest foes during a strike, fighting the movement they started. Abe Cahan, who still prefers speaking Russian to any other language, came to this country at about the same time as L. E. Miller. In fact, they were members of the same group. Several of his books in English, especially "Yekl, a Tale of the New York Ghetto" and "The Rise of David Levinsky," though thoroughly in the Russian manner, deal with the most despicable characters of American Jewry.

"Forward" is one of the most feared papers on the East Side. It can make or unmake people according to its whim or appreciation. It can make and unmake plays. Woe to the one who has ever antagonized it, politically or in any other way! Two eyes for an eye and ten teeth for a tooth. It is feared more because of its power than because of its strength.

Further below is the office of "The Day," a paper founded by Herman Bernstein but now edited by William Edlin, "Gentleman Edlin," as he is called in the neighborhood. Mr. Edlin was the friend of Jack London during the latter's school-days. The readers of "The Day" are those who have more or less assimilated themselves in America and are still desirous of holding on to everything that is Jewish. It has also a wide circulation among the newly arrived intellectuals from Russia.

Next door to "The Day" is the office of the "Jewish Daily News," the oldest paper, the first owner of which used to sell his paper himself on the streets of the East Side, after having written and printed it, meanwhile peddling also other things. It is now one of the wealthiest papers.

There is another paper also, the only morning paper, the "Jewish Morning Journal," which has been inherited by the sons and nephews of the original founder. It is an orthodox religious paper, the policy of which is directed by Peter Wiernikl, whose book on American Jews in this country is probably the most authoritative one. But these nephews and present owners are hardly able to read what is being printed in their own paper, ignorant as they are of the Yiddish language. To the founder it was an ideal, to them a splendid business.

There are also a number of other Jewish publications, magazines, all clustered down together along East Broadway, within a stone's-throw of one another, forming the Yiddish Park Row and facing Seward Park, across which is the largest American public school in existence. Seward Park is like an open-air forum, where from early morning till late at night bearded men with their tool-bags under one arm and prayer-bags under the other are discussing the policies of the world, as well as the interpretation of passages in the Talmud and the Bible; while the youngsters of the neighborhood do their courting, between games of baseball and football and foot-races that are being organized by the teachers from the neighborhood schools.

Across the park, at Jefferson Street and East Broadway, is the brick building of the Educational Alliance, founded by German Jews in the Russian Jewish district in order to help the assimilation of the people. How far it has succeeded can be known by listening to the people talking on the street. Like St. Mark's Church, which in order to attract people has had to give itself over to the advancement of the arts, the Educational Alliance has had to do the same. The youngsters of the neighborhood are much more interested in art than they are in religion of any kind. There is a very ably conducted art school in the Educational Alliance. Abe Ostrowsky and Auerbach Levy are staff teachers. Its drawing and painting classes are frequented by hundreds of people in the evening, working-men returning from shops and factories, some still in their overalls, anxious to work before they have taken their evening meal. The whole neighborhood is teeming with young artists, the future great artists of America. It is from this district that came such celebrated singers as Alma Gluck and Sophie Braslau, players like Mischa Levitzki, Max Rosen, and Maximilian Rose. There is not a house, no matter how poor it be, where there is not an easel, a piano, or a violin, and where the hope of the whole family is not pinned on one of the younger set as a future genius. Indeed, the question in the neighborhood when two fathers meet is:

"What is your son?"

"A player of the violin."

"And who is his teacher?"

Or:

"What is your daughter?"

"A player of the violin."

"And who is her teacher?"

And teachers . . . but that is another story.

But this is only the intellectual Main Street of the East Side Jewry. Back of that, on Henry and Monroe Streets, and Cherry Street, Madison Street, and 'way down to the East River, there live the sweat-shop workers of the million and a half Jews in this city. They sleep in windowless rooms after a day of terrible toil. Airless, cold, underclothed and undernourished, they are the ones who form the block-around line at every concert, shivering in the cold, wet to the skin in the rain, waiting to hear this or that or the other opera, with which they are more familiar and from which they derive more genuine pleasure than the people in the horseshoe. Watch a performance of Heifetz, of Mischa Elman, of Zimbalist, or any of the other great players, and you will feel what great desires animate these shop-workers.

On Second Avenue, which is the white-light district of the Jewry, there are several Yiddish theaters, which, though originally started in the lower East Side, have moved further up town. The farthest one is the Jewish Art Theater, which has won its spurs with our English-speaking audience also. Half of the audience of the Jewish Art Theater is frequently Gentile. It is in this theater that its director, Joseph Schwarz, himself no mean artist, has given plays by Andreev and Ibsen and Chekhov long before the Moscow Art Theater had appeared. It is from this theater that graduated Jacob Ben Ami and Celia Adler, and this is where played the Schildkrauts, father and son, and a host of others too numerous to mention. And Mark

Schweide, undoubtedly the best character comedian, combines the profession of actor with that of essayist and poet.

Among the Jewish theatrical critics largely responsible for the present better class of plays acted in the neighborhood theaters is I. Friedman, whose witty and trenchant pen has been the cause of the elimination of many a trashy thing from the theater.

But this is largely Russian Jewry only. Its district is apart from the Jewry of other nations living in this city. Below them on the other side of Grand Street and below Avenue A is the Galician and Polish district, with men and women who still believe in miracle rabbis abounding in the neighorhood, the men with side-locks and long caftans and the women with wigs over their hair, which was shorn the day of their weddings. And farther up, encompassing the district from Delancey Street to Houston Street and First Street, and westward to Second Avenue, is the region of the Rumanian Jews, distinguished from the others by the number of cafés and dancing-places, and also by the number of libraries, one of which, the Rivington Street Branch, has the most complete Rumanian library in the city.

At Greenberg's and at Moskowitz's you can hear Rumanian music, haunting melodies, tripping dances, while you eat the highly spiced food waiting for Mr. Volstead's amendment to be forgotten. But nothing is as typically Jewish, typically because it is of all nations, as the market-place under the Delancey Street Bridge or the push-cart section of Orchard Street. Everything under the sun litters the sidewalks and the push-carts: expensive overcoats, pianolas, jewelry, radishes, onions, silk shirts, stockings, corsets, and even the most intimate wearing apparel is sold in the open by the bargaining dealers, whose asking price is at least three times the selling one.

You can pick up some beautiful Russian candelabra and other antiques, brought by families who have discarded them in favor of some trivial New-York-made thing. Bits of rugs and lace, Paisley shawls and other things, brought from the far corners of the earth, are to be found there; not always at reasonable prices, for there have been too many amateurs who have descended lately upon that district, and the venders have learned the value from the increasing demand for such things.

The Delancey Street Fish-market on Thursday or Friday gives one the impression that all the seas in the neighborhood have suddenly been emptied upon the slimy cement floor under the bridge. Fishmongers of all nations are proverbially alike. Fat, ruddy, coarse, and quick. Although it is in the Yiddish district, people come from everywhere on Thursday and Friday. The wares are hawked in a hundred different languages, shrilly in every possible voice, by men and women and children.

The poorest of the poor live right and left at the foot of the bridge, on Goerck Street and Lewis Street, where the lower floors are occupied by rag-sorters, with the stench of all the garbage-cans of the world in one's nostrils, and in dilapidated houses, from which the next habitat is one of the consumptive hospitals of the country. Really it would be a great public saving for these institutions if they were to obtain means to raze that part of the city. It could be dumped into the barges of the D. S. C. at the near-by East River to great advantage, with the garbage of the city.

Lewis Street was originally an Irish district. When the Jews began to occupy it there were sanguinary battles, until by sheer numbers and because they offered higher rents the Irish had been pressed up further. But now the Italians are doing the same thing the Jews have done. They are pressing further and further. Upon the painted signs of former Jewish grocery stores can still be seen the Hebrew letters under the Italian "Grocerias."

It would be idle to say that this district has only furnished artists and cultured men. It has also been the home or the stamping-ground of gangsters and thieves, some of whom have already paid their debt to society. The wonder is that there have not been many more, if one takes into consideration the conditions of life there. I know of one home in which the eldest son is a doctor of theology and the youngest son is a pickpocket, while of the two daughters one is a celebrated pianist and one a street woman. I know another home where out of nine children three are prominent business men, three died in consumptive hospitals, and the last three moved away with their families to Riverside Drive and have become charity workers.

The Henry Street Settlement, the Rivington Street Settlement, and all the other settlements in the neighborhood, because of the poverty of the newly arrived, bewildered immigrant, can do very little. There is little one can say to men and women who work in impossible sweat-shops twelve hours a day for less than a living wage, or to people who have to make out of their homes a workshop, carrying from the large factories bundles of trousers and coats to finish at night. There is little that can be told to a child who has to help his mother to work on coming from school. Charities only pauperize the people they try to help. The only thought of those who still have strength after a few years of living in this country is to get on commercially and get on financially, and to run away from where they are. The Jews in Harlem, the Jews in the Bronx, on Morningside and Riverside Drives, are the ones who have left all that behind them. It is they who have built up the Bronx from a wilderness into a borough. It is they who have built up the tremendous apartment-houses on Riverside Drive.

A million and a half of people of one race, though of different nationalities, in one city. All the faults of a whole nation are to be found within them, as well as all the virtues.

The Moroccan and Greek Jews living under the elevated along Allen Street, Allen Street where the sun never penetrates and the night is only a little darker than the day, and which was not long ago a red-light district, have apparently little in common with the other Jews. They have their own synagogue, their own newspaper. They are in touch with the original Portuguese Jews who came to this country first and who have now spread all over the city, the home of these Portuguese Jews having originally been around where Washington Square now stands. These Moroccan Jews, looking as unlike the other Jews as if they were not of the same source and origin, indeed looking like Moroccans themselves, are slowly filtering westward, spreading toward Third Avenue, mingling with the Italians with whom they seem to be nearer akin than with any other people.

Of the numerous synagogues in the neighborhood there are many which were once churches, and were abandoned by their congregations, who moved further up town, driven by the Jewish invasion. A number of these churches of different denominations, though still nominally in existence, have less than a handful of active members. Indeed, St. Mark's Church, until it had got on to the spirit of the people about it, had had its pews practically abandoned and empty. To-day with its statuary in the churchyard and its pointed façade which makes it look more like a medieval French building than a modern one, its pews are steadily occupied by those who think more of their own intellectual advancement than of religious segregation.

Hemmed in between the East River that runs from the south to the east of the city and that other river of steel, the elevated, that runs upward on Third Avenue, in that voluntary Ghetto called the East Side, is perhaps the best reproduction of what Jerusalem was once and what Jerusalem might be. Here are to be found men of the type of Isaiah and Jesus, preachers, self-immolators; and the Sadducees and Pharisees who pray on the street corners are here represented by the soap-box politicians holding forth each near the other.

As after a long thirst the traveler is never satiated with the water he has suddenly found, so have these East Side Jews never satiated themselves with their newly granted political rights. Socialists, Republicans, Democrats, and Progressives, Anarchists, Bolshevists, Communists, ists of all kinds are in continual dispute, shouting imprecations across the street to one another from the platforms or the rear ends of trucks at election time. And yet those same elements, so vitally interested in the politics of the country, find their real recreation in dreams of the times in which they lived in the countries of their birth. There is a Hungarian coffee-house in which Reigel, the celebrated Gipsy violinist, is playing Hungarian songs to those who did not fare any too well in Hungary. At the Russian Bear, on Second Avenue and Thirteenth Street, they crowd the place to hear the Russian Balalaika Orchestra play the Russian folk-songs, the songs sung by the same muzhiks who only yesterday killed so many of the relatives of the ones singing them here now. At Moskowitz's on Houston Street the Rumanian Jews sing at the top of their voices the songs of the country they left for more than one reason. There are Polish music-halls where the Jews of Poland gather and sing. There are book-stores, carrying books exclusively each of a particular language, the language of the people in whose neighborhood the book-store happens to be. And though there are other Ghettos they are but the arm stretched out, grasping at something, while the body remains there on the East Side.

In the hectic going and coming, in the continual whirl and noise, and the babble of buyer and seller, there is too much movement for any sensation of sadness. Houses of that district, which only until yesterday were mostly dilapidated old shanties, are slowly growing up and becoming modernized, owned frequently by those who formerly lived in the dark basements of the selfsame places.

And stretching across the river, through the Delancey Street Bridge and under it, the arm still goes further, rounding up on the other shore as if it were merely across the Jordan, making of the quiet and peaceful Williamsburg district in Brooklyn another wing of the great Ghetto. It pulses of its own life. Poverty there is not as prominent as in any other district. It is less than one generation between shirt-sleeves and shirt-sleeves. True, it vomits forth from time to time the worst that is in it. You may have to guard your pockets tightly while passing along its densely populated streets, but they are densely populated because of the toiling many going back and forth. The East Side, which to many, and to most until a few years ago, was akin to the slums of a city, is now fast becoming something else. Poverty is absorbed much faster here than elsewhere.

Already one can see the strong mixture of several peoples; propinquity is doing its work. Children of mixed marriages, marriages between Italians and Jews, Poles and Jews, Russians and Jews, and Americans and Jews are no longer a rarity anywhere. The curious mixture of black hair and blue eyes, and of blond hair and black eyes, of high cheek-bones and round chins, is becoming more and more an every-day occurrence among those people. But the other half never seems to count with such children. No matter what the mixture, they still remain Jews, partly so because they are considered such by the people with whom they come in contact, and partly because of other reasons too manifold and complicated to discuss here. Though the up-town and the Riverside Drive Jews have abandoned the outward appearances by which they were commonly recognized, eager as they are to assimilate themselves with the rest of the population, the street inhabited by them is as easily distinguishable from the next street inhabited by another nation as if one had suddenly passed

from one country into another. Nay, even when the people are not on the street a glance upward to the windows would surely in some way betray the building which houses the children of Israel.

A million and a half of Jews of all nations and of all degrees of culture, assembled in one city, most of them thrown in one district. A whole race, with all its elements, the worst and the best, most of them, though yearning for a new condition, still longing back to the old one, the present generation nothing but a midway station between what has been and what is to be.

The first Italian ice-wood-coal cellarman who located on Cherry Street gave ample warning to the neighborhood, which was Jewish, of what was to follow. A few months later an Italian grocer moved in. And shortly afterward the old, bearded fellows of the neighborhood dared not go out after dark. The Jewish barber, who knew how to give a hair-cut without violating the ritual by shortening the side-locks, also had to make room for a mandolin-playing son of Napoli la Bella. And in a year all the street, except one block, was thoroughly Italianized.

In that block, very near the East River, lived Nathan Berman. He was there before the invasion. In fact, he was left over from a group of immigrants of which every one had become wealthy. He alone had put the left foot first when he stepped on these shores. Not a single thing that he had undertaken but went to the rocks. His old friends had tried in vain to lift him out of the mire of poverty. His feet were as if glued to misery. It got to be known that there was no use helping him. A curse preceded and followed and hung over everything he did or intended to do.

It seemed that the same curse also followed his children. Though they were healthy and of the average kind, they had no luck. In school the teachers paid no attention to them. The other children did not chum much with the red-haired Bermans. When Bessie was sixteen and worked at shirt-waists she was idle half the time. Strikes and city ordinances closed up the shop. She was not to be thrown away either, Bessie; but the boys did not take to her. She was without a sweetheart until she was eighteen, when she married a widower thirty years older than herself.

The Berman boys, two of them, had no better luck. Sad-eyed, slow, plodding printers both of them.

Mother Berman had no time to think of her misfortune. She had too much work to do. She kept the rooms so clean one could mirror oneself in everything.

Nathan Berman sold coal and ice to the Jewish families of his block. When he was not delivering a bag of coal or a chunk of ice he was chopping wood for kindlings. He had settled down to such work for the rest of his life. He never smiled, never laughed. In fact none of the Bermans ever smiled or laughed. This may even have been the cause of their misfortune.

As the Italian invasion became more pronounced, the Italian coal and ice men began to take over the cellar trade. In the summer they threw crusts of watermelons after Nathan Berman. In the winter they bombarded him with snowballs. The little slate and pencil that hung on the cellar door for customers to write their orders on during Berman's absence disappeared every day. It was nothing but ill wind and curses and attacks from the invaders. The Jewish coal man became even sadder than before. He was continually surrounded by enemies. Every non-Jew was his enemy. He began to fear for his life as well as his livelihood. It was with great difficulty that his block held its own.

Then one day Nathan Berman wandered out from his

dark hole into the sunshine. It was a cold and crisp morning. The windows of the Italian stores of the neighborhood were resplendent with colored glazed confectionery set between green pine twigs. The street had taken on a different air. Joe, the terror of the neighborhood, greeted him with a friendly, "Hullo, you old Jew!"

A little further Berman's business competitor, a swarthy Sicilian, stood in front of his cellar in his best clothes and smiled at him.

"Hullo, Nathan; come have a drink." He dared not refuse.

In the coffee-house everybody was friendly. They slapped him on the shoulder. They begged him to drink with them; and before he had left the place Marino, the barber, had filled his pocket with long, black cigars.

Berman walked out into the sunshine again. There was something gay and green in every window. There was something friendly in everything and everybody. He thought of his wife as he lit one of the cigars that were given him.

It was a gift. He had never before received a gift. People had helped him with loans, and even if he had never paid them back, the debt was still there.

He had never made a gift to any one. He had given when it was his duty to give. He had never experienced the pleasure of giving—giving only for the pleasure of giving.

A smile dawned faintly on his face. He felt so nice and warm. He had never made a gift to his wife. Of course, he provided her with what he could, but he had never given her anything unasked.

"Oi! Oi! Oi!" wailed his wife a little later, when Nathan Berman appeared in the doorway with a few packages and a Christmas tree under his arm. "Oi! Oi! Oi! He has betrayed his faith!" she yelled as she barred the way.

The neighbors assembled. Nathan Berman tried to explain but only succeeded in smiling. It transfigured him. That red beard of his shone as if it were oiled with gold. His wife looked at him. His children looked at him. They did not recognize him. They had never known he could smile!

He smiled as he begged them to take his gifts and the Christmas tree. But nobody wanted to touch any of it. Still smiling, he slowly descended the stairs to see his friend Marino, who had given him the long black cigar he was smoking.

It was midday, and I was on Second Avenue, watching some excavation. There were mysterious thuds within the empty bowels underneath the street—drillings—hissings, hoistings, and the "hey-ho" of men pulling at a rope.

Suddenly a whistle blew and gray overalled men appeared from below, peered upward like so many prairie-dogs, blinked in the light, wiped the dirt off their hands on their trousers and the sweat from their brows with a movement of the back of the hand, and sat down, some on thick pipes, others on the edge of the sidewalk, to eat their tin-pailed lunch.

Meanwhile two young fellows had erected, at a little distance from each other, two portable speaking platforms and were busy performing the usual faker tricks to attract a crowd from the hurrying host of people rapidly filling the street.

One of the fakers was pulling unending lengths of colored ribbons from his mouth; the other one was playing a funeral march on a trombone. In a few minutes each of them had the nucleus of a crowd round himself. The ribbon-pulling gentleman had the youngest of the crowd, ones who would be the first to arrive at a circus.

He closed his mouth with a sharp bite, swallowed hard, worked his Adam's apple up and down comically as if he were choking. When the giggling had subsided sufficiently this wiry faker uncoated himself in one movement, appearing in a sleeveless athletic shirt, rubbed his hands, and began:

"Ladies and gentlemen, I am so pleased to see a young audience to-day. Why is it that the other kind goes where a funeral march is played? Why do they think of death? It is because they are sick. Why are they sick? Because they have not taken care of themselves. Why have they not taken care of themselves? Because they do not know how. I am the only man in whose possession is the Ponce de León elixir of youth, of eternal youth. It is not a drink, it is not a medicine——"

As he spoke his hand worked a cardboard box open, and in a second he had gripped the handles of a gymnastic apparatus and was demonstrating its possibilities.

"Five minutes of this every day, and you will be eternally young and happy."

"My brothers," shouted the other faker, "my brothers, I am just out of a sick-bed. I have been ill all my life, and did not know it. Then, last year, I broke down and the doctors gave me up. I should not be here now. I should be buried seven feet below the ground. But I met an old Hindu, and he gave me something that saved my life. And now, brothers, because it has saved my life I have decided to devote myself to saving yours. You are sick, you are ill, all of you. Not one but——"

"Only fifty cents and you shall never lose your vigor," shouted the ribbon-pulling man. "Here, thank you, thank you."

"You are sick, you are mortally sick and don't know it. I don't charge for the medicine, only for the bottle, fifteen cents. If any one of you has a bottle— You are all sick! Maybe consumptive, as I have been. Asthmatic! You can't sleep. Thanks. Fifteen cents. Who wants another one? Here, thanks. You are all running fast to your grave. You don't digest well. This medicine will give you health, will save you," hoarsely shouted the funeral-march man and grabbed his trombone again.

"Shut up!" shouted the other one. "What you sell is good for the dead. Nobody needs medicine. What you need is exercise, proper exercise. Shut up. Ladies and gentlemen, this little apparatus selling for only fifty cents——"

And so it went on for about an hour. The two men

debated at a distance about gymnastics and medicine, each winning away from the other's crowd those who were convinced for prevention and those in favor of cure.

And there were some who had bought both medicine-bottles and gymnastic apparatus. Meanwhile the two enemies shouted at one another, mocked each other, and it looked once as if they were coming to blows.

The lunch-hour was dwindling rapidly. The crowds thinned out. At the stroke of one the two men folded their platforms, put on their coats, and walked away in opposite directions.

A little later, entering a little lunch-room in the neighborhood, I saw them at the same table eating. I sat down next them.

"What do we do to-night, George?" asked the athlete.

"To-night? Well, let 's see. It 's Thursday, eh?"

"Yes, of course it 's Thursday."

"How about socialism?"

"How many books do we have?"

"About a hundred."

"You take it, then."

"And you?"

"I 'll do the corn-removers."

"Too bad you have n't got another book to sell against mine!"

"Books is rotten, anyway. I hope we get rid of them soon."

Then each counted his money from the hour's sales.

"Sixty bottles."

"Fifteen Sandorfs."

"Rotten."

"Rotten."

"Do you know those fellows?" I asked the waiter a little later, as the two were leaving the place.

"Them? Them is two brothers. The best men in their business."

## CHAPTER V

### CHINA

FROM Russia, if you were going up through Siberia and Manchuria, the road to China is not a very long one. If you are retracing your steps through Canal Street, going westward, have another look at the Manhattan Bridge to the left, tear yourself loose from the pullers-in of the clothing stores, and turn left again to Chatham Square, which had once been a suburb of New York. The dilapidated building of the old Thalia Theater, once the pride of the city and now a colonnaded shambles of stone and brick, housing cheap Italian vaudeville, stares you in the face. Don't let curiosity tempt you into Baxter Street, where is the open-air market of old clothing. Go straight to Mott Street.

In the morning little Chinese children play in front of the gilded pagoda-like house-fronts; children with faces like cameos cut in amber, as unreal to the immediate surroundings as if they were little dolls that had been stuck in for bizarre effect. There is an air of utter abandon and freedom about these tots—so very much unlike the preoccupied mien of children one meets anywhere else, the unreality is still more heightened. Unafraid and undaunted, they look every one square in the face with their almond-shaped, downward, well-set-apart brown eyes, certain that no one would molest them. For nowhere in the world are children brought up as freely as among the Chinese. A passing man in blue silk cassock and felt slippers, with drawn face and a long cue hanging on his back, looking the very personification of evil, stops in front of them and watches their little game on the stoop. He raises his hands within the long sleeves, crossing them over his breast, and remains long to gaze at them, smiling and encouraging them. Then he reaches into his pocket and throws them coin more liberally than any other children ever get from parents or uncles. The manner these children receive the gifts, as if they were due grace, is another indication of the relation between children and the older ones among the Chinese. It is not only because there are so very few children in the Chinese quarter, the immigration laws having long forbidden Chinese to come with their wives here; it is characteristic of the attitude of the Chinese to children everywhere under all conditions. In the few Chinese households I have visited, most of them very poor, where there are children, it is safe to say that seven tenths of all the family's earnings are spent in luxuries for the little ones. The garb of a six-year-old little girl costs fully five times as much as the whole expense of dress and clothes of the father and the mother. Silks and satins in profusion, and the best of everything at all times.

Mott Street is a narrow, curving street, on which the lower floor of every building houses a business of some sort. Numerous novelty shops, with all sorts of Chinese and Japanese embroidered wares, kimonos, robes, fake jades, chop-sticks, dishes, tea-sets, dolls, knives, and a lot of other similar things the "rubberneck" coming to visit

Chinatown in one of the sight-seeing cars is bound to buy as souvenirs. Between those large stores, right and left, are other stores catering to the Chinese of the neighborhood. In the windows are nondescript things of which no white man knows the use, but which under the expert handling of the Chinese become excellent savory dishes. Even the fresh vegetables in the windows are strange things to the average visitor.

Farther down is Doyer Street, where the Doyer Midnight Mission is. It was up to not long ago the Chinese Theater. The inside of the theater was left much as it had been, with the broad wooden benches disposed in geometrical figures on a slight incline toward the blind stage. Instead of the actors we now have the droning of the preachers. Next to the Doyer Mission is the Baptist Mission House and the kindergarten, with carved teak-wood tables and paper lanterns hung on the low ceiling, and the walls decorated with dragons and serpents in bas-relief with green eyes and mysterious golden manes. I wonder whether the good these missions do will ever offset the value of what has been! I wonder whether Kindergarten No. 30 has anything it can teach Chinese children except the tyranny of the older over the younger . . . and a few English words. But—it was pointed out to me that they are becoming civilized. A door from the Doyer Mission House is a real-estate agency, conducted chiefly by Chinese brought up in the American way. The paper posters on Pell and Mott Streets used to be announcements of plays and concerts; to-day they are real estate ads.

There are numerous places especially conducted for the

benefit of a sight-seer. For a consideration, one is shown, in a room of a rear house, rows upon rows of beds on which lie the stupefied opium-smokers. But most of these men, and sometimes women, are hired by the hour to simulate conditions Mr. Poodle and Mrs. Grundy are going to denounce in their home town on their return from wicked New York. They are created specially for their benefit. Opium-smoking goes on of course, but not where it is shown to sight-seers.

There used to be one place where the murder of one of the guests was staged nightly. It was done with such realism the guests would fly after having paid for dinners they had only ordered but not eaten, afraid lest the police on coming would arrest them. Some white woman would get up from a table and begin to execute an Oriental dance. Dancing, turning, she would reach the pianist and put her arms languorously about his neck and draw him to her lips. One of the Chinese, somber-eyed, supposedly her lover, acting as if he were half stupefied with dope, would rise from another table to tear her away from the pianist. There would be a scuffle between the white woman and the white man and the Chinese; a knife would flash in the wicked hand of the yellow man; there would be a loud scream, and the woman would fall to the floor. The attendants of the place would drag her away into a back room. A few other Chinese would spirit away their compatriot while the hubbub created by the screaming visitors and guests would be at its loudest. The pianist would continue to bang away on his instrument as though nothing had happened. And the visitors, thrilled, scared, horrified, would run to the doors, not without leaving their watches and pocketbooks in experter hands than theirs. It is no longer staged as frequently, but occasionally it still takes place to satisfy those who come for thrills in that district.

When the tongs—those secret societies of the Chinese, the difference between one and another unknown and non-understandable to anybody else—when the tongs are fighting a few bullets are whistling past the narrow streets, and a man or two may be found lifeless in a hallway, but the Chinese quarter remains outwardly the quietest in the city. A hundred Chinese, walking back and forth silently along the walls in their felt slippers, so thoroughly merge with the surroundings you neither see nor hear their movement. The quiet color of their clothing so well fits in with the grayness of the sidewalk and the dull-brown reddish color of the outer walls they seem not to move from one place to the other. Their mincing, effeminate gait, while the upper body remains stiff, makes one think they are automatons, not human beings. At a joss-house, while a hundred men are conversing with one another passionately, or praying, it is so quiet one could hear the buzz of a fly in the middle of the heavily scented, teak-wood-walled room.

The upper floors, above the business places in the district, when they are not occupied by soul-saving stations and mission-houses, are mostly club-rooms of the Chinese. A man can go in any time he chooses and sit all by himself in a little corner and doze off the little poppy that he has put into his pipe, or seek that inner quiet, that dumb quiet within himself, so precious to the children of China.

The few households with families and children are

usually on a floor above, or in one of the rear houses on Pell Street, Mott or Doyer Street. There is my friend Me Tom, who has married a white woman who for years tried to convert the heathen Chinese to Christianity. She has more than become converted herself to her heathen religion. Me Tom had given in to her ways at first, and eaten her corned beef and cabbage, and permitted her to furnish the apartment as she chose, with ugly mahogany sideboards and brass beds and French mirrors and cretonne hangings. She had even put in a davenport in the dining-room. It looked for a while as though Me Tom was becoming reconciled to the taste of his American wife. He never protested, and let her do what she wanted. Little did Mrs. Me Tom know, having come from Boston to New York to do uplift work, that her husband was maintaining a separate bachelor apartment just across the street, which was furnished in his own Chinese way, with low-burning lights and round, teak-wood tables and backless round taborets incrusted with mother-of-pearl. For three years Me Tom kept on furnishing that apartment with the beautiful things from his own country he could lay his hands on. And when it was all finished he asked his wife to come and

see it. And even she, antagonistic as she was to everything that was not Anglo-Saxon, had to admit her heathen husband had furnished his apartment much more beautifully and much more comfortably than the one she had arranged. And they moved over into Me Tom's establishment, abandoning the other one to another mixed couple.

For such things happen only too frequently. Those who come to convert become converted themselves. There are three little Me Tom children now. The oldest is nine years, a little girl, blond and slender, looking very much like her mother except for the somewhat slanted eyes and oversensitive hands. The other two children, Chris and George, look exactly like their father. So far the only disagreements in the family have been because of the children, the mother not being inclined to let them have as much their own way as the father intends them to have. The other day Me Tom told me, "Little childlen in Amelica vely unhappy." And pointing to a Chinese woman walking on her heels because of the stump-like feet that have been compressed in bandages since birth, he added, "Feet of Amelican woman not nice."

There are of course other couples in the district not as happily mated. Those of the Chinese who cannot live alone and were unable to get women of their own kind have married colored women, particularly from the West Indies. The offspring of such couples have inherited the worst there is in both of them, with the cunning of the one and the cruelty of the other, with the rapacity of the one and the shiftlessness of the other. The Chinese have no confidence in the result of such mixtures and keep away from them. But there have been other mixtures, particularly with the Italians, which have proved more successful; and there is one Chinese man, Chon Loei, who, claiming he was a Chinese Jew, had married a Russian Jewess. They also have two children, boys both of them, named by the mother Israel and Moie. And although they look very much like their father, with only a little of the mother in their noses, they speak the most perfect Yiddish I have ever heard children speak, and even sing Yiddish songs. Their mother has lately become a very active Zionist. It is side-splitting to see these two children among the other children, and hear their noisy singsong talk, so different from the speech of the others. The mother sends them both regularly every day to a Hebrew teacher in Henry Street . . . that they may become men of Israel.

As you come out from Mott Street and go into Doyer Street you will see the walls plastered with yellow papers upon which are printed a hieroglyphic script running downward. These are the announcements of tong meetings and other meetings that are being called. It is part of the social life of the district, a small world in itself, with its own problems and troubles, leaders, statesmen, and gossips. The forward young Americanized Chinese use these bill-boards for free real-estate advertisements.

Most of the houses of the Chinese district are owned by Chinese themselves. Through whatever hands these houses have once passed, they are now Chinese. The architecture, the material used, the laced iron of the balconies and fire-escapes, the projecting garret-hoods from the wooden shanties, the painted brick, the narrow crooked stairs, the dark hallways, and the flagstone yards, it is all Chinese; transformed, rebuilt to suit the general taste. No other people have changed their environment as much to suit them as the Chinese. The Catholic Church of the Transfiguration on Mott Street is architecturally out of place and looks like an intrusion. How much more in taste with the surroundings is the balconied building housing the joss-house, the house of public worship, facing it! Below the joss-house is the home of the Chinese Free-

masons. There seems to be no contradiction between the two institutions. The efforts at Americanization are evident in the large signs over the American Citizens' Alliance, but they are nullified by the Chinese National League. Wherever one Chinese lives is China. He carries the country, its traditions and customs and laws, with him.

If you are lucky enough to see Rose, otherwise known as the Angel of Chinatown, and she can usually be met in one of the soul-saving stations, she will conduct you into places where many of her friends live, where you will see more of the intimate life of Chinatown than can be seen on passing the street—except for such sights as are especially prepared for the sight-seer. It is true that on Doyer Street and on Baxter Street there are several opium-joints. I have visited one several times myself, and counted eight white people out of eleven in the place; people whose names are very frequently blazoned in the papers as principals of this and that. There they looked more like disemboweled creatures from whom everything that had a semblance of real life had been taken out. Their brains seemed to have been scooped out from within their skulls. Their eyes were bleary and partly closed. The twitching lips, and the arms hanging over the edges of the narrow cots on which they lay down, made them a picture of contemptible distress portrayed to horrify. The Chinese lay in a trance without in any way giving the impression of disgust and horror given by the others.

When I asked one who knew what caused the difference of appearance between the opium-smokers, I was answered: "Because the Chinese know and the white man does n't.

White man hog. He eats much. He drinks much. He smokes much."

You cannot fail, from whatever side you enter Chinatown, to see the missions of the neighborhood. I do not know how many souls they have saved to justify their existence or the cost of maintenance. But it were interesting for them to know that the Chinaman sees no objection to worshiping at six different shrines at the same time. There are such who are Confucianists, believers in Laotsze, Mohammedans, and Christians at one and the same time. How they can be all that together is clear only in their own minds, and cannot be made clear to ours; no more than a Chinese puzzle is as readily understood by a white man as it is by a yellow one.

Chinatown in New York is also the central traffic-station of the underworld commerce of narcotics that goes on throughout the continent. No matter where it is carried on, in California, in Canada, in Florida, or in Mexico, the trails forever lead back to the gates of Chinatown, where they are lost never to be found. For the one who would divulge a single thing is through some peculiar method of the Chinese immediately found out and silenced forever.

Of the many crimes that have been committed in that district, very few of the guilty ones have ever been found out. The justice of the Chinese is meted out by themselves as swiftly if not swifter than any other justice. Most of these crimes are committed for commercial reasons. The honesty of the Chinaman in his direct dealings with people is too proverbial to need any repetition here. Any Chinaman can get any reasonable amount of money from any other one, by paying usury, without giving any other guarantee for the payment than his word, which is also his life. Failure to pay is not aired in the courts of justice. There are swifter means than that, and the example is a much more efficient one.

I once ducked several revolver-shots while walking with Chuck Connors through Mott Street. They were aimed at a man passing along the street. Connors looked at me, and, with his knowledge of the people more intimate than that of any one, he told me, "That man will never reach the corner of the street."

And he did n't. For before Connors had finished his phrase the lifeless body of the man was dragged into one of the hallways. There was no outcry. There were no screams. Several Chinese passers-by, or lookers-out of windows, or whatever they may have been at that particular moment, turned their backs immediately and entered their homes. The street became deserted for a few minutes. By the time the vigilant policeman from the corner had rushed upon the scene with his menacing club and drawn revolver, there was nothing to be seen.

Connors turned around and told me: "You won't say a word. I vouched for you."

A little later I asked my companion why and how he had vouched for me, since it had been a chance meeting between us two! Connors answered, "I gave them the sign."

Still later he explained to me that he had made several signs with his raised arm after the shots had been fired. The dead body was never discovered. It was disposed of Chinese fashion.

There are fewer Chinese wearing their cues down their backs than there were a few years ago. This was due to the change of the government in China, permitting them to do so. At first only the youngsters fell in with the new order of things. But slow as the Chinese are to accept any new thing, this particular reform they hastened to adopt as rapidly as our young ladies accepted the knee-length skirts a few years ago. The fights, the revolutions in China have their echoes here, echoes and partizans.

But Chinatown never looks as much like China as at New Year's or at some other Chinese fête, or when a new treaty of peace has been signed between the different warring tongs. Then the colored paper lanterns are hung across the sidewalk from every floor of the houses, bits of quaint paper masks appear in the windows, silks are hung from here and there, blank cartridges are being exploded, and the fireworks for which the Chinese are justly famous the world over are being let loose everywhere, changing the narrow, crooked streets into a fairy world. From the windows of the joss-houses, club-houses, and restaurants float curious, plaintive, screeching melodies from the zither-like instruments which carry the melody, while the people sitting around it sing harmonies to the song.

Now that peace has been established, members of the different tongs play fan-tan together; fan-tan and not mah-jong, which, although widely known as the Chinese national game, has been denounced to me as a game foreign to the Chinese people. Playing fan-tan a man may lose his laundry establishment, for which he had worked twenty years, in a few hours, and depart outwardly as peacefully from the table as if the game had been one in which a toothpick was involved; for he has the hope of winning another laundry back very soon. As a matter of fact, Me Tom explained to me that the Chinese laundries over the city are never sold by one Chinaman to another, but only lost at fan-tan.

Here, too, the same as in the other districts of foreign population, the Chinese known to us under one name live in groupings of people of different cantons. Because of the numerous Chinese dialects, totally different from one another, very frequently Chinese do not understand one another as well as they are commonly supposed to. I was having dinner one night with my friend Me Tom and remarked that he was trying to speak English to the Chinese restaurateur, which the other man understood with great difficulty. I thought at first Me Tom did it for show, or because he wanted the other to learn the language of this country, but Me Tom explained to me: "He comes flom a fal-away canton in China. I do not understand his language."

Me Tom is a very emotional and temperamental gentleman. More than once he had refused to serve me tea or even admit me to his sanctum when I was accompanied by people he did not fancy at first or second glance. He simply barred the door of his little place, which is a-tremble every time the elevated train stops at Chatham Square, and said:

"No, no, no have tea, no have nothing, no, no. Come other day."

Or he folded his arms, standing near the counter, if we

had succeeded in getting by him at the door, looked askance, and intrenched himself behind that Oriental impassiveness which is refractory to all appeals. And when Me Tom does not want to do or answer something, he does not know a single word of the English language. He is deaf and dumb then. The best and the only thing to do is to leave the tea-house as graciously as possible. For it is known that Me Tom's place is not altogether a public place. He serves only such people as he likes.

The food, the tea, the manner of service, the price, are altogether a matter of emotion, of temperament. Even the color of the dishes is a matter of Me Tom's choice. He has more than once refused to serve tea, to a friend at my table, in a cup of the same color as the one from which I drank. Explanations? If you care to have them in Chinese you will be welcome—sometimes. In English he gives none.

So, as you see, we have to deal with a peculiar sort of a man, and the story here offered may sound as strange as the man himself is. But then you must remember that Me Tom is a Chinaman of refinement, a man of taste, a philosopher and an artist. Thought is Me Tom's art medium, as words to a writer, sound to a musician, color to a painter, or solid mass to a sculptor. Me Tom is an artist philosopher. Would there were many like him!

The day previous to the one I am telling about, Me Tom had refused to serve some friends of mine.

"I don't like them," was all he had said.

As I was sipping my tea the following day, I decided to

turn the tables on Me Tom. Calling him over, I pointed to a group of gentlemen from the Flowery Kingdom sitting at another table, and said:

"Me Tom, I don't like them. Put them out."

"Why don't you do it yourself?" he answered.

"This is not my place, Me Tom."

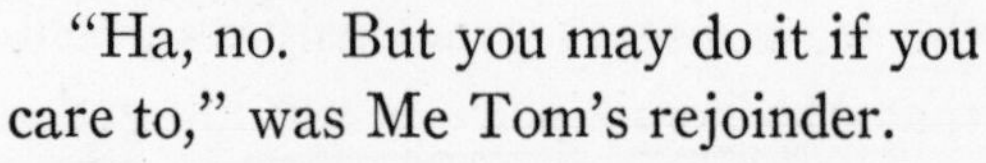

"Ha, no. But you may do it if you care to," was Me Tom's rejoinder.

He waited a long time and looked so searchingly into my eyes that I felt very uncomfortable. Finally the guests left of their own free will to play a little game of fan-tan elsewhere.

Me Tom first cleared the table they had left. The work done, he closed the door so as not to be disturbed, made some tea for himself, and came to sit next me on the upholstered teak-wood bench under a Buddha, close to the wall. A flickering movement in the incense-bowl had revived the insinuating odor and submerged the scent of sandalwood which had dominated till them. It was Me Tom's way of letting me know that he demanded absolute attention.

I gave it, and here is the story he told me.

There is a province deep down in the interior of China. It has not yet been penetrated by whites. And in that province they once had a judge who was very severe.

But one day the people rose against that severe judge

and decided to kill him and choose another judge. So one man said to them:

"Choose the wisest. One who has lived with his body and mind. Not one who has never sinned, but one who has sinned and repented and therefore knows that if he should have paid for his sin with his life he could never have repented."

Then an old man asked to be heard. Said he:

"Let us keep the same judge. But dispense with the executioner. Let the judge also execute his judgments."

And so the following day the executioner was sent away from the palace and the province, and the judge was vested with a new power.

That day he ordered a man flogged. Fifty lashes was the judgment. But having given as far as the third one, and heard the shriek of the culprit, he let the bamboo fall from his hand, and was so faint that he had to be carried home.

When he returned to his bench the next day he was a much milder man, and people heard him admonish like a father where formerly he would have ordered the most cruel tortures.

Then one day a man committed such a heinous crime that the populace of the whole province clamored that his life be taken to pay the penalty.

Tremblingly the judge pronounced the fatal sentence.

The people were determined that the judgment be executed.

The judge, sword in hand, went down to the subterranean execution chamber, but returned with head bowed so low that it seemed as if he and not the other one were the culprit.

"Let him live another day," the judge said.

The following day the judge was ill.

On the third day he first heard all the cases before him. Then again he thought of the criminal in the dungeon. But he could not act; he could not. Not that day.

"Oh, let him live another day," he said to the people.

Another day, and another day, and another day, went by. The judge's hair turned gray, his hands became feeble, his knees weakened, and he could think of nothing else but of the man he had to kill. And whenever he postponed the duty for another day, it was as if he were postponing his own death by that length of time.

"Oh, let it be for another day," he now begged each morning. He pleaded with his wives and his children, and the passers-by on the streets, and the people who came to him for judgment. At last life became such a burden to the one-time severe judge that he died.

"And for all I know the man who has committed the heinous crime is still alive," added Me Tom, as he looked me straight in the eyes.

"When I object to some one's presence I put him out myself, friend. I execute my own judgments."

There was too much incense-smoke in the room; so Me Tom opened the door again, and went to wait on a high stool behind the counter. His immobile face, his heavy small eyes, and the rigidity of the pose he assumed told me plainly that my friend wished to be alone, all alone with his memories and thoughts and the Confucius statue up in his private room over the restaurant.

But at the door Me Tom called to me:

"Man should be more like to a match than to fire-stone. He should burn and consume himself when he produces fire."

# CHAPTER VI

## LITTLE ITALY

THE down-town Italian quarter extends on the east as far as Forsyth Street, with small infiltrations into Rivington, Houston, Stanton, and Delancey Streets, southward to Pearl and Oliver Streets, and west from Bayard Street through Elizabeth, Mott, Mulberry, and all the streets that run westward to Seventh Avenue, and northward to about Tenth Street, encompassing almost all of Greenwich Village, which was, and still is in a measure, the American quarter of New York. On Bayard Street the Chinese quarter fringes off. The sign of Chon Tu Fa swings in the wind against the sign of the Italian *levatrice,* the midwife, next door to him. Wherever a few Italian families come to settle, among other evidences the sign of a midwife springs up immediately. And so if by some order all push-carts and names on windows were to be suddenly wiped out, these *levatrice* signs would be a perfectly safe guide through an Italian quarter.

In former years, before the first generation of Italians had somehow acclimatized itself to conditions, a night visit through Little Italy was not a very safe one. There was too much revolver- and knife-play in the neighborhood. Whether it has been due to stern police reprisals, education, or Americanization, or perhaps prohibition, I do not know, but the fact is that Little Italy, which furnished such a large percentage of the criminal elements of the city, is no longer entitled to that infamy. And if prohibition has done one thing, it has emptied the streets of the Italian quarters of their dangerous gangsters and of their houses of ill fame and their votaries. One is no longer pulled in by women standing in open hallways, offering sensual pleasures within, in the same tone of voice hardware or fish is offered in Turin or Naples. It is, I am told, much more difficult and expensive than it ever was to hire a gangster for some dirty work. These women and men have settled down somewhere to a much more lucrative and safer profession. They have become respectable citizens, building homes for themselves and raising families. Prohibition has done all that. Bootlegging has reduced the number of prostitutes and gangsters in New York City.

You go down through Park Street, sloping down from around the corner of the Church of the Transfiguration on Mott Street. Mysterious Chinese signs hang on both sides of the street. You come upon the open square of Mulberry Park, deserted in the daytime, and the place of trysts at night. You are in Little Italy, Elizabeth Street, with fruit push-carts on the sidewalks, groaning heavily with all the colors; with deep cellar stores and cellar restaurants, and the odor of fried fish and oil; the cries of the venders in that open-mouthed Latin of the southern Italians are hurled at you. In the upper stores are banking-offices and export-houses combined with cheese and olive wholesalers. The tooting from a boat on the river near-by completes the illusion that you are in Naples. The men, tall and blue-eyed, with coal-black mustaches and sonorous voices, and little tufts of hair over the forehead, are mostly Neapolitans. One can easily distinguish them from the rest of the Italians. There is something gay and easy about them, something of the blue sea of their homes. Even as they call out their wares, whether fish or peaches, apples or oranges, dates or figs, they interpolate little phrases from the Italian *canzonettas,* "O Sole Mio" or "Santa Lucia."

Go as far as West Houston Street, or better still to Bleecker Street. Don't pass hurriedly by the former residence of Thomas Paine, the Revolutionary patriot. The wash of several Italian families, colored, patched, and clean, fluttering in the wind, hangs from the window he used to lean out of when tired reading and smoking. Bleecker Street was once a great residential center. It is now just like any of the shore streets of an Italian port, with music stores combined with barber shops, and dressmaking shops combined with grocers. You may want to stop at one of the music stores where some new *canzonetta* is tried out. There will be no objection. These *canzonettas* are turned out by the hundreds weekly, sentimental love-songs, or clever ditties about the eternal subject of mirth, mothers-in-law.

Pass under the elevated station and hurry down further, until you come to Elizabeth Street, then turn back to your right. Pass the old Paradise Park, with its brick-inclosed walls, and you are in the heart of one of the most extraordinary industries of the city.

All that has come out of garbage-pails—old forks, old knives, broken plates, collar-buttons, old shoes, worn coats, trousers, vests, women's dresses, all that has been discarded by the rest of New York as unfit, as unusable—is being hawked and sold by men dressed in the very things they buy and sell. It is here that those who have lingered too long in the Bowery come down to change their "good" coat for a worse one, so as to get a few cents in exchange. Vests and hats are being sold from head and body. Shoes are being taken off from feet and sold; pocket-knives, cigarette-cases, everything that can bring in a penny. Things that have been stolen, small things not valuable enough to be pawned, are being disposed of in this way. Across from the power-house, there are several saloons where all these buyers and sellers come together, and in the back rooms the old clothing exchange, where things are thrown in a balance-scale, weighed, and paid for across the counter, remind one of the old Moulin de la Galette and the old Place Maube of Paris. The smell of dirt and sweat, and a hundred other indefinable odors, the appearance of the merchants and the sellers, drive one out into the street, despairing of ever breathing fresh air again. The whole street is lined with stores and sweat-shops where bearded old men, bent and half blind, work away to put these old things in a wearable condition, whereupon they are shipped south, after being washed and steamed, for the colored trade.

Turn around and go into Mulberry Street, where both sides are lined with fruit-stand push-carts. What strikes one first is the beauty and the variety of the vegetables and fruits sold there in what is supposed to be one of the poorest quarters. Peaches with blooms on, and the softest and the most luscious plums, the largest apples and most beautiful pears, the cleanest salads, are sorted and handled in the most expert and delicate way, lying near and between each other so as to form a color-scheme—the most

unusual vegetable leaves and roots, coming from the Italian gardens around New York and grown especially for the people here.

Whether winter or summer, the Italians of the district live much more on the street than in their houses. In the summer the houses are almost completely deserted; mother and children, mostly very numerous broods of small ones, wait outside on the steps, or at the hallway, until the last minute before the return of the paterfamilias. And as one looks up and sees the green growth on every window-sill, it makes one think these houses serve no other purpose but to hold these flower-boxes on the windows, and the fire-escapes to serve as poles for the wash-lines hanging between them. It is as if the street were in continual holiday, with the wash of all nations unfolded and fluttering in the wind. And all the time there is the cry of the vender, and the *canzonetta* sung by the idle merchant, and the sound of the mandolin and the guitar coming from the numerous barber shops in the neighborhood. Oh, these barbers! Each one a cousin of Caruso and a nephew of Verdi.

You may still be able to get a passably good glass of wine in some of the restaurants. It is extraterritorial as far as prohibition is concerned. And a good many Italians speak now with contempt of those who left the country after the enactment of the Eighteenth Amendment. Those fools feared not to be able to get their glass of wine with their meal, and did not know how they could live without it. I met an old friend of mine not long ago who had returned to Italy then, swearing never to come back to America. When I asked him what he was doing here again he answered:

"Me did not know 'prohibish' was one of the best laws for the poor in this country. You no need no lis', nothing at all."

That is the manner most of the Italians view prohibition. The best law for the poor . . . bootlegger.

It is in these houses that for years the first inrush of Italians thought the bath-tub was a coal-receptacle, and wondered profoundly when the real use for which the tubs were intended was explained to them. They were outraged to know that children could not go to work before they had reached a certain age, and resented any interference when they had transformed the homes they were living in into sweat-shops, mother, grandmother, and the whole family, to the little suckling, working at something or other. And until a branch of the Garment-workers' Union had been specially formed from them, ameliorating conditions of work and standard of living, I have no doubt that many diseases, the white plague especially, were frequently carried in the garments finished in these decrepit homes. To this day hundreds of homes are really sweat-shops, factories where Fifth Avenue lingerie and the finest of silk gowns are being made for less than one twentieth of the price obtained for them in the big stores.

It is to be expected that the Italian native population, although it has shown a tremendous advance over the native population of any other group till now, will be reduced, though the number of *levatrices* in the neighborhood is increasing. But I have heard a woman singing the praises of one *levatrice* as follows:

"She is one good *levatrice.* I know twenty women, her customers, and in five years they did not get one child. She one good *levatrice.*"

The priests of the neighborhood thunder and cry. Greater powers are competing with them. There is an inverse relation between the increase in the cost of rent and the birth of children. A family of ten or twelve, living in a three-room apartment, is not considered overcrowded by the Italians themselves. On visiting one family some time ago, I expressed wonder to the lady of the house that she was able to live with eight children in a two-room-and-kitchen apartment, whereupon the good woman exclaimed:

"We no live in all the apartment. My husband's sister she got four children and she live with us. Half my children, half this room, and half the other room."

"And how do you get on?" I asked.

"Not so very bad," the lady replied. "Only my sister-in-law she take in boarders. They got children. That makes too much noise, a little bit." Of course rent in the Italian quarter is, considering space and service, higher than on Riverside Drive.

The saying that children should be seen and not heard is not a dictum of the Italians. Their children are more frequently heard than seen. There is a continual shouting up from the children on the street to the mothers at the windows and vice versa. There are no curtains to Italian windows. The people are too Latin for that.

There is very little effort on the part of the Italians to learn the language of the country. Being over a million in the city, they are so complete an entity that they do not find it necessary to learn English. Indeed, those who have any business with them must learn Italian, if they intend to get along at all.

The colored people living in Carmine Street speak Italian as well as the Italians. There is an occasional intermarriage between Italians and colored people, as well as between Italians and Jews, the latter because of their proximity and because of the garment factories abounding in the neighborhood. On a visit to Little Italy with my friend Maria Lombardi, who was in search of some *canzonettas,* we found a colored man, black as pitch, in the store. And it was he who tried out the songs for her, singing them in a full-throated voice, phrasing the Italian much more roundly than the best singers at some of our operas. Upon expressing her wonder she was told the son of Ham was partly Italian.

Of the hundred *societe,* mutual-benefit lodges, political groups, named after famous prize-fighters and politicians, most of them are joined for the handsome burials they give their members. Not an Italian family but is indebted to its neck for burying some one. If you are lucky enough, on turning from Mulberry Street to Bayard Street, you will hear from a distance the blare of trumpets and the roll of drums, playing some funeral music. The musicians march ahead and are followed closely by the members of the *società* to which the deceased belonged. Some of them are dressed in gala clothes, and others are in their working-garb; they have been just able to jump out for the two or three hours that it takes to accompany the deceased to the Brooklyn Bridge. Then comes the gorgeous-looking hearse and a number of caparisoned carriages, with the undertaker acting as major-domo. Burial seems to be held in much greater honor by the Italians than either birth or marriage. People canvassing for such *societé* are continually putting forward the number of members who, because of the heavy fine imposed upon those who refuse, will eventually follow the deceased one, and the number of carriages after the hearse, as well as the funeral decorations over doors and windows.

Each street has its own patron saint, sometimes several saints, for whom festas and processions are being given at stated days of the year. The particular street, or part of the street, as the case may be, is then decorated with flags and lanterns, and rows of colored oil-lamps overhead. The image of the patron saint is placed on a high pedestal against a wall, with tens of big, tall wax candles burning right and left, and a large collection-box near-by. The *società* which had arranged the festa, to which every merchant and every family has contributed, each according to his wealth, is marching to the blare of fanfares in front and in the rear of the procession. Different floats, naïvely and childishly crude in their arrangement, pass back and forth. Behind the holy image, carried in a baldaquin by bareheaded men holding colored wax candles six feet high in their hands, are carried stretched-out flags for the collection of different moneys supposed to go for this, that, or the other charitable institution.

There is great rivalry between the organizations in charge of the different saints' processions. Many of them are really nothing else but grafting gangs to whom the religiosity of the ceremony is nothing but an excuse. To hear a discussion between such opposing gangs, when the respective saints are being reviled, is a Homeric treat.

Architecturally, Little Italy gives the impression of a town that had suddenly been left by the native inhabitants following an invasion. The invaders, having occupied the

houses, let them go to seed, not knowing how long they were to remain there, lest the vanquished suddenly return to their own homes. The whole district presents the most pell-mell throwing together imaginable. There is not the slightest order in the alinement of the streets or in the residential qualities of the adjoining houses. Crumbling-down brick houses lean on wooden barracks which were erected temporarily and have remained so for the last forty or fifty years. Shanties lean on million-dollar industrial buildings. Crooked archways built on ten-foot frontages bulge in the center like a card-house ready to fall.

On Broome Street near Elizabeth Street, where the Ogden Hall once was, between a saloon and a fire-engine company, stands the beautiful Salvatore Church with windows painted loudly, audibly, in red, green, blue, and yellow, as if it were a Village tea-shop. The Broome Street Tabernacle, a most magnificent brick building, ornate and aged, faces Police Headquarters on Center Street, and leans on houses that seem to have been blown there by some wind from the east. From a distance the tall, angular buildings, erected on narrow triangular strips, look like toys built too tall, ready to topple over at a first shake.

There is St. Patrick's Church on Mulberry Street, going through and occupying a full block to Mott Street, squat and square, as though sitting on the ground, surrounded by a brick wall with iron-clad doors pierced through the brick that time has somewhat worn. The broken windows of the colored panels, running all around and almost to the ground of the edifice, the leaking roof, the patches of repair on the cracked walls, leave one with the feeling that this church was built within a fortress, as though in inimical territory, though the few trees within the fortress are the only ones in the neighborhood. Fantastic, the cracked toy building, as if erected by the hasty hands of some children playing at building, stands a little brick house on the corner of Houston Street leaning on the church. The window-frames are oblique; the doors are hinged on a side, with a little toy balcony over the first roof. And as if to mock the whole thing, the enormous Puck Building, with its severe and magnificent doorway, looms up near-by. Crowding one another as if drunken and afraid of falling, trying to support one another, stand all the houses on Mott Street from one end to the other. A little further up is Colonnade Row, in Lafayette Street, from one of whose houses President Tyler married Julia Gardiner of Gardiner's Island. John Jacob Astor was once a resident of Colonnade Row. . . . Colonnade Row, like the architectural survival of some remote past.

There is a passageway about four feet wide between 311 and 313 Lafayette Street, between two tall buildings. Half the bootleg traffic of the quarter is transacted there. Not very long ago, the meeting-place of the C. K. Club of the neighborhood was here. The C. K. Club, which I joined many, many years ago, was the Captain Kidd Exploration Club. It was composed of about twenty-five Italian boys of the neighborhood, who met regularly every morning with demountable spades under their coats, to go down to Liberty Street, to the supposed site of the home of Captain Kidd, and dig under the buildings in search of hidden treasure. Those were exciting days, and my little friends hoped to some day . . . but time is cruel, more so than age. . . .

When I last visited the C. K. Alley, most of my old C. K. "brothers" were there, only in spats and expensive fur coats, with goggles and leather gloves, while the running engines of their big cars were waiting for them outside. They were still out for treasures, and they had found an easier way than to dig for the ones under Captain Kidd's house, the house of our dreams.

"Where is Pietro?"

"Pietro was shot dead," Moreno informed me.

"And Joseph?"

"Joseph is in jail."

"And Amato?"

"Amato is all right."

"All right," also were Cordova and Charles, and Nardo. And "all right" meant he was in the Volstead business.

Next to C. K. Alley is Shinbone Alley, the dirtiest shame of the whole city. One can literally wallow in dirt to his knees after a rainy day. A suffocating stench vapors from the ground on the warm days; children play in the gutter; the little mothers in charge of the tots, left with them by the mothers who have gone to work in the factories around, play in the dirt, and black flies cover their pale, sickly faces. It is just across from the Speyer Hospital for Animals. Really there is much greater concern for the welfare of dogs in this city than for children.

As if to show that there is still something of old romance and adoration left in the hearts of men, there is a brick building on Lafayette Street with the word "Mary" in big gold letters over it. Cleveland Place is a little square between Kenmare and Lafayette Streets, just facing the office of "La Folia," the humorous Italian weekly. It still presents some appearance of orderliness, for it was until not very long ago inhabited by a survival of the great number of French people who had once occupied that district.

As early as seven o'clock in the morning numerous children wait on the door-steps of the public schools in the neighborhood. Their parents having gone to work, there is no other place for them. For their delectation and edification there are daily dog-fights in the street, between dogs of rival kennels, kept in the cellars of the neighborhood.

The beautiful Church of Our Lady of Pompeii, with most magnificent round panel windows, is a near neighbor of Jimmy's Restaurant, from which emanates so much interesting news in the daily papers—news of battles and fights and scandals. It is not very far from the Garret, now Grace's Tea-room, in which Washington is supposed once to have lived. It is in this garret that the first Village newspaper was published. When a fire destroyed it partly a few years ago, many original manuscripts of Wilde, owned by the man who inhabited the place, were burned, as well as several original drawings by Aubrey Beardsley. To-day the Garret, once a meeting-place of artists of all branches, is the rendezvous of those who come "to see" the Village.

Then there are the dark streets of Mercer, Greene, and Wooster, dark and deserted at night; for they are occupied mostly by factories in which work fourteen nationalities elbow to elbow, hatting, dressing, and clothing the rest of the country. The streets are completely dead after nightfall except for the hollow sound of the hickory club of the night-watchman on the sidewalk, an occasional fire, and the unsupportable odor coming out from the windows of the factories being cleaned for the following day's work.

By reason of a thousand causes, little barracks on ten or twelve-foot frontages separate huge buildings. There are empty places in which all the refuse of the neighborhood is being thrown.

Coming upward, there is little Congress Street, back of the old Republican Club on King Street, with an old brick stable that was built in the days when this was still Greenwich, and horse-carriages were a necessity and in style. A minute's walk from there is a beautiful row of buildings erected by Frenchmen, with love for vine-covered fronts and lace portals, now occupied by Dante Alighieri pastry-shops, pleasure-clubs, and such like. Across from it, on Macdougal Street, where the invasion has not completely destroyed all the old homes of the only American quarter of the city, stands a new row of studio buildings, just below Bleecker Street, in which some of the old architecture of the neighborhood has been revived. There are any number of magnificent doorways and windows in the vicinity that should be retrieved and conserved, which are now being hacked to pieces every time one of the old buildings crumbles down and a new one goes up in its place. Such doorways and windows will never be made again.

At the left of the entrance to Macdougal Street, on Spring Street, where is the Butterick Building of granite and a wooden shack facing it, is Vandam Street with its gay small red-brick houses, with white doorways and clean-lined windows and arches on the wide street. Little flower-boxes on the window-sills of the houses, greening and blooming, outside in the summer, inside in the winter, seem to smile at one the hope that more of them will yet come. These houses had already gone to pieces a few years ago when a movement sympathetic to the return of old things in Greenwich Village revived them. The houses were rebuilt or put in order, with a feeling for the old lines that had been. But of this later when we shall pay our visit to America.

At the Antica Roma in Baxter Street at noon I frequently meet my old friend Onorio Ruotolo, whose bust of Caruso is in the lobby of the Metropolitan Opera House, and whose Dante adorns the library of Columbia University. A hundred of his other works adorn different buildings and institutions in the United States. Tall and swarthy, handsome, his voice rings even when he speaks in whispers. Forever embroiled in some big political or artistic dispute with this and that one, mincing no words, siding definitely with one faction or the other, he may be thundering one day at a Fascist whose host he is for lunch, and thundering against some of his old friends of the extreme Left the following day.

Arturo Giovannitti, the Italian-American poet, whose book, "Arrows in the Gale," attracted considerable attention sometime ago, and who was one of the mainstays of the great Lawrence strike, for which he was put in jail—blond and vigorous, sarcastic and spoofing—is generally shouting his repartees to Ruotolo from the other end of the restaurant.

It was at the Antica Roma that I witnessed one evening the following incident: The Società del Ditto, a more or less musical organization headed by Halpherson, the veteran musical critic, and presided over by Galinele, a celebrated Italian lawyer, with members in all walks of life, painters, artists, judges, lawyers, etc., was dining Chaliapin, the Russian singer, as the guest of honor that evening. The conversations at the tables and all the speeches were carried on in Italian. Galinele—short, stout, with a goatee beard, rubicund, and a laughing face, looking very much like a drinking monk cut out from a Rembrandt picture—is one of the few men I know who can talk interminably and yet be interesting.

Chaliapin, the big Russian, whose gray hair in no way diminishes the impression of youth given by his panther-like body, was continually on his feet telling stories. An assistant district attorney, whose name may remain unmentioned, was constantly interrupting the great basso, asking him to talk American; for he was the only one who did not understand Italian. There was no way of quieting him. He was forever on his feet telling of the green Emerald Isle from which he came, and damning these "foreigners," who spoke "Wop language" instead of "good old American."

This assistant district attorney was not a member of del

Ditto; only a guest who happened to have been invited by some one. Chaliapin turned around to him from the opposite end of the table and begged him, in his very broken English, to be so kind and not to interrupt. I could see the repressed flame in the eyes of the angry Slav. The Latin element was turning around, wild-eyed. Many a man would readily have silenced the intruder in a more or less permanent way. Again and again the man interrupted and insulted all present. Chaliapin as well as the others begged him to desist, and when some one had tried to apologize for him to Chaliapin, telling him that this was not an example of an American, the man of law grew angry and raised his fist against the apologizer.

With a panther-like leap Chaliapin had jumped across the table. Bottles, dishes, and forks clattered on the floor, and although twenty men tried to halt his leap, clinging to his arms and tall legs, he shook them off like a football tackler. One big shove and he threw the man through the door to the sidewalk. The district attorney was lucky indeed that the rest of the people had interposed themselves between him and the infuriated Boris. Attorneys Wolfson and Neuberger spent the rest of the evening convincing Chaliapin that this assistant district attorney was *not* the best example of an American.

The Società del Ditto dines some celebrity every week. The food is . . . well, the food is divine. The company human and male exclusively.

There is a barber on Mott Street. Galifero is his name. He works from early morning till late at night at his trade. Between work he spends his time at a tiny little piano at the rear of his store, reading scores of operas and singing the heroic tenor parts from them. Every once in a while his old ambition to sing in public gets hold of him. Galifero is one of the musical barbers. Every once in a while some

fake impresario canvasses the numerous Galiferos with operatic ambitions in the neighborhood, and, after having them invest all theirs savings to give them the privilege of singing and showing themselves, the company is wrecked somewhere in a little town around New York. Seldom if ever has such a company lived long enough to appear in the city. And yet there is no end to the gullibility of the Galiferos. Perhaps the same or another impresario will turn the trick again with the same man next year or the year following, when he thinks the barber has accumulated some dollars. Since the advent of Valentino all the youth of Little Italy try to look as much as possible like the moving-picture hero, and to haunt the moving-picture studios of the city, having in their Americanization somewhat abandoned the desire to become grand opera singers. Caruso is the idol of the older relations of the young Italians.

I have always been rather lucky in my choice of artists of the shears and razors. My first barber was Max Rosen's father. In those days Max was a nice, blue-eyed little devil practising the violin after school hours, or after he had come home from wherever he had been instead of school. There was a back room in the barber shop which was kitchen, sleeping-room, and dining-room to father and son. It was on Delancey Street, near the Williamsburg Bridge.

Beril, Max's father, was the teacher himself. He had studied the violin with Enesco's former teacher, and considered himself teacher enough—himself and the razor-strop. Of course, Max played better than his father even then, but you know how artists are—jealous, terribly jealous. Father, son, brother, mother, it does not matter. Front stage, by any means.

Beril Rosen probably imagined we came because we liked to hear him play or discourse on music. It certainly was not my reason for walking twenty blocks. I liked Max, still like him, and think a lot of his great playing.

After the Rosens had gone from Delancey Street to capture Europe I looked around for another barber. It took me a full year to discover him, on Mulberry Street, between a pastry-shop and a grocery store—a good barber, an excellent one, and with a beautiful tenor voice. Bonatesta was and is his name.

And every time I came I found him singing—good, jolly, round Bonatesta, perhaps a little over-perfumed, a little overfed, a little bit too flashy, but perfectly groomed and teethed.

Busy? From early morning to late at night. For everybody liked the singing barber. And Bonatesta was no robber.

He shaved you or trimmed your hair without forcing the "best" scalp treatment or the "special" face-massage on you.

But last summer I remarked something very unusual in my man. He sang less frequently, looked worried, and began to extort the usual little extras from me and from all the others.

Then one day I found him much agitated; indeed, too agitated to perform any work.

"What's the matter, Bonatesta?" I asked.

"Wait, wait; you see to-morrow," he answered. "Something big, big!" And was unwilling to give further information.

The following morning Mulberry Street was covered with large posters announcing the opening of a grand opera company of which my friend Bonatesta was the chief tenor. Indeed, his name was smeared over the whole of the large red poster. Knowing the basis on which such companies are organized by shaky managers, I understood at once the basis for the little extras, the hair-balsams and the massages and the sudden increase in price of all work in Bonatesta's shop.

Very soon after that the place changed owners. Opera is so very expensive!

And now, Bonatesta being only a salaried man in the place which he formerly owned—before the venture in grand opera—he no longer sings while working. He has lost his sleekness, his sure-footedness, his joviality. His forehead, which was so innocent of any sign of thought or worry, is now deeply furrowed.

He does not sing.

"Why don't you sing, Bonatesta?"

"This is a barber shop, no opera-house," he answers.

Formerly he considered himself a barber with a beautiful voice, but now he thinks of himself as an unhappy great singer who has to work as a barber. So he has become a bore.

He is now trying to rake together enough money to appear anew in some "opera."

I am already in search of a new artist of the shears and razor.

Further down on the Bowery stands the old Thalia Theater, in which all the old and the new farces by Italian masters as well as the tragedies and melodramas are being repeated. Across from it is the Mori Theater, the former Miner's Theater of old fame, and still another theater where the Lipzin Theater once was. There are occasional presentations there of plays and players that for artistic merit have no counterpart anywhere in the theatrical history of New York. I am speaking of Mimi Aguglia, the Sicilian actress, whose performance of Oscar Wilde's "Salome" ranks with that of the greatest actresses of all time. She and Grasso, whose stay in the city was such a very short one, are at present the greatest living exponents of the Italian school of acting. It is curious that Mimi should have failed on Broadway because of her slight accent in English, when so many others whose English is in no way better than hers, but whose accent belongs to a different nationality, have succeeded so well.

There was another Italian theater, the old Garibaldi Theater, on Fourth Street near Third Avenue. It has been demolished. A shirt-factory stands on its site. Alla Nazimova saw her start in this country there. I well remember her playing there with Orlieneff, the Russian actor, who was also her teacher. Emma Goldman, the anarchist writer and orator, had acted as the impresario. The hall was not heated, and as some of the seats were broken or had been completely torn away, people sat on overturned lemon-boxes, with their coats on, their collars up, and their hats well over their ears. I shall never forget the performances of Ibsen's and Gorky's plays in that cold theater. There was no scenery and no lighting, to speak of . . . but what acting, what sincerity, what enthusiasm!

There are four daily newspapers and one weekly, all of them in the Italian language. Unfortunately, the writing is so badly sprinkled with English that the more cultured of the Italians of the neighborhood are continually protesting against it. "La Folia" is a humorous weekly, and by far the best paper of the five. There used to be another weekly, edited by Hugo d'Annunzio, the great d'Annunzio's son. Quiet and unassuming, Hugo, who is an engineer and an aviator, is the most modest son of a great man I have ever met. As engineer, he works quietly, winning his spurs by his labor instead of deriving any advantage from his lucky birth. I do not know but that, given the choice of spending a few hours in the company of son or father, I should not prefer spending it with the son. No living literary man is so honored, spoiled by his own people as Gabriele d'Annunzio is by the Italians.

It is not correct to speak of Little Italy as the only Italian quarter in the city. Over a million Italians could not, no matter how densely they would populate the area, be crowded in such a small few acres as the district described. There are several other Italian settlements; one on Twenty-sixth and Twenty-seventh Streets and Eighth Avenue down to the river. There is a large Italian settlement in Harlem, another one in the Bronx, still another one in the Morningside district, not to speak of the Italian districts in Brooklyn and East New York. As the Italian population grows it continually extends northward and eastward, pressing out other populations, notably in the Polish and Austrian districts, making incursions into the Greek and French settlements, gaining footholds everywhere, steadily, mercilessly. But Little Italy seems to be the central body, the others outgrowths and tentacles, which spread only to repeat within themselves the same characteristics as the central body. Like any other nationality, the Italian, too, is moving upward as he Americanizes himself, abandoning sometimes the outward characteristics, shaving off his long mustaches, and giving up some of the color about him, yet

forever retaining that foreign something which characterizes him everywhere. *Levatrice* signs spring up wherever he comes to live.

At Tenth Street and Second Avenue, in old St. Mark's Church, is housed the art school Leonardo da Vinci, presided over by the sculptor Onorio Ruotolo. At night hundreds of pupils working in the daytime in factories and shops come to study their favorite arts. The teachers attempt with great devotion and love a renaissance of art and artisanship among their people. It is one of the most interesting places in the neighborhood, and visitors are welcomed in that loud Italian fashion which makes one forget he is intruding.

A. Walkowitz, the musician of the palette, he who uses his brush as a violinist uses the bow, first introduced me to Darino, the sculptor.

We were walking one early morning after an all-night session with Horace Traubel, who has recently joined his great friend Whitman; as I say, we were walking up Fifth Avenue and were silently drinking in the shadow of light thrown by the rising sun when Darino, tall and thin, coming from the opposite direction, called good morning to his friend.

The introduction was as unceremonious as the breakfast we had a few minutes later was simple.

"Will you come to see me one of these days? I am always home after six in the evening," Darino told me before we separated.

"During the day he works in some shop, but at night he models. And what a wonderful artist he is!" So mused Walkowitz.

That very evening I went to see Darino. His studio was a small room on the lower part of Eighth Avenue. A bed, a piano, a table, two chairs, a sculptor's easel, a barrel of plasticine, and the walls, the four of them covered with drawings. Marvelous, delicate drawings.

I found Darino at work at his easel. He was modeling the curly head of a child. His long, thin fingers caressed the wet clay with such lightness one could hardly realize they left any trace where they passed. Like a master pianist evoking a pianissimo passage from the keyboard, he passed his fingers on the lips of clay.

In the evenings that followed I climbed the stairs many a time to see my new friend at work. That curly head he was modeling had entered into my life. I was always thinking of the pure and holy lips of the child, of the clean brow and the almost imperceptible line descending from the throat to the dawn of a bosom.

A month later Darino was still working at the same head. Every night after six, and Saturdays and Sundays the whole day, he worked on that head. The lips became holier. The brow cleaner. The oval-ended chin finer.

"Won't you come out for a walk?" I asked him one Sunday. "You look worn out. A walk would do you good. Come, Darino."

No, he could not come. He had to finish his work. Another few weeks and he would be through with it. Only once or twice had I heard him play on the piano.

He had to play, he explained, to sensitize his fingers. They were coarsening because of the work he was doing in the locksmith's shop. The touch of cold iron was thickening the epidermis. A Mozart sonata was very helpful. He had learned to play the piano for that very purpose.

It was the same with reading great poetry. He had learned to appreciate great poetry. It was very helpful. One's mind had to be so nimble to perceive fine lines. Nuances of line and curve.

And then one day, when I had come up to see him, Darino told me that the curly head was finished. Such loveliness, delicacy, purity of line! The sight of such beauty gladdened my heart—overpowered it. One could almost feel the little mouth breathe, the throat throb.

I said little. Darino, too, was silent. He had wrapped his shoulders with the only blanket, sat on the edge of the cot, and chewed nervously at his thin blond mustache. There was just a hint of fever in his large, blue eyes. The room was cold. Warmth softened the clay too much.

The following morning I climbed the rickety stairs again. I was not alone. I had brought a friend with me to view the masterpiece.

"Come in!" called Darino.

The easel was empty.

"Where—where is curly-head, Darino?"

He showed me the barrel in the corner of the room. "There."

"Why?" It was almost a cry.

"Well? Had not I told you yesterday that it was finished? I have no other plasticine. I am beginning another head to-morrow."

And for years and years he had done the same thing over and over again. He was found dead of starvation the other day.

And speaking of interesting places, one must not forget the famous Barbetta at Thirty-ninth Street and Eighth Avenue, where most of the Metropolitan song-birds come for their meals. Caruso had his steady table there. It was draped in black and remained so for two months after the great tenor's death. A favorite stunt in former days, and it can still be done to-day, was to bet as to who could eat a dollar's worth of food at Barbetta's, the food is so cheap. But there used to be Chianti and Lacrima Christi in mat-covered cool flasks. . . . It is well Caruso died before the best in life was taken from him . . . from us.

Noon-time, after a rehearsal of "La Juive" at the Metropolitan Opera-house, I was waiting in a dingy little hallway of the office at Thirty-ninth Street. That entrance for the artists looked more like a waiting-room on the elevated railway or one of the D. S. C. section offices, where the white wings leave their brooms and shovels after work.

What a contrast between this entrance and that other one for the patrons! And that other one is not extraordinary.

I was waiting to see my friend Carlo Edwards, the chorus leader. I admire him because he has changed his Christian name only to wedge himself into America's great opera-house. Others have made greater concessions for things of lesser importance.

The rehearsal over, the chorus, the principals, and the leaders rushed through the door as boisterously as school-children. A word in French to one another, an Italian greeting, a good-natured slap on the shoulder, "Au revoirs," "Rivedercis," thrown right and left, and the hallway was empty again. Empty, save for a white-haired old gentleman who had come in at the last minute to pick up some smoldering, half-consumed cigars from the floor.

I had turned my head away in pity. The man's clothes were passably clean, though the once black coat had turned green, and the holes in the felt hat showed evidence of innumerable battles with wind and rain. The whole of his countenance stamped him as one of the profession, one who had either dreamed of appearing or had actually appeared on the boards to shout the fatal words, "Alas, poor Yorick! I knew him," or the toreador aria to the gallery. Such dreams leave indelible traces on a human face.

I followed him to the street. He walked slowly to the corner, lit one of the cigars, cocked his hat jauntily on one side, and blew the smoke in full blast to the wind as he closely scanned the passers-by.

"Good morning, Harry," he called to a nattily dressed young actor passing hurriedly by.

"Good morning, old man," was the answer.

A little later another acquaintance passed and was greeted in a familiar fashion. An hour, two hours later, the old man was still on the corner of the street, calling greetings to bediamonded young men and to over-painted women in fur coats.

The following day, before Broadway's business began, he was at his post. He buttonholed a leisurely strolling young man, locked his arm in his, and walked with him to the office entrance.

"Bonjour, signor; bonjour, maestro."

Left alone, he looked to the right and left, eager to know

whether somebody had seen him walk arm in arm and shake hands with the maestro. He planted himself again at the corner, in the middle of the sidewalk and, as he saw one of the singers coming, walked over to greet him.

"Bonjour, Martin. I just had a long conversation with the maestro. We spoke about you."

"So!"

"Yes. I told him that in my days the orchestra was kept more subdued. It 's no use—we old fellows know."

"Excuse me, I 'm in a hurry, old man. Many thanks for mentioning me to the maestro."

"Have you a dollar, perhaps . . ."

"No, no, not a centime, old man." And as he walked away he called over his shoulder, "Thanks for mentioning me to the maestro."

"I did, Martin. I told him your voice did not carry and that you sang off pitch."

But the other was already within the door of the office.

A little later the gray-haired old fellow buttonholed another man.

"I was just talking to the maestro. . . ."

"I have no time, old man."

"I mentioned your name to him."

The other slowed up.

"So! That *was* nice."

"Can you let me have a dollar?"

The most interesting family in the city is that of d'Angelo—builders of churches. The father is an architect, the oldest son is a sculptor, the second one a painter, and the third one, the youngest, a sculptor again. They live and work together. It has been so in their family for several generations; some pretend since the Renaissance in Italy. They have always been builders of churches. Only one name is signed to the work of all of them. And theirs is beautiful work, honest, faithful as work is seldom done at present.

At their shop visitors are not welcome. These people, like the old builders of cathedrals, live only for one thing: their work.

## CHAPTER VII

### THE AMERICAN QUARTER: GREENWICH VILLAGE

IT is right that the only distinctive American quarter in New York should be where it is, on the site of the old Indian village, the Sapokanikan, where the Indian planted tobacco on the sweet meadows that lay between the North River and the Minetta Waters. Though so near to the Italian quarter, once part of the village, now practically merging with it, it is so distinctive that the streets which still belong to the Village are easily distinguished from the others. The Village has not been made after a definite plan like most of the other streets above Canal Street, which have been laid out in advance by the city engineers, but it has grown. Lane after lane between neighboring houses was widened out in the most convenient way, without thought to the future development of the streets as at present. It is why this part of New York presents such a resemblance to the network of streets in the Montmarte in Paris, to certain quarters of New Orleans and Philadelphia, and has not been affected by the city plan of New York.

From a bird's-eye view, the haphazard winding of streets and alleys is that of a wild garden grown without much aid by the hand of man. No twenty-story buildings rise suddenly on the land between shacks. No industrial cupolas darken and danken the streets; for the Minetta Water, though no longer on the surface, is still lustily flowing underneath the ground, thus making it impossible, or too costly, to erect tall buildings on the shallow foundations, as those who have attempted to do so have learned much to their annoyance and cost. The East Side branch of Minetta flows underneath, less than fifty feet below the surface, east of Fifth Avenue through Twentieth and Twenty-third Streets, in a straight line to the southwest corner of Union Square. Another branch crosses Washington Square and flows through Minetta Street to the North River between Charlton and Houston Streets.

On the ground encompassing Fifth and Sixth Avenues, the Minetta Water was not so very long ago a very sweet lake, on which the Dutch burghers, when Greenwich Village was yet the Bossen Bouerie, fished for trout. A little further westward, and up to the present docks of the Cunard and White Star Lines, there was good duck-shooting in the wooded land this side of the shore.

From a few houses erected there by thrifty farmers because of the quality of the land, after the settlement of New Amsterdam, the Bossen Bouerie grew to a good-sized village by the time Governor Van Twiller decreed it was his own property and used practically the whole of it for a tobacco plantation.

There is something indefinable that has remained about this part of New York, which distinguishes it from any other quarter in the city. That sweet smell which emanated formerly from the tall poplars and the woodland about it, and the sweet earth and clear water, still lingers in the air. A slow tranquillity, as if one were away from the mad industrial rush about the few acres which form this district, seizes one as soon as he dips into one of the narrow curving streets winding capriciously hither and thither, with that old carelessness that hath no regard for time, and no hurry to get somewhere by the straightest line.

So much has been written about the Village in the papers and magazines that now every visitor from the Far West or the North or the South, upon coming to New York, wants to take a look at it, as if it were a menagerie or a show-place. Booths and tea-shops and stores, cabarets, dancing-places, and all sorts of fake attractions are dotting the lips of the Village and poisoning them. Only the heart remains pure, as it has been, of all this pretense. To the stranger who has only heard about it but not lived in it, to the occasional slummer and passer-by, Greenwich Village means a sort of wild place where pretended poets, pretended painters, and pretended writers prance about with their bob-haired, bare-legged women in extravagant dress, playing at art, fooling away time with no care or regard for their own morals or the morals of their neighbors, exhibiting themselves, so to say, to the ridicule of the rest of the world. Even New Yorkers, who should know better, look upon Greenwich Village as strange territory, as upon an exotic growth which has been allowed to remain where it is. New Yorkers treat the Village as if it were a foreign country, when as a matter of fact it is the most American of all districts. It may not be the most New Yorkish of all, but it is certainly the most American, for here you find people from all over the country, frequently the best from everywhere, working, laboring, to voice the spirit of the country.

Greenwich Village has been the artistic center of the country for more than a half-century now. Poe lived here, Washington Irving, Mark Twain, Thomas Paine. Of the present generation of writers and artists I know of no center in the world where there are gathered in one locality as many as there are here. There is Theodore Dreiser, living in St. Luke's Place, facing the St. Luke's Park, working with his heavy head, too heavy even for his big body, held in his hands at the open window, trying to capture a mood or a color, laboring with words, arranging and rearranging them, with seldom a respite from his labors. I have never yet met Dreiser in his studio without a feeling that though he was pleased to be interrupted, to have an excuse not to work for the little hour that I spent with him, he also resented being interrupted from doing his work. No, you cannot get him to live anywhere else but in the Village, of which he knows every house, every inch of ground, acquainted with most of the people about him, with his landlord and the landlord's agent, and the janitor and the children of the janitor, knowing what each one of them is doing and how each one of them is getting on in this world. And had I no scruples of robbing Dreiser of one of his stories, I could tell a most extraordinary tale he told me about the scullery tramp he employs to clean his room from time to time.

And should you find out where Dreiser lives you are next door to the working-room of Sherwood Anderson, whose work has attracted so much favorable and adverse attention from all sides. He, too, is a hard worker. He, too, is a great lover of the Village and has come directly to it from Chicago, as Dreiser has come, without even dreaming of taking up his abode elsewhere. You can occasionally meet them both, walking one behind the other, Sherwood the younger one, with the big black eyes he has inherited from an Italian grandmother riveted to the ground. His forehead is partly covered by the blond tuft of his Scotch ancestors. A muffler is wrapped well around his neck, under the heavy coat tightly buttoned over his sturdy body.

I am yet to know a better raconteur than Sherwood. Breakfasting with him across the table at the French Pastry-shop, I have many a time forgotten that it was a working day which had only begun. Tales of the Middle West, imitations of conversations with farmers and working-people, anecdotes of his friends in Chicago; of Ben Hecht's innumerable business ventures, upon which he grows so enthusiastic until they fail; and of Carl Sandburg's strumming upon the ukulele while he shouts with a thick tongue the verses he has just written; and of wanderings with his father, who knew the slang of every trade and the craft of none and obtained temporary jobs on his conversational charm.

And to go from this heavily masculine type to the lightest, there is the little home Edna St. Vincent Millay has just built not far from Cherry Lane, a crooked, narrow little street that reminds one of Venice, a toy house in which none but she, tiny, light, and skipping, as aërial as her own verses and as harmonious in movement, lives. No one, on passing her slight, modest, gay little figure, hopping down one of the streets, in her bare head and with a shawl negligently thrown across her narrow shoulders, would suspect that he is in the presence of America's most charming poetess.

On Macdougal Street near Washington Square is the Provincetown Playhouse, celebrated now because it was the original home of Eugene O'Neill's plays, before their phenomenal leap to Broadway and fame. O'Neill, too, is a Villager. I remember when some years ago, just returned from the sea, he had brought with him some of the plays which have since made him famous, and some germs of plays he is still writing. We were having breakfast together in the Washington Square apartment of John Reed —Jack, big Jack, beloved by all, who has since died in Russia and was buried in the Kremlin at Moscow. Floyd Dell was there, also. We were discussing plans for a new theater. I do not believe the total capital of all present then was a hundred dollars. And yet what enthusiasm! This enthusiasm made it possible for the one-act plays that were first presented in the lecture-room of the Liberal Arts Club. The stage was nothing but the speaker's platform elongated and widened a little. A play by Floyd Dell, a play by Reed, and a play by O'Neill were presented to an enthusiastic audience of friends. And because of the interest aroused immediately, the stable next door, which had come into disuse because of the advent of the automobile, was rented for a larger theater. It seemed a very dangerous undertaking then. But the young men put their hands to the wheel. Within a few weeks the stable was transformed into a theater, and where the horse-manger or something else had been, a stage was erected. The Provincetown Playhouse is the most significant thing that has happened in American dramatics. The Washington Square Players, the Theater Guild, the Little Theater Movement that has since spread over the country, received its baptism here.

I met O'Neill again the other day. How well he wears success and fame! He has remained the same unaffected, quiet soul. The same passionate seeker of truth. The same uncompromising artist that he has been. A little mellowed but just as enthusiastic, with as much confidence and as much interest in the Provincetown Playhouse, which does not bring him a cent, as he has ever had; forever writing a new play for it, directing its destinies, much more concerned with what happens there than with his Broadway audiences and Broadway managers.

Many other efforts have seen their beginnings here. Djuna Barnes's plays, Edna St. Vincent Millay's plays, first of which is her now famous "Aria da Capo," Schnitzler, Strindberg; whatever was too good and too uncommercial for Broadway, and yet had artistic value, has seen its first production there.

Another former Villager, who now is too busy to come down frequently, is Charles Edison, Thomas Edison's son. Witty, whimsical, poetic, he is the friend of many whose names were not known until a few years ago. And his little theater that was, on Ninth Street and Fifth Avenue, the little Thimble Theater, has also been an effort toward something better on the theatrical stage. There is Jo Davidson, the famous sculptor, with his studio in the heart of the Village. And Mrs. Whitney's studio with the perpetual exhibition of the work of young artists from the neighborhood.

Of painters there are no end living in the Village. There is Jerome Bloom, Maurice Becker, Popini, Paléologue; and that most charming and playful of all cartoonists, Al Frueh, whose home is on Perry Street. Cesare, Stengel, Auerbach Levy, Jerome Myers, and a hundred others whose names are not on the tip of my pen.

You can meet any of these masters and worshipers of clay, the palette, and canvas hurriedly going down the street in their working smocks, to breakfast or lunch, or on a sudden excursion to a paint-shop in the neighborhood. I do not believe there is any other district in which people labor as faithfully and as constantly as in the Village, despite the vulgar opinion to the contrary. Almost fifty per cent of the literature in America is written here, and a far greater percentage of the painting done in this country is by people living in the Village. Almost all the sculptors' studios are within its radius. All that is real in modern music—I am not speaking of jazz and rag—but most of the members of the International Composers' League and the Guild of Modern Musicians, Varese, Ruggles, Salzedo, Eve Gauthier, are Villagers. And if you happen to be on an afternoon in Washington Place between Sixth Avenue and Sheridan Square, you will meet a short, graceful lady of uncertain age, walking slowly up and down, wrapped in a fiery red mantilla, with her bobbed golden hair hanging loosely and uncovered. It is Madame Georgette Leblanc, Maurice Maeterlinck's former wife, in her own right an interesting artist, writer, poet, singer. She came from Paris to . . . the Village.

The various stories and articles about the Village that have spread have helped to root the idea that the Village is composed of the idlers of the country. The contrary is true. The Village may not be and is not the most New Yorkish of all the quarters, but it is the most American, as a glance at the above-named celebrities will prove. Few of them are native New Yorkers. They have come from the Middle West, and the South, and the Northwest. But on coming here and on trying to find their own milieu, they have gravitated toward the most likely place. It is unjust, criminal almost, to libel the numerous serious artists who have wasted their lives in hunger and starvation in cold garrets, and refused to abate their artistic standards. Every once in a while an item in the paper ends such a struggle. No road is as hard to travel as the road to artistic fame. For one who succeeds, five hundred equipped as well if not better, but with less luck or personality, perish by the side.

There are, of course, as there are in Paris and in other big capitals wherever artists congregate, a number of men and women who play at art. Those who have read Murger's "La Vie de Bohême," or who have seen the opera with the same name, will think of the number of professional students in the Latin Quarter, young men grown old on their parents' monthly allowances, wearing their students' caps on their gray heads, who have danced and visited cabarets in school hours, consorting with women as light-footed and gay-hearted as themselves. Surely *Musette* was as light as she was portrayed, and there are a thousand sisters of hers doing the same thing the world over. But no one in France thinks that this is all that is being done in the Latin Quarter and Montmartre. For almost every bit of literature of France has come out from there; every bit of art in all the branches. Montmartre and the Latin Quarter was the home of Zola and Anatole France, and Balzac and Maupassant, and Debussy and Vidor and Rodin. They, too, have undoubtedly had their hours of gaiety and abandon, but who dares look at all they have produced, their tremendously prolific labor, and reproach them such recreations?

Like Montmartre, the Village needs no apology, and this is after all a travel-book. But for those who may be tempted to visit the Village, attracted to breakfast at a piggery or a crumpery, and dine and dance at a Green Horse or a Black Moon, or shiver among pirates on Christopher Street, or look into the fireplace of Romany Marie's shack, I want to say that this is not the "goings on" of the Village, but merely the fringe of it. The young men in flowing neckties and long hair they will see exchanging jokes and kisses at the tables with the bobbed-haired, smocked young ladies are not students, but those who have come there to masquerade as such, little clerks of the neighborhood, or young students from the adjoining New York University, who come here to play the devil smartly. Those who belong to the Village, the real ones, are not to be seen, or are seldom seen, in any of these places.

Until publicity was given to the Village, say about ten years ago, I remember when there was not one single place of the kind. We used to go down, a group of us, to Polly's on Macdougal Street in the basement of the Liberal Arts Club, and by chipping in we got a common breakfast or a lunch. Some unfortunate colleague of ours, on needing money, once described this place and sold the story to a newspaper, whereupon the Village became a newspaper source and center of attraction. In time people began to go to the Village for lack of something better to do, and thrifty New England ladies changed the aspect of quiet into a fair where all things are bartered and sold. Many of the New England ladies who have come here to study are the cause of it, for they saw immediately how an honest penny could be turned, and opened their bead-shops and toy-shops and antique shops and tea-shops. I venture to say that nine tenths of those shops are in charge of Bostonians.

"Where is the Village? Where does it begin and where does it end?"

Hypolite Havel, an inveterate Villager, once answered this question, "The Village has no geographical delineation; it is a state of mind."

The Village extends from the south side of Washington Square and Macdougal Street, clear across to the North River, swerving off on the side to comprise King Street and Vandam Street from the beginning of Macdougal Street to the other end, and northward practically to the river at Thirteenth Street, and down again to Sixth Avenue.

Its streets, except a few, and the avenues, Sixth, Seventh, and Eighth, were not cut originally. The houses, most of them, had not been constructed in one street line with some definite plan in mind. As there were large tracts of land between farms, the original inhabitants built their homes on the best sites of their particular plots of land, turning the entrances and windows whichever way they thought best. As the adjoining plots were occupied and new houses were built, lanes were formed between them. And when still more houses were built they somewhat faced these lanes, although not in any regular fashion. The result was that when Greenwich was incorporated into the city of New York, and the streets were being made to conform, it was found that the extension of Fourth Street

from the East Side crossed Tenth and Twelfth Streets and ended at Thirteenth Street.

There are streets in the Village that suddenly leave off and run away from you, and you have to dodge and turn until you pick them up again three or four blocks away. There are others that stick to the traveler, no matter how hard he tries to avoid them. You leave them and dodge into another street, only to find out that you are still in the same one. There are any number of wooden shanties left to fall apart by themselves, by the grace of wind and rain. Litigations, because the different inheritors are at odds, and because of lack of order in the title-papers, make them belong to nobody. Indeed, not long ago nine families on Commerce Street discovered they had paid rent to some one who, having seen the house vacant some ten years before, had moved into a part of it and had rented the rest to tenants. For eight years these people had paid rent before they became aware of the fact that the house did not belong to the man from whom they rented it, and that he himself did not know to whom it belonged. Had the Building Department of the city not protested against the lack of fire-escapes, that man would still be collecting rent. It can be done again and again.

Most of the houses in the neighborhood cannot be sold because of litigation. Some of them are twenty or twenty-four inches outside of their ground limits. Most of them are at odds with the rules and regulations of the Building Department. But all of them are beautiful to look at, with something about them which makes them distinct from the houses anywhere else. Age mellows the color of brick and copings.

It is easy to see that these houses were built by their original owners with a view of inhabiting them themselves and not of renting them. These are houses made to live in and not to speculate with. Long and beautiful French windows and wide oak doors, hung on hammered hinges, are a delight to the eye. Everything feels a regard and care for beauty of line—the roof, the chimney-stacks, and little flower-gardens in the front yards of a good many of these houses. It is a pleasant surprise, on coming from up town, suddenly to see that row between Twelfth and Thirteenth Streets on Seventh Avenue, with wide wooden balconies and verandas in front of the houses set back forty feet from the sidewalk, and beautiful flower-patches and trees in the little front yards; and this in New York, where every inch of ground is appraised at big amounts of money. There are beautiful green vines creeping over the old moldy wood, and though the insides of most of these houses have been remodeled and changed, still enough of the old is left to show what it has been.

All through the Village one frequently encounters such sights. There are trees in the back yards, old poplar-trees and acacias which emit a sweet smell on their blooming days, and patches of green everywhere. There is less hanging of wash-lines fluttering in the wind here than anywhere else. And the curtains in the windows, in sheen-colored gauzes, are a study in themselves. There is the Cherry Lane district, with the Cherry Lane Theater built on the site of one of the old stables; and situated on it and spreading from it a multitude of little one-family houses with large studios on the top, for painters and sculptors. There is Washington Mews with its row of little blue-painted houses, with a large iron gate toward Lafayette Street, in itself a little gem set apart from any of the houses in the city. Another similar artistic corner which makes you forget where you are is Macdougal Alley; and on Eighth Street is Cat Alley, not in New York's Baedeker, but well known to Villagers. From midnight to sunrise it is the rendezvous of all the cats in the district. And what battles for supremacy are fought here!

There is a profusion of originality in building everywhere. Even those who build to-day, artists and writers who have succeeded in getting enough money to do so in these days of expensive construction, build according to their own dreams and their own necessity. Nest-holes, or whole floors with only one room, large and wide, so as to give one space to walk around while he thinks or dreams.

There are a great number of good old folks, old inhabitants of the Village who have lived there for generations, who would not change or think of leaving it for any other district. The old folks of St. Luke's Place, or Commerce Street, or Barrow Street, seem to have been considerably disturbed by the sudden inrush of visitors and slummers in the neighborhood. And rents, too, have gone up considerably. Garrets which once rented for eight dollars a month now rent for twenty times that amount; because some up-towner has taken it into his head that he, too, should have a litttle "nest" in the Village. There is one particular house on Bank Street, in which I lived for several years, paying what was then the large rent of thirty dollars a month. To-day it rents for exactly eight times that sum. And Bank Street is anything but in the center of the Village.

There used to be a French bakery shop just around the corner from where I lived, and several other French families were living in the neighborhood. The Village was once a center of the Parisians living in New York, probably because it reminded them so strongly of their own Montmartre. But on visiting my former habitat I found that the French bakery shop, which had stood there for over a hundred years and had been in the family for several generations, had suddenly become a tea-shop. My old French friends were compelled to leave. And because the other French families could not get their *croissant* and their long, crisp baked bread, they, too, have moved away to other places where such things might be obtainable.

The building where Thomas Paine died, on Grove Street, although there is a bronze tablet on the wall commemorating this fact, is now a restaurant gaudily painted outside. The home of Mark Twain is being torn down to make room for some tall tenement-house. The Garret on Washington Square still lives, but it, too, will soon be torn down for some industrial edifice that is to be erected in its place.

Because of the tremendous rentals asked now, the artists have had to move elsewhere, leaving their rooms for those who are in a more lucrative employment than theirs, advertising illustrators, jazz-players, and bubble-makers, who want to live in the Village. Only those who own their homes in the neighborhood, and the old inhabitants who have lived there, are in a position to remain, to withstand the inrush of slummers and sensation-seekers, and keep the only American quarter in the city a distinct entity.

On West Thirteenth Street an old wooden house, No. 38, marks the slanting line of the old Union Road, which was

frequented by the stage-coaches connecting Greenwich Village with New York. There used to be a monument to General Wolfe, the hero of Quebec. It was this that gave the street once the name of Monument Lane. But evidently the English soldiers at the close of the Revolution took away with them the memorial to their gallant countryman, afraid lest the victors might mishandle it. There are no definite data as to this fact. Some assert that the monument was in the form of an obelisk and was taken back on board by the English; some, that it has never left the country. At any rate, it has never been traced. It may be resting somewhere in an underground cellar in the neighborhood.

Where the Washington Arch now is, on the site of the old Potter's Field, was the old public gallows, from which much less than a hundred years ago culprits were swung in the air. Looking on from the front stoop of an inhabitant of Washington Square, an old man still living has recorded how he saw the execution of Rose Butler in 1822, a negro done to death for murder or for witchcraft.

There were many French farmers who had neat gardens a little southward from what is known as Greenwich Village proper, and toward Franklin and Leonard Streets, in the old South Greenwich. There are still many houses on West Eleventh Street which retain their old French cottage building characteristics, with wooden stairs away from the street, from what was once a lane, inclining terraces, with little trellised gardens within. On a summer's day, peeking in through the wooden fence, one can still see leisurely French families dining on warm evenings outdoors under their trellised arbors.

In memory of Thomas Paine, Barrow Street was once named Raisin Street, a corruption of "Reason," to commemorate Thomas Paine's most famous book, "The Age of Reason." And the records of John Randall, the city engineer who prepared the present city plan, speak of how he used to see the old philosopher sitting at the south window of the first-story room in a house on that street. The sash was raised, and a small table or stand was placed before him, with an open book upon it, which he appeared to be reading.

"He had his spectacles on. His lower lip rested upon his hand, and his chin rested between the thumb and fingers of his hand. His right hand lay upon his book, and a decanter containing liquor of the color of rum or brandy was standing next his book or beyond it. I never saw Thomas Paine at any other place or in any other position." Thus writes the careful Mr. Randall.

And there are other records speaking of the old philosopher, who, when he escaped from the surveillance of Madame Bonneville and her noisy children, would rush to the ale-house for another supply of rum, his hat well over his brow, and his silent face grimly set in defiance.

What tended mostly to develop Greenwich Village from a farm to a city was its excellent natural drainage. The soil underlying it for fifty feet is pure sand. Every time an epidemic of smallpox or yellow fever hit the city of New York, below Canal Street, the inhabitants, loading their household goods and their merchandise, would rush away to the country—to Greenwich Village. The thrifty burghers would then put up shanties to accommodate them. Upon the farms and meadows little wooden stores, selling provender, were erected. Where Bank Street now is there used to be a corn-field, but at the corner of it, during one of the last great epidemics, one of the city bankers erected a branch of his bank in order to continue his business with the people who had fled in great masses to the more salubrious part of the island.

From every epidemic a number of people remained to

live, so as to insure greater security against disease and pestilence for themselves and their children. During the great pestilence of 1822, not only did people come to live in Greenwich, but even the custom-house, the post-office, the banks, the insurance offices, and the printers of newspapers located themselves in the upper part of Broadway, building houses, some temporary and some permanent, in the heart of the Village. Indeed, on West Eleventh Street an enterprising Mr. Sykes erected a wooden house capable of accommodating three hundred boarders. Even the Brooklyn ferry-boats began to accommodate Greenwich Village at the foot of Eleventh Street.

Perhaps one of the most interesting land romances is the development of the Sailors' Snug Harbor. Captain Randall bought the twenty-one acres of land lying east of Fifth Avenue as far as the Bowery and Washington Square, east and north, in 1790, for about twenty-five thousand dollars. It was a beautiful piece of farm land. He bequeathed it in 1820 or thereabouts to the Sailors' Snug Harbor, with the provision that the grain and vegetables grown on the place should be sufficient to nourish its inmates. It produced then food in the value of about four thousand dollars. Within a short time the executors saw that they could derive greater profit by leasing the ground to others. To-day the ground-rent of this twenty-one acres brings more than half a million dollars a year profit; the whole thing was accomplished in less than a hundred years. There are still men who remember the free and wide meadows on that site. There are still such who have eaten vegetables grown on that place, where to-day stand innumerable houses, erected at the leaseholders' own expense; for not an inch of ground owned by the Sailors' Snug Harbor has ever been sold.

There are any number of houses in the Village which are not sold for similar reasons. It is why they remain as they were a hundred years ago.

An interesting bit of old New York can be seen at Eleventh Street and Sixth Avenue, back of the French Pastry-shop. It is a small triangle with the ground raised above the level of the street, in which is part of what was once the second Jewish cemetery. When Eleventh Street was cut through to the West Side, the rest of the cemetery was swept away by the street. Another Jewish cemetery was then formed at Sixth Avenue and Twenty-first Street on the West Side. From the rear windows of the dry-goods stores which face the street the leaning old gray tombstones can yet be seen, for they are still, in a desultory way, cared for. The Hebrew inscriptions and the dates plainly marked on the tombstones are witness to the early date at which the Jews lived in the city.

Stretching down to what was once Love Lane, Twenty-first Street, going directly eastward, is another branch of the American quarter of New York. There are conflicting dates as to when it was first established. I mean Gramercy Park proper and its neighborhood. I doubt whether any house there is more than a hundred years old. Many very tall apartment-houses have already been erected on the southeast side of Gramercy Park, thus destroying a good deal of the former enchantment of the place. For there are any number of houses in that neighborhood with little gardens in front and in the back yards. Doubtless it was the later merchant nobility that came to settle around there. A good many of the houses on Gramercy Park have changed from private dwellings into clubs, and some of the old inhabitants have found it much more convenient to rent their homes at the exorbitant prices they command than to live there. If instead of a district it were a pottery, one could characterize it as Late American. In spite of its air of distinction, it has something foreign about it, something mixed in its brownstone, florid architecture smacking of our architects' visits to Italy and the more stately France.

Of course no one passing through East Nineteenth Street could miss the residence of Robert Chanler, familiarly known to his friends as Sheriff Bob Chanler. It suffices but to glance to the left side, until one sees a painted giraffe in bas-relief over his portal, with its curious heavy set-in door, looking very much like the entrance to a fortress, to know immediately one is before an original existence. But this is not half as interesting as the man living within. Big, curly-headed, heavy Bob Chanler, looking very much like the picture of the elder Dumas, is one of America's greatest decorative painters and the scion of one of the oldest American families. Weary and tired, I have many a time knocked at his door and been received in as friendly a fashion as if it were an oasis in the desert and he the Arab owner of the tent. And something better than dates and camel's-milk has always been offered to me.

What a man and what a house! From the stairway to the studio in the garret, it is decorated and painted in the most fantastic way, with serpents and grotesque animals crawling over one another in the most vivid and subtle colors, red tongues hanging from leaping dragons, and porcupines embossed in gold jumping over one anther—Naiads and sylphs and giraffes and elephants, pell-mell, grouped only because of harmony of color and movement and not because of the natural proximity of their habitats. All that is weird is painted on that stairway.

The rooms are full of costly furniture, old and antique, just holding together. The walls are done in sudden patches of yellow and black, and the color-scheme of the ceilings is deliberately a mystifying one. And then suddenly the large studio on the roof, in which Bob is working away at the most unusual hours, leaving occasionally a gathering of friends at the dinner-table, in the midst of the most hilarious or serious conversation, to go up to his studio and daub a few brushes here and there, on one of the numerous huge decorative canvases at which he is working simultaneously.

And there is no telling what Bob might say or do. Garbed in a pair of loose denims, over which hangs an ample Russian blouse buttoned securely at the neck, with a sash around it, a pair of loose *babouches* on his feet, he sits for hours on his heels upon the couch, apparently oblivious to all that is going on about him. But suddenly something strikes. He jumps up. He slips away into his work-room or to his bed to sleep.

I do not want to say that visitors are welcome. But they are very frequently welcome when there is one of Chanler's exhibitions of his screens on the lower floor of the building. And if one should be so favored as to be invited for one of his evenings, one may be certain of meeting what is most distinguished in the world of art and letters.

And now that we have jumped about in such a hasty way through the American quarter, I must apologize for having treated it in so intimate a manner. For it may be very unbecoming in a comparative stranger. But it is done in love. I know of no other quarter on this continent where I would rather live and labor than this one. So much of what has been done stimulates one to work. The Village presents itself like an unusual romance. A romance of action. Come into being because of recurring pestilences in another part of the city. Come into being where there had been lakes and fields and woods, only yesterday.

Yet there is nothing of newness, no odor of fresh varnish and no polish, to assail one's nostrils and eye. No shrill cries in an unfamiliar language. It is all mellowed by time, and saved from industrial invasion by the nature of its very soil.

Greenwich Village. I love it!

# CHAPTER VIII

## THE GIPSY QUARTERS

GEORGE BORROW, relating his wanderings with the Gipsies, makes them speak frequently of the "affairs of Egypt," when they want to refer to intimate things relating to the essentials of their life. He makes his Gipsies consider Egypt their original home, gives the impression that they still have secret ties to the land of the Pharaohs, and thereby confirms the original error which gave to the Gipsies their name, from the corruption of the word "Egyptian." Had he made the Gipsies speak of the affairs of the Balkans instead of the affairs of Egypt, he would have been nearer the truth. For of the total number of Gipsies living to-day, more than three quarters live in the Balkans, the greater part in Rumania and Hungary. That is why in New York the Gipsies quarter themselves chiefly among the Balkan peoples. The Rumanian Gipsies live in the Rumanian quarter, the Polish Gipsies in the Polish quarters, the Hungarian in the Hungarian quarters, with a continual migration from one country to another, from one quarter to another, which frequently is marked off only by an intermediate street or by the width of the sidewalk. And yet there is a great difference in the character and language of those Gipsies. Only the older ones understand the Calo of the Balkans, which is the speech of the European Gipsy. The younger ones, especially those who have learned English, are fast forgetting their original tongue, much to the annoyance of the older ones, who denounce them constantly as traitors to the fold.

To speak of Gipsy quarters is, however, a bit dangerous,

for there are Gipsy quarters only in the winter. Spring sees them off, departing as suddenly as they arrived, leaving no trace behind them other than a few disappointed old women whose cures they have undertaken, a few grieved maidens to whom they have promised love-potions which they have never given, and a few superstitious men who have been in the habit of going to them regularly to have their fortunes read and advice given on how to confound their enemies. For it is the delusion of every Balkan man or woman, including the Poles and the Russians, that some enemy, a horde of enemies, in league with the evil one, is continually dodging their steps, undoing what they have done or attempted to do. And even the white plague, which so frequently overtakes the Balkan younger element in the narrow, unsanitary quarters in which they live in the city, transported from high mountains to dark cellars, is attributed more to sorcery than to lack of air and proper nourishment and to work under unendurable conditions. The Gipsy promises to confound the Satana, the Dracu, the Strigoi, or whatever name the evil one carries in a Balkan tongue.

But go they must, as soon as spring comes. And their departure is as sudden as it is unobserved. The curtained empty stores in which they have lived along the streets are suddenly discovered in the morning uncurtained. The big downy beds in which they rolled themselves for the night, the only furniture except trunks and bundles in a Gipsy's house, are removed as quietly as only feathered downs can be moved. When the neighborhood wakens in the morning the Gipsies are gone. Gone to haunt the roads, to weave baskets from the rear end of a wagon to which a lean nag is harnessed. Gone to tell fortunes to the villagers and farmers while the men are dealing in automobiles. Since the horse has gone out of fashion the Gipsies have become itinerant automobile dealers. Forever moving onward, though in circles, westward, trading, the Ford that was ridden in the morning becomes a Rolls-Royce in the evening, and will again be a Ford the following day, leaving the difference, by no means negligible, in the pockets of the children of the Ganges River. And clever as they have been at horse dealing, they are still cleverer at buying or selling a car.

In October I had gone to visit my Gipsy friends who should have come in from the west at about that time. There was no trace of them anywhere. Although they had come to the city in September, they had returned to the road, feeling that there were yet three months of good weather ahead of them. And when a Gipsy can be outdoors he is never to be got indoors. When I returned again, three months later, Fourth Street between Avenue A and the East River, Third Street, Second Street, First Street, the heart of the Balkan quarters in New York, were full of them. Not an empty store which had formerly housed a butcher or a grocer but had been taken by them. The windows were curtained off to the top with Turkish patterned gauzes and calicoes; and a beautiful dusky maiden, with her black tresses hanging loosely over her shoulders, and her golden necklaces and bracelets dangling from her neck and arms, was standing outside awaiting her lover from the other street. An old woman, loaded down by the numerous dresses she wore, one on top of the other, and a wolfskin fur coat on top of all, was walking about, followed by a number of impudent gamins, on her way to gossip with friends who had just come from some other part of the country, to learn the tidings of the road.

Big, tall Mathei, fully six feet four inches high, proportionately broad and weighing about three hundred pounds, whom I had known ever since I was a child, had frequently encamped within sight of my home on the Danube. Here he received me with open arms. He had news for me from the other side. But first of all he wanted to show me his new wife. Fully thirty years younger than he is, a beautiful Brazilian Gipsy whom he had married in Mexico and for whom he had paid eight thousand dollars in gold. And so proud was he of her he had weighted her down with jewels and silks. Of course marrying a Brazilian Gipsy had ruled him out of his clan. But he was in love. He expected them to come to their senses. His own family had already forgiven.

The long store, which had once been a butcher's place, was carpeted. Even the walls were hung with thick Oriental rugs, some two inches thick, of all colors and hues. The back half of the store had been curtained off to serve as a bedroom and dining-room. A huge, billowy down mattress was lying on the floor. A coal-stove, red-hot, stood in the center. Two fighting-cocks, which had never left the side of the lady, were peaceably cackling to each other.

Mathei stretched out on his back and asked his wife to dance to the rhythm he was beating with his palms. It was indeed a great delight to him; for no Gipsies dance as well as the Brazilians and the Spanish do, and Mathei was eager to show her off. I had not been there long when his son came in, with his wife, and his daughter with her husband; and also two of his former wives made their appearance. We were a gay company that evening.

"This is a good country," Mathei told me, "except for one thing. Why is the wine so expensive?"

When I told him about the prohibition laws he opened his eyes wide. He had never heard of such a thing. He had thought that because of certain taxes imposed upon the wine—and this idea has been current among all the Gipsies—the good juice had become more expensive.

Across the street from Mathei lived Lupu, a Rumanian Gipsy, the chief of the Rumanian clan in New York. His home, as befits a chief and as if he were still on the road, was a larger one than that of any other Gipsy in the neighborhood. It had formerly been a tailor shop. It was larger and more luxuriously furnished than any other home. By that I mean to say that there were more down beds and thicker layers of carpets, both on the floors and on the walls. A great number of silver trinkets, bells and bracelets, and a considerable number of weapons, swords and blades from Damascus and Teheran, Yataghans from Turkey, Spanish florets, Greek sabers, and muskets and carbines and flint-locks from all countries and all times decorated the walls. A young Gipsy fiddler was sitting near him, ready to play at command. For Lupu had only reluctantly come over here during the late Balkan War, and was pining away,

longing for the more familiar stretches of roads and rivers that he had known for years. And so he kept a young fiddler to play him home songs, to smother his home-sickness.

"But look, Lupu," I said to him, "you are making more money here, I am certain. You are warm in winter. You are not molested. Why should you be so morose?"

"I am a Gipsy chief, supposedly without a home or a country," the roamer and rover answered. "But when the summer is over do I return to Galatz or Braïla, next to my own people, to hear the language that I have always heard, and dance to the tunes I have always danced to, and listen to the people talk about the great deeds of my father or forefathers, or what? No, I come to live in a street populated with people who are themselves strangers here. And my children, you will see them soon. My grandchildren are taken to schools where they kill them so as to teach them to read a few words in a book which they will forget anyhow." And after a few moments' silence he added: "But what is worse, what is much worse, is that there is no joy in our trading. It is not money only." Rising to his feet, he yelled at the top of his voice: "I am a horse-trader! We have been horse-traders for hundreds of years, and there are no horses to trade with here! And I hate the boiling, smoking, horseless things people run around in, which we buy and sell!"

"Why don't you return home?" I asked him. "You have enough money. There will be no difficulty."

Lupu sighed deeply. And then he told me another secret.

"The women won't go. Every one of our women is

making three and four times the amount her man is making. You thought that because people go to school there would not be any fortune-telling, ha? If I told you that my wife is making sixty dollars a day telling fortunes, and that the older they are the more money they make, would you believe me? And women do not care to leave a place where they make money. To them money is everything. If we were to listen to them we should be living in the city here all the time."

As we were speaking an automobile stopped in front of the house, and two well-dressed ladies came in timidly. Had they understood Lupu's glance as he welcomed them and asked them to go beyond the curtained part of the store, they might have hesitated. I heard low murmurs, the broken singsong of the old Gipsy woman who was telling them things in a mixture of French, English, and German. Sighs, gasps, and the clinking of money. I smelled a little incense mixed with sulphur, and heard talk of a black cat at midnight. The whole thing lasted less than five minutes, and the two ladies rushed out with flushed faces and bent shoulders. Lupu's wife came out to greet me, literally licking her chops.

"Cate? How much?" Lupu asked, without turning his head.

"Dece; ten," and she turned her back proudly.

The old chief pulled out his watch, his old Turkish watch which he wound with a key, and pointed with his fingers on the hands. "In less than five minutes, and she only tells me half of what she got."

Another woman followed these two. She was from the neighborhood. She carried a little baby in her arms which seemed to be wasted with some disease. She was behind the curtain. A Hungarian. I heard Hungarian words in the conversation. She remained there for a few minutes. Lupu did not trouble to ask how much that one had given. Then suddenly he leaned back, closed his eyes, and asked the young Gipsy boy to play.

A few minutes later twenty or more Gipsies came in, for in that store lived the whole of Lupu's clan, which virtually formed four families; and the youngsters who did go to school looked pale and emaciated, indeed so pale you could hardly have distinguished them from the other boys of the neighborhood.

But only the older men took it so to heart. The younger element did not seem to care much where they lived, as long as they could have their loves and their drinks and their dances and their music—as long as they make so much money themselves, and their wives always making more.

The women-folk of the coppersmiths and kettle-makers are visited in the daytime by the musicians, whose work is only at night. The musicians, better dressed than the other men of the tribe, in fancy shoes and red neckties, with waxed and oiled hair sleekly combed, carrying their fiddles under their coats, begin their visits from about noon. And there is music in every coppersmith Gipsy household while the man is away, interrupted only by the arrival of some superstitious hunter of fortune-telling; very few of the Gipsy women find it necessary to go abroad to hunt for customers.

At night when the Gipsy musicians have gone each their way to play at weddings, some of the more fortunate ones to cabarets and restaurants, the coppersmith clan is walking around entertaining the wives of the musicians until the small hours of the morning, entertaining them with songs and tales and dances and interminable quarrels and talks. Arranging marriage matches is the chief occupation of the coppersmiths and kettle-makers. And it is no small matter to arrange such a match, considering the love of bargaining of the Gipsies. The mother of the young man transacts the business with the father of the young girl. She generally begins by offering for the bride a mere pittance, a thousand dollars in gold, whereupon the father of the girl takes umbrage, as if it were an insult to his daughter, and he hurls threats that he will kill them all for offending him so.

"Does anybody know something about my daughter that I do not know? Has she misbehaved? Is she sickly? Has her mother ever been ill? And have not my children all lived to be big and strong?" And he points out four stalwart, husky sons with their offspring.

The tumult grows until the people in the neighborhood, thinking the Gipsies are about to kill one another, call the police. The patrol-wagon appears. The neighborhood is abroad and curious. A hundred bronzed vociferating men and women suddenly rise like ghosts from everywhere and make their way into the store. "It is notheeng, just talk." They pacify the policemen.

After such an initial scandal the mother raises her offer with five hundred dollars. Meanwhile, hand in hand, the youngsters, whose fate they are settling, make the rounds of the moving pictures; visit friends, in absolute certainty that within a day or two the affair will be settled satisfactorily; for the mother would be proud to pay a considerable sum for a bride for her son. Or, as one of them told me when on a visit with Miss Fillmore and Mrs. Champenois: "You pay six thousand dollars and get a big, nice healthy girl. You pay three thousand and you don't get a big, nice girl. And a big, nice healthy girl gives birth to big, nice healthy children. And the not nice, big healthy girl does not give birth to big healthy children. And they cost much money for doctor and everything. And then when their papa wants to marry them nobody gives much money for them. It is cheap to pay much money at the beginning."

Of course, nothing is ever said about the bride's dowry —equal if not surpassing the amount paid for her—in silks and jewels and down beds.

They showed me a pretty girl, asking me whether I would not myself be willing to offer even more than six thousand dollars for her. This manner of mating is the cause of the Gipsies' survival. The mating is that of the careful stock-breeder.

A Gipsy wedding in a hall on St. Mark's Place, or in another hall in the neighborhood, is something never to be forgotten when once seen. Such a wedding lasts at least three days. It generally begins on Friday and lasts over Sunday, with four bands of music succeeding one another. The women come to the wedding arrayed in the most gorgeous costumes—in silks and brocades from all the ends of the earth, and jades and rubies and diamonds studded in silver belts and in bracelets hanging and dangling on the brown bare arms and from the red sashes that hold together on the hips the two halves of the ample, colored skirts they wear.

And the men, the older ones especially, wear their own national costumes, the white shirt hanging over the sash, and the wide trousers embroidered at the seams tucked into the high patent-leather boots, and tall, beribboned astrakhan caps on their heads. And they dance and yell and sing and drink in a continual swaying motion, changing rhythms and tempos with sudden interruptions for solo dances and solo songs. The older men and women, always anxious to show the younger ones that they are still alive,

execute the most intricate steps, to the great admiration of the circle of onlookers, who stand with backs bent deeply over them in a circle, clapping their hands and yelling their "Ohe! Ohe! Ohe!"

At midnight of the second wedding night the bride dances. The dance usually begins in a slow walk, but it ends an hour later in a terrifically furious step, in which all those present finally join in a frantic hysteria of limbs, until the bride swoons in the arms of the groom, who himself, not having danced a step, is the only one capable of taking care of her. And he carries her away to his home while the others still dance on.

The wedding festival still continues. The mother and father of the bride are conducted home by part of the guests, who remain with them to continue the festival. And the mother weeps and cries. She has lost her child and berates her husband for having sold her to an unworthy man. The mother and father of the groom have to be brought home, and part of the guests remain with them to continue the festival. And then the nearest relatives are brought home, marching through the streets with the musicians at the head of them, singing softly so as not to disturb the sleepers. Such is a Gipsy wedding in New York—or in Damascus, or in the Carpathian Mountains.

The Gipsies live unmolested in New York, until something happens in the neighborhood. But when the police find no clue to some crime, suspicion is immediately directed toward these mysterious strangers. A number of them are called to the police station, harassed, questioned; and the usual wind-up of such an affair is an order compelling them to leave the neighborhood within twenty-four hours, without the slightest consideration of the hardships it may entail upon them. The Gipsies here are without any protection. No voice is ever raised to defend them. They are also the prey of numerous welfare societies. The Prevention of Cruelty to Children comes to bother them, compelling them to send their children to school, or to dress them in such manner as befits future American citizens, which these children will never be. The truant-officer of the adjoining school is a continual trouble to them. For after he is once inscribed and enrolled, the young Gipsy *danchuck* thinks that he has done his duty and is likely never to appear again until forced to do so. When Lupu or Stan or Vladislav finds himself haled before the judge, the whole clan appears with him, and they cry and weep and gesticulate in a half-dozen tongues to make themselves understood. And the father is fined and ordered to punish his son for truancy. One might as well ask the seal to punish her young for diving.

On First Street, below First Avenue, live the Russian Gipsies, headed by Mishka, who is chief violinist of the tribe. Mishka, met on one of the principal streets of the city, would never be taken for a Gipsy. He is most immaculately dressed. And although swarthy, with a small ear-ring hanging in his left ear, his peculiarities would be taken as the eccentricities of an artist rather than as the characteristics of a race. He speaks French and German fluently, is suave, and has the best of manners. He has played at the Hermitage in Paris and has made his fame on Piccadilly. In Moscow and in Petrograd he was one of the most favored leaders of Gipsy bands in the midnight cabarets. His gifts from his admirers are many. It has taken him a long time to make his peculiar art of playing valuable in New York. But so many of the Russian aristocracy arrived here that numerous Russian inns and cabarets sprang into existence on upper Broadway. The

democratic American is paying for the privilege of being waited upon by a Russian nobleman who serves caviar at two dollars and a half a sandwich and tea at fifty cents a glass. Mishka plays in one of these places to give atmosphere. Two or three hundred dollars a week is as nothing to him. In a good mood he buys a few thousand dollars' worth of jewels for his wife, to subdue her anger when he has been too long away from her; for many are the temptations put in his way. As at home, the Russians who can afford it are anything but niggardly, and their women are very charming.

But when his work is over Mishka returns to his *gadzhika* and his *danchucks,* a half-dozen of them, ranging from ten years down, in a basement store which had once been a coal shop down on First Street. He takes off his Tuxedo and his immaculate white shirt and collar, and dons a Russian blouse, and is at home. He had once, in an attempt to become a regular citizen, moved into one of the apartment-houses of the neighborhood, dressing his wife and his children American fashion and giving himself out as a Russian. He had even bought furniture on the instalment plan from a dealer on Avenue A, with stiff missionwood chairs and rockers and regulation sideboard and brass beds. But before a month was over he had returned to the basement. His quarters had been too much like a house, while the basement is much more like a subterranean tent.

I expect Mishka to make several such attempts in the near future. His American friends, musicians, urge him to become an American. Mishka himself urges his children to go to school, and has indeed made his oldest, a girl of ten, teach him to read and write. It is the beginning of the end of the Mishka clan. I suspect and am afraid that his playing will greatly deteriorate, once he is cut off from his habits, which have been the habits of his ancestors. He already speaks of marrying his daughter to an American boy. The girl herself is trying to subdue the colors of her dress and is ashamed of being known as a Gipsy by her schoolmates. Indeed, the whole Gipsydom of Russian musicians on First Street has been tainted by Americanism. These Gipsies are being mentioned to the other Gipsies of the neighborhood as an example by well-meaning ladies urging the welfare of the children, and by the truant-officer. And because of that there has been a good deal of friction between the Rumanian and Hungarian Gipsies and the Russian Gipsies in New York. The outside world knows nothing about that.

There is not a thing that happens to be against the Balkan *tzigan,* but it is immediately imputed to the intrigues of the Russian ones. As it is, the Gipsies of one nationality have none too much friendship for the Gipsies of another, in spite of Borrow's contention that they form a secret society the world over. It is indeed a rare thing when a Hungarian Gipsy woman marries a Rumanian Gipsy man, or vice versa; and it is still a rarer occasion when a Brazilian Gipsy or a Spanish Gipsy is permitted to enter the clan. A white man or a white woman will be much easier welcomed than a Gipsy of another nationality.

On Third Street, below Avenue A and down to the East River, are housed the Brazilian Gipsies. There was some commotion not long ago when, after a fire in one of the houses, in which Cordoba and his family lived, a mother bear and two little cubs were suddenly seen dragged out into the street. The Cordobas had brought the trio into their home while the neighborhood was asleep. Every stitch of clothes the whole family possessed went up in flames. But the bear and the cubs were saved, much to the later annoyance of the Gipsies, who suddenly found themselves in Dutch with a hundred laws and regulations. The firemen had no sooner gone than the Gipsy family returned to the store, boarded up the broken windows, and began to moan. But it did not take very long before the other Brazilian Gipsies of the neighborhood had rented another store for them and fitted them out. For the wealth of one Gipsy is the wealth of the tribe.

The Brazilian Gipsies are less colorful than the other ones. They sing less than either the Hungarian, Russian, or Rumanian Gipsies do. And they are not as given to fortune-telling, are not as skilful at it, as their brothers of the skin are. Their doors are not as open to strangers. You can open the door of almost any Gipsy family and be received hospitably after wishing them good morning or good evening. They will offer to show you their costumes and their bric-à-brac, and let you finger the jewelry that hangs on their necks and from their arms. But the Brazilian Gipsy, like the Spaniard, living under curtained windows, will only open a crack of the door, peer at you, ask you what you want, shake his head, and close the door before you have answered. They are neither as wealthy nor as large-handed as the other Gipsies and are suspected, by the Rumanians especially, of all sorts of evil things. Indeed, I have been assured that neither cat nor dog is safe in their vicinity, and that they eat even other things. But this is another Gipsy peculiarity, of accusing one another and thus confusing everything.

On Fifth and Sixth Streets and on Ninth Street live the Hungarian Gipsies. Tall, slender, curly-headed, with long, black, waxed mustaches, musicians all of them, they stroll about like the lords of creation, with utter contempt for their wives and women-folk of the tribe. The men make their quarters apart from the women's quarters, very much in the manner of the Mohammedans, who separate their harems from the living space.

You can easily recognize a Hungarian Gipsy's home. The curtains are much lower, and the people have even taken to living in apartment-houses. Should you pass the street slowly and listen, you will perceive the curious fiery sound emitted by the cymbalom, their favorite musical instrument. Furious waves of music, made so familiar to the cultivated ear through Liszt's Hungarian rhapsodies and Brahms's Hungarian dances, will let you know that you are in front of a Hungarian Gipsy's home. You may, if you feel like it, go in and wish them good morning. No pretext is needed. They are accustomed to visitors. You will be asked to allow them to tell your fortune, and before you know it you will be separated from some of your money, and, seated comfortably on a low divan, you will be smoking a cigarette while the lady of the house is urging her daughter to play for you something on the cymbalom. After she has played, there may be another girl in the family who can sing, and you will be asked to listen to her singing. When she has finished singing and you have

given her something, another one may suddenly begin to turn somersaults and do all sorts of gymnastics for you. You will seldom see any male member of the family. If they are at home, they will not even deign to rise and wish you welcome or look at you. And if they should happen to come in while you are there, they will pierce you through with their small black eyes, a question or two will be asked, and woe to the one suspected of having looked too tenderly at any of the women of the household.

The men congregate in innumerable Hungarian restaurants of the neighborhood, restaurants and *Weinstuben,* where there is great talk of this and that great musician. When the Hungarian cymbalist, Yanosh Barti, who has played for years at the Capitol Theater, died recently, there was almost a riot because of the disputes between the other musicians as to whether he was a greater cymbalom player than another one still living. It is strange, but the *pusta* children who have for centuries lived in the deserts of Hungary, so isolated, so within themselves, are adapting themselves most readily to city conditions. I have seldom heard talk among them of a desire to return home.

And so through the winter these nomadic races, here in great numbers since the late war, have dotted the lower East Side streets, the Balkans of New York, with their winter homes, thus helping the other inhabitants to feel more at home. Indeed, were it understood, those who are so anxious to Americanize southeastern European people would welcome the Gipsies among them, if it were for nothing else but because they give that touch so necessary to the hundred thousand people living, pining, and longing for their homes. They can endure Anglo-Saxon civilization much easier with the presence of their Gipsies about them. They can forget, when it is necessary to forget, that they are not at home. The dash of color, the dash of song they bring, is like the special condiment needed in order to make food palatable. There would be no festivities among the Rumanians and Hungarians and Poles, or the Russians, if it were not for the Gipsies. It would be impossible for them to have any festivity, christening, or marriage (the first frequently before the last) while jazz was played or rag songs were danced, such music being not only meaningless to them but insufferably cruel to their ears.

There are about thirty thousand Gipsies roaming over the United States at present. Of that some twenty thousand are natives, in Louisiana and New Mexico. The other ten thousand are almost evenly distributed between the Russian, Polish, Hungarian, and Rumanian Gipsies. In the winter, between the months of October and April, about four thousand of them live in New York. Five hundred or so of the men are occupied playing nightly at cabarets and at the weddings of their co-nationals. Others are in continual demand in the neighborhood show-houses and vaudevilles as dancers and performers. The rest of them are fortune-telling to fortune-hunters.

They have neither church nor any other religious institutions. Each tribe has a different religion from the others. They have no literature and care for none. And when I lately read to them what celebrated gipsologists had said about Gipsies, there was great merriment among them all.

And yet, impossible as it sounds, it seems to me that most of them who have come here will be absorbed; but in the following manner: The Rumanian Gipsies will intermarry with the Rumanian people living here, the Russians with the Russian, and so forth. By the time these nationalities through intermarriage absorb one another, there will be little left of the original Gipsy blood. Such things have already happened.

We went down one day to buy some costumes for a theatrical production. Most of the Gipsies refused to sell. But one family with which I am fairly well acquainted was easily persuaded to take gold in exchange for gorgeously patterned, ample, blood-red, canary-yellow, and field-green silken dresses. The bargain concluded, we were still short a wedding dress for the second act. After much palaver, the old lady consented to show us her wedding dress, which she has kept these fifty years. It brought forth gasps and cries of delight from Miss Mary Fowler and Mrs. Jeanne Cassel. Gossamer spun and woven by fairy hands in the shadow of a golden evening. But she would not hear of selling it, the old lady. I entreated and begged. No, it was hers. She had refused even to include it in the dowry for her daughter. After many hours, and when I had explained that we should be compelled to show a Gipsy bride in an unbefitting dress, she draped it on one of the ladies. Tears came into her eyes as she looked at her. "Even as I looked in that myself." And then she suddenly exclaimed: "Take it as a gift. But I will not sell."

We made to leave, afraid she might change her mind. At the door she stopped Miss Fowler. I trembled. The old woman's face became entreating. Her lips and eyes had that curious shrewd smile I know so well.

"Cross your palm with silver, and I will tell your fortune."

And she who had so magnificently given was begging—swindling—out of habit.

It is east of Third Avenue above Twentieth Street. You will find the place easily enough in daytime. Horses are tied out on the street, while a peculiar kind of people line the sidewalk, some flourishing long-handled whips over their heads, others with their riding-crops under their arms or sticking out of their leggings.

In good days, early in the spring, the block resembles a

horse-fair in a far-off country—in any far-off country of the world. For this is the peculiarity of the business. Horsemen are the same the world over. McTurk of Dublin, Ciorcani the Gipsy of the Hungarian plains, Mr. Sire of New York, and Mahbub Ali of India in Kipling's "Kim" are one and the same person. And where horses are sold the same methods are applied, the same language is used in different tongues, and the environment changes to suit the men who fill the circle.

"This heah hawse is lame. The right foh leg drags," says the would-be buyer.

"Lame nothing. He just favors that leg," answers the dealer.

"Lame" is eliminated from the language of the seller. A lame leg is a "favored" leg.

A horse is never older than thirteen years, because after that his age can no longer be read in the age-worn teeth. And when it comes to price, a horse is worth what you can get.

Inside one of the half-cement, half-brick buildings the auction is going on. The auctioneer is standing on a bench, the buyers in a wide circle. A horse, tagged and numbered, is held in place by a young hostler, who hangs on the short halter with all his weight to show off the spirit of the animal. If it is a plow-horse, he stands loosely by to impress people with its meekness, kindness, and docility; for a runner or a trotter he has different tactics. A really good boy is worth his weight in gold.

There is old Tom, a horse-dealing Gipsy. Everybody knows Tom.

But he never even lifts his head when a pedigreed horse is offered for sale. He never hears the introduction of the auctioneer when a "blood" is brought out. He does not care to know what the dam or sire was, and he does not want to listen to the tale of records set on the track by brothers, half-brothers, sisters, and half-sisters of the horse in question.

"Them are horses for them that know nuthin' about horse-flesh and ain't horsemen at all," is Tom-As-Is's dictum. "It 's for amatchures. That knowin' for sure all about the animal is disgustin'. Listen to him!"

The auctioneer was reciting, refreshing his memory from written notes: "Dam retired from track with two-ten record. Sire with two-four. Brother now in training for big Futurity. Winner of——"

"Do you hear him? Come out of here. I ain't in the market for no machines. It 's horse-flesh *I* buy. And it 's up to my eye, to my experience, to my horsemanship to know all about a horse when I see it. The rest is gamble, excitement. What 's a man in the business for if not for that? Why buy it if you know all it can do?"

A magnificent young colt with a long pedigree was put up for sale. Its sensitive head was kept erect on a thin, long neck. The red nostrils spurted fire, and the taut veins on the buttocks and legs were quivering with excitement.

"Tom," I said, "what do you say to this fellow?"

"It 's all in the pedigree; I ain't got nothing to say."

"Could I make something out of him?"

"Well, it 's in the pedigree. Figure the record of the sire and dam. If you 'll keep him well and train him well you 'll get a fair average of the two. Nothing to get excited about." And Tom left me.

The young colt was sold for a very small sum. There were no "amatchures" at the sale.

Then, toward the end, No. 64 was brought out, a young colt, part Arab, part mustang, and with a dash of thoroughbred and some other breed thrown in. There was no pedigree, and the auctioneer called out: "As is—sold with no guarantee."

Tom was outside the stable, but the sound of "As is" brought him running to the circle. Instantly he was at one of the legs and felt it knowingly and slowly from the hips down to the hoofs. When the operation was over Tom saw three other men, each busy feeling a leg.

He had to wait for his turn on the other legs. What a quartet of horse-dealers! How much alike they looked to one another! Finally they were given a chance to buy a horse on their own personal knowledge. Then each tried the horse for its wind and kept his observation to himself.

"Nice young colt, two years old, as is. What am I bid for him? How much to start with?" chanted the auctioneer.

"Twenty," said Tom-As-Is.

"Twenty, twenty, twenty, who gives twenty-five? Twenty-five I 've got. Who gives thirty, thirty, thirty? Thirty I 've got. Who gives forty? Forty . . ."

Tom bid higher and higher. The others kept raising the price. At the end the non-pedigreed, non-guaranteed horse sold for three times the amount the pure-bred colt had brought.

"It 's not knowing what goes into the making of him that makes us expect something extra," explained Tom, as he led the awkward creature to his stable. "He mebbe won't make more than a tram-car horse, and mebbe he 'll break records! Who knows? But in them pedigreed things it 's machine-like. I 'm a *horseman,* I am."

A horseman he is, Tom. Of the same tribe as El Zorab in Arabia, Mahbub in India, Ciorcani on the *pusta* of the Magyar land, and Mehemet Ali in the swamps of the Dobrudja.

# CHAPTER IX

## AFRICA

UNTIL ten years ago Harlem was a district of New York, a suburban section within the city, inhabited by second-generation Germans and German Jews. To-day it is a city in itself. Negro Town. The heart and the pulse of the colored population of Greater New York. Harlem cannot hold the whole colored population of New York. Neither can the older negro district, the Fifty-ninth Street section. Neither would Brooklyn. There are obstructions and objections and restrictions everywhere against them. The center of the colored people is in Harlem. Indeed it is the center, the intellectual center, of the colored population of the United States.

There are between three and four hundred thousand colored people in Greater New York. In the last census there were not one tenth that many. But Chicago rioted after St. Louis had gone on a "nigger spree." Atlanta, Georgia, had its dance. Lynchings, burnings, persecutions, are the main reason why colored folk have been flocking to New York, where a "nigger slaughter" is not so frequent an occurrence.

All shades and all sizes. Woolly-haired, immense, half-lumbering Africans as black as pitch. Brown-colored, bronzed men and women, mahogany blonds, down through all nuances, and the almost white negro, straight-haired and blue-eyed, whom nobody suspects.

Not all white men of Europe are of the same race. Of the same blood. Of the same faith. Not all negroes are alike, although most of their ancestors have been ravished from Africa. Since their arrival in this country there have been many intermixtures into their blood. I have seen perfectly black negroes of long Spanish faces, with the cruel penetrating eyes of the Moor and the elegant gait of Iberians. I have met red-haired negroes with a wistful Irish smile. I have friends of a lighter shade, from New Orleans, where they have so thoroughly mixed with the French they are hardly to be distinguished, with all the love of color and softness of one race and the precision of mind and clarity of the other. The Italians have mixed with the negroes, and so have the Slavs and the English and the Mexicans and the Indians.

Of these mixtures the ones with Indian blood are the finest. The women especially—of skin like golden bronze dyed in deep-red blood. The big gala eyes swim in clear-white pools, and the hair is like shavings of ebony; lustrous and rich, plaited down over trim and beautiful necks. And there are Jewish negroes, Abyssinian Jews squat and long-bearded, hook-nosed Falashas, real Jews, who because of their color are compelled to live among people of an alien faith instead of among their own coreligionists.

Four hundred thousand negroes in New York. There never has been such a number of negroes in any one place, either on this continent or on any other continent. Every twelfth person in Greater New York is a negro or has negro blood. Four out of five negroes have white blood in them. And they are none the better for it. The best the race has achieved was achieved by pure-blooded Africans. They have their own life, their own dreams. More isolated in their social relations than any other single group, their dreams and ideals may be sectional but they are their own. Thicker walls separate them from any other population. Not only of color. A thousand and one aversions. A thousand and one superstitions. A thousand and one traditions. We have been taught the negro is a different sort of an animal. Because of his color. Because of his particular odor. Because of the coarseness of the grain of his skin. Because of his speech. Because of his taste for certain foods. Each of our major senses has been prejudiced against him. And yet . . . Four out of five negroes have white blood. There is at least as much white blood in the American negro race as there is black. And that is so not because of black immorality but because of white immorality and the inhumanity of our ancestors. The whiter a negro the weaker he is physically. The pure blacks are giants. When slave-dealers went to Africa they selected the strongest specimens for work and breeding. Only the strongest survived transportation on a slave-ship.

And yet almost everything we have of true native art in this country is of negro origin—folk-lore, the spirituals, jazz, the dance, and some of our best poetry. The negroes brought that in their souls from Africa. The origin of native American art is African.

Some of the greatest art the world has ever possessed has grown out of slavery and oppression. Greece in her imperial days, Rome in her strength, Egypt in her glorious period, have had their art produced only by slaves, by those who suffered and endured. Those who had comfort and leisure enjoyed what the others produced without appreciating its value. Had it not been for the great suffering in Russia I doubt whether any of the arts which the Muscovite empire has produced would have flourished. Pushkin was a negro. Shevchenko a slave. Any one who could remain with dry eyes and calm heart during the singing of spirituals by negroes should be avoided for callousness. Any white man who could gaze into negro eyes without horror for the wrong done them during centuries should be . . . condemned to read the prophet Isaiah's fifth chapter for the rest of his life, mornings and evenings.

Four hundred thousand negroes in one city. It has not increased immorality. It has not increased crime. They have their own proportion of vice and their due percentage of criminals, neither more nor less than any other single group in this city. They have their gambling-dens and cabarets and houses of prostitution and corrupt politicians and swindlers and saints and institutions and churches and artists and novelists and musicians, exploiters and exploited, and bankers. Not one quality, not a single vice of modern civilization is missing. They are as a matter of fact living as separately from any other group as any other group lives separately from them. The pity of it! For so much lightness, so much gaiety, so much naïve merriment is lost. Nowhere in the city does one hear so much frank laughter as in the Harlem or the Brooklyn negro sections. Nobody can laugh as engagingly as a negro. It is one of the first things that strikes a visitor that New York is a laughless city. Somehow one leaves his ability to laugh frankly at the outskirts of the city. But there is laughter in Harlem, in the Brooklyn negro quarter in Bensonhurst, on Fifty-ninth Street, and even in the narrow Carmine Street and Minetta Lane where the congestion is such one is able to cut the air with a knife. There is laughter and song and dance.

A friend of mine recently said to me: "Harlem! The old Harlem is dead. I lived there all my life until not long ago, when I was squeezed out by the negro population invading the old section. All the *Gemütlichkeit* of it is gone. Gone are the comfortable *Weinstuben,* where one could smoke his pipe and peacefully drink his glass of Rhine wine. Gone is the old *Liedertafel* and the hundred and one social organizations, and the *Turnvereine* and the singing-clubs, where one could pass the evening peacefully. They have all moved elsewhere, and the new places don't have the atmosphere of the old ones. Gone the old restaurants where one could have his *Knackwurst und Sauerkraut,* served by a golden-haired, white-skinned, blue-eyed Margaretchen. Gone the agreeable homes where the rows and rows of long-stemmed meerschaum pipes hanging from the wall gave to every home that manly quality so dear to the Teuton race. It used to be so pleasant to pass a Harlem street on a summer evening. The young ladies were accompanying their *Lieder* with the twanging of the soft zither, and the stirring robust melodies from the Lutheran churches used to fill the air on a Sunday. It is all gone now."

It is all gone. But in my recent long perigrinations through the Harlem streets I have failed to see the little notice under the "To Let" signs, "No Jews need apply," or the other little notices in German, "Keine Juden, und keine Hunde." An American city with such signs on doors was a shame. The absence of them largely compensates for the absence of the other things my friend so much regretted.

At 138th and 139th Streets, between Seventh and Eighth Avenues, are two rows of houses that were designed by Stanford White. Built in pre-negro days, they had been the pride of the neighborhood, houses of fairly well-to-do white people until not very long ago. In my eagerness to see what the negroes had done to Harlem I visited these streets again. They were still there, the houses, and, although inhabited every one of them by negroes, still as beautiful, still as tasteful, still as clean. The little bits of color in the curtains, the flower assortment on the sills and in the cement urns of the broad sidewalks, made them more agreeable than ever.

The story of the passing of those houses into negro hands is the story of negro Harlem. Below the surface of that story is the story of the negro migration from the south. When the Fifty-ninth Street district around Seventh and Eighth Avenues was no longer able to hold the negroes of the city, even after they had been sardine-packed, Harlem was in one of her periodical real-estate slumps. The old-fashioned railroad flats, mostly dark and cold and uniformly built, were being vacated steadily for the better houses built in the Bronx and elsewhere. There was not a house but had several empty apartments. But the owners would not rent to negroes.

In his eagerness to cover his carrying expenses, one of the shoe-string landlords rented an apartment in the middle of the block to a mulatto family. By the end of the month the rest of the tenants living in that house had vacated their apartments. By the end of the following month the whole house was occupied by negroes. They had been living packed four and five families in one apartment in the Fifty-ninth Street negro section before that. Tenants of houses adjoining, to right and left and across the street, began to abandon the block. Before winter that whole block was a negro block. And as the negroes were not in a position to pay rents as high as the whites who had abandoned them, the houses were up for sale very soon. They passed into the hands of negro owners and of such white owners as did not object to having negro tenants, expecting to increase their rents as soon as conditions permitted. In this respect the negro owner has, like *Emperor Jones,* learned a thing or two from the white landlord.

The white population fled as if in dread of a contagious disease. Block after block was deserted by the white tenants. Negro realtors, seeing their chance, infiltrated in other blocks by buying a house and going in to live themselves. No one refused to sell. Dollars were dollars. Some of the strongest objectors to negroes sold their houses. It was enough that one negro family should come to live in a house for the whole block to be abandoned to them. And because of this invasion 138th and 139th Streets, and Seventh and Eighth Avenues, though distant from the steady biting in of the infiltering colored population, were being steadily abandoned. White people vacated in advance of the invasion. The beautiful houses designed by Stanford White stood empty for a long time, until the bank owning the mortgages, which had been allowed to become defaulted, decided to tear them all down and sell the ground. The houses were a useless burden and a loss on their hands. They could then have been bought for five or six thousand dollars apiece, although they had cost fully five times that amount to build. Upon the advice of Mr. Jacques Nail, a negro student realtor, the houses, instead of being torn down, were sold on small payments to negro tenants. The invasion, which had till then only been from the south to the north, began to run from the north to the south, until at present hardly a house in that section of Harlem, between 120th Street and 140th Street, and between Lenox and Amsterdam Avenues, is not inhabited by colored people. Churches, banks, stores, theaters, the power to grant political offices, municipal offices, everything has passed into the hands of negroes. A city in itself, brown, black town, Harlem. And the negroes have not left Harlem as they found it. A visit to Harlem would help dispel the idea that "niggers" are shiftless—when they have an incentive for their work—something more than corn and sow-belly. But it will also teach how prejudice might, because of enforced congestion, cause one of the most serious holocausts this or any other city has ever experienced. As it is, the infant death-rate is just keeping pace with the birth-rate among the negroes of Harlem.

The beautiful Abyssinian Baptist Church on 138th Street has the Rev. Dr. Powell as pastor. It was designed by a negro architect, built by a negro contractor, with negro labor from and moneys collected from negroes in the city. Not a thing within the church, but it has been done by negro hands. The pastor, a tall, colored man, with a thunderous voice and big curly head of hair, looks very much like the picture of Alexandre Dumas, who was himself of negro blood. I am yet to listen to a better choir than the one directed by the choir-leader of that church. I am yet to listen to a better church organist than the colored woman treading the pedals and combining the stops of the magnificently voiced organ of that church. This church, like most other negro churches, is really more than a church. It is a social center. At a service on a Sunday the pastor comments upon the political events that have taken place during the week, and sways the audience to his view by his thunderous oratory. He speaks as much of earthly events as he praises the Lord. Not a thing that has happened in the world escapes him; and he is not afraid to denounce the things he does not agree with.

At one of the recent services Dr. Powell announced the church was going to have classes for instruction in sex conducted by capable physicians. Children of all ages were urged to come, and there were also classes for the parents. As far as I know it is the first time that such a course has ever been undertaken by a church. Dr. Powell does not hold that ignorance is bliss in all matters. "Why dodge the sex question when the living are a testimony to its existence?" he thundered. "It is because of ignorance that so many diseases have spread."

There are numerous courses and classes within that church. It has an employment bureau, sewing-classes, cooking-classes, a gymnasium; and the Rev. Dr. Powell showed me with great pride his home. "Furnished very much as the best homes on Riverside Drive, so that a colored girl coming here looking for employment in one of the better homes might, by helping to take care of my apartment, learn how to work and earn her wages elsewhere," he explained. "The Southern negro girl on coming here must be helped to become a capable worker."

At the revival meetings, while hymns and spirituals were sung, the old folks "got religion." The women, in shrill, piercing voices, screamed out: "Yea, Lord! Yea, Lord! Yea, Lord!" while the droning voices of the multitude moaned and wailed. Voices break out, self-denunciatory and praying for the Lord to come to their aid and save them and protect them against the evil spirit that is within. The whole congregation joins in prayer, only to be interrupted by another rousing voice citing a whole chapter from the Bible and commenting upon it. Rising to his feet, another man is so moved that he completely loses control of the tongue he has been using, and passes on to an incomprehensible gibberish, into a language and tongue he himself no longer understands, a subconscious language if one may say so, which has been stirred from centuries past, beyond the time of other days, like under-enharmonics of life—the base of all emotions and reactions. Really, these

CHURCH

people have religion. They go to church not as an obligatory call, a duty, a formality. It is part of them.

I saw a young white boy of splendid physique and beautiful blond hair and blue eyes distributing literature to the folks between hymns. "Surely," I asked Walter White, who was with me, "this young boy is not colored."

"He is," Walter, who is himself blond and blue-eyed and fair-skinned, answered me. "Only one drop of colored blood makes a white man a negro, but nine tenths of white blood in a colored man do not make him a white man. It has been so decreed. See how white he is. Should he live among white people and should they find out he is of negro ancestry they would draw away from him as if he were the worst kind of criminal."

At another time, on coming to services at the same church, in company with Miss Rebecca West, the English novelist, we saw a number of white women and white men in the church who could unsuspectingly pass anywhere as white people. At St. Philip's Church, on 135th Street, in the Bible class of the Rev. Mr. Bishop, who himself looks more like a patrician Italian than a negro (this church was also designed, built, and constructed by negro labor), I saw a beautiful, golden-haired, blue-eyed girl. She was as fair to behold as any golden beauty I have ever seen.

"And is she a negress?" I asked the Rev. Mr. Bishop.

"Of course she is," he answered in the most matter-of-fact tone.

"But golden-haired?" I questioned, and passed on to other matters.

And then I understood a good many other things. I

understood why there are so many supposedly white women married to colored men in the negro quarters! Why there are so many white men married to colored women in the negro quarters! I remembered a girl friend, whose desk had been next to mine on a local newspaper, whom everybody had condemned because she had married a colored man and gone to live among colored people. I remembered the case of a man whose wife, seemingly white, gave birth to a colored child, and the woman, rather than confess her race, preferred to be divorced on the ground of infidelity. She wanted to free herself of the negro Ghetto, free herself of persecution and restrictions. And I also remembered another case where, in spite of the opprobrium of all who knew him, a friend of mine took his blond wife and negro child abroad, for he was the only one who knew; the wife had confessed her race to him. And I was told of another man who had crossed the line and married into a white family, but who committed suicide when his first child was born, not because his wife had withdrawn her love but because he had hoped to free his offspring from the opprobrium.

But there are many more negroes, men and women, who have successfully crossed the line, many more than we care to know or to admit. And, oh! the tragedies caused by nature's playful and wilful ways with these people. A blond child will be born to two perfectly matched negroes, a black child to two perfectly matched blonds.

There are a hundred little churches housed in apartment ground floors, with little window-pane pictures of the saints pasted on the panes of the windows and gold-lettered wooden signs on the wall. Some of them have the most fantastic names—Eureka Church, Oasis Church, and the like. And services are announced in the quaintest possible language, in removable enameled letters. The reason for these many small churches is to be found in what follows. A colored man after having lived in New York for a little time returns home, South, on a visit. Going to church on Sunday the brother is asked by the preacher to step up to the front and to tell to his brethren about the great city. The visiting brother is well dressed, looks prosperous and happy. He generally draws such a glorious picture of the opportunities, the tolerance and the economic conditions here that the whole community, including minister, doctor, and undertaker, follows him to the city within a week or two. The hardships they encounter could only be braved and vanquished by laughing, gay-hearted folk. Any other kind would succumb.

Within the last year close to five hundred thousand negroes have migrated from the South. It is because of this that housing conditions in Harlem and in other negro quarters are appalling. Really no one would dare publish the result of investigations on the density of the population in some of the Harlem districts, or the Brooklyn districts for that matter. The danger of the colored invasion once past, because these houses had passed into colored hands, rents were raised until they are to-day, relatively speaking, probably the highest in the city. Apartments for which white people had paid a few years ago forty dollars a month are now rented for a hundred dollars or more. Families have doubled up, and tripled up, to pay the exorbitant rents from the wages obtained in such occupations as are open to the negroes. One must not forget that only a very few occupations are within their reach. Trade-unions have long refused them membership. Whenever they have won such privileges, it was only for fear lest they be used as strike-breakers during an industrial war. As it is, many trades have barred them from the possibility of earning a living.

There is greater privacy in the low dives and cabarets, in the streets, in the dark hallways, in the numerous saloons which flourish in spite of white prohibition, than in the homes. Because of high rents less than a hundred colored children graduate yearly from the high schools of the city. They must work. There would be starvation in many a home of negroes if child-labor laws should be strictly enforced. High rents caused by segregation are the cause of the black immorality and lawlessness and of the blind pigs leaning on the walls of the police stations. The white messenger who collects the protection money has his drinks served in his own cup which he carries in his pocket, and complains of black immorality! Most of the expensive dives in Harlem are supported by white customers, who complain of black immorality. If the blacks should do to the whites what the whites do to the blacks for insults to women there would be a hundred lynchings daily in New York.

Chris Matthews, formerly one of Harvard's greatest athletes, related to me the other day on his visit from Boston how for a year he had been refused by his team-mates permission to eat at the same training-table with them.

In Annapolis they had drained the water from the pool after he had taken his swim, in spite of the fact that he had been instrumental in winning the championship for his team. I have listened for hours to tales of riots and lynchings, as told by Miller and Lyles, the co-authors of "Shuffle Along" and "Runnin' Wild," and to the tales of Walter

White and Wendell Johnson; but the tale of the lynching of Matthews' soul seems to me the most tragic one. Though his body still lives, they have killed him.

And in spite of that, and in spite of all the misery they have endured, what joy and gaiety and merriment the negroes are capable of! What full-throated laughter, what spontaneous giggling, in which every limb and the whole body takes part in an expression of joy or merriment! Heinrich Heine in one of his essays said that the dance is the song of the limbs. The colored people have made laughter the dance of the inner voices.

There are some six weekly newspapers edited and published by colored people for colored people in the city, not to speak of several magazines of more serious import. The professional men of all walks meet and know one another thoroughly. There are numerous lodges and groups and societies where they come to discuss things. Like the intellectuals in other districts, they also have their coffee-houses, where they stay till the wee hours of the morning talking about this and that.

At the Abyssinian Jewish Synagogue the black-bearded, dusky-faced men affirm that Moses, Jesus, and Solomon, and David were Ethiopians like themselves. They point to numerous passages in the Bible, interpreting them this way and that to confirm their views and opinions. They sit day after day, night after night, discussing the Old Testament, which they have at their finger-tips, in the old Hebrew. With that curious separatist spirit so marked in the Orient, the few hundred Abyssinian Jews are split into a hundred factions, because of the interpretation of a verse in the Bible. They are the butt of the ridicule of the other negroes, who take their religious argumentation but lightly. Yet these people come to dispute religion even in the Christian churches. Their propaganda fervor holds perhaps the explanation why the Jews are so disliked by Gentiles. The apostles must have been as insistent propagandists. And those who finally accepted the creed continued to dislike them for their methods. How little color has to do with the marked characteristics of a race or a nation! In their studiousness, their sad humor, and their lack of ability to laugh as loudly and as frankly as others, they show themselves to be much more Hebrews than the white Hebrews are. And when I asked one of them what he would really wish his condition in New York to be he said, "To live among the other Jews." They resent the epithet "negro," and their inability to mingle with their white brethren of the same religion makes them bitter against their privileged coreligionists. And one of them told me, "There is no chance of any of us ever crossing the line; for there is no white blood in us."

And his wife stood up in her enormous corpulence and added, "And there shall not be."

To which her husband replied, "Except if a white coreligionist marries into our fold."

They are very poor, for their children also are forced into poorly paid professions because of their color. Most handicrafts are closed to them. The negro is not persecuted in New York. He is segregated and tolerated. Only the poorest-paid work is open to him whose skin is not white.

One night I was sitting at a table with two negroes and their wives at one of the "protected" cabarets of the town. There were about a hundred people in the establishment, but I was the only man in street-clothes. They were all immaculately dressed. The women were resplendent in gorgeous gowns. Rivers of diamonds were displayed shining brightly in the subdued lights of the place. They danced, frantically, joyously, with the most sensuous abandon of body and spirit, to the jazz played by a gyrating band, the musicians actually dancing on the platform while they played. The drinks were unusually expensive, and though because of their profession, which I suspected, the visitors should have known better, the only difference in the wine, in spite of the different prices, was the color and the shape of the bottle in which it was served.

My male companions at the table did not wait long to strike up friendship. A tall, corpulent man leaned over to me and questioned gently:

"Your name, please."

I told him. Whereupon he rose and ceremoniously introduced me to the rest of the company. He eyed with displeasure the bottle in which my wine was served, for it was not of the highest priced. It shamed his table. The other tables topped one another in the costliness of the drinks that were ordered. He asked me politely to consent to partake of his wine. When I had consented he spilled my wine in the brass bowl and put the empty container under the table out of sight. As the waiter did not appear quickly enough to suit him, Mr. Smith raised his eyebrows and said:

"Is it not remawrkable ho' these ma-an servants are procrastinating?"

"They are procrastinating!" the other assented, happy to mouth so high-sounding a word. "Yes, sir, they is procrastinating; yes, sir!"

While the music played and the dancing women exhibited their diamond-studded garters through the slit in their gowns, and the phosphorescent white combs in their hair were gleaming, he inquired of my profession. And then he spoke of his.

"The other gentleman, Mr. Jones, and I is partners. I 's

a sci'ntist and di'tishon and chemist. A sci'ntist, that 's what I is, a di'tishion. There are plenty of learned folk in Harlem, sir."

"Is that so?"

"Yes, that 's what I is. We two, my partner and me, is going to change the color of our race and make it happy. We are going to make 'em white, so they can live everywhere and go everywhere and be even the President of the United States. The only trouble with the colored race is that it ain't white. Not that I says we is inferior! No, sir! Only when you are in Rome you 've got to be like Romans, as Lincoln said. So we will make 'em white."

"Is that so?"

"All this straightening out hair business, permanent wave, is not the thing; ain't near the real thing. The hair is like tassel on corn. To change it you must change the seed. It is not sci'ntific. I am a di'tishion. I believe in doing things fundamentally."

Suddenly he raised his voice and looked to the people about him. People crowded our table now, though the music played.

"Why am the Northern people blond? Why am they blond, I asks." And his large belly shook like jelly while his black eyes rolled furiously in the white pools. "I say they am blond because they eats fish; cold-blooded animals they eat. And because of that they have fair skin and blond hair. Color comes from within, and not from outside. That is sci'ntific. But you cannot change the whole colored race into a white race at once. Burbank he ain't done changing the nature of fruit by paintin' it. You 've got to do it sci'ntifically. And through the mothers especially. None of the hair-culture is the real business, although it does come in in my scheme, for religious purposes. And so when a woman has got sense enough to come to me I look at her and study the grain of her face. Then if she is very black I prescribe a diet of fish with a little vegetables three times a day. And I give her the right kind of face-powder. And it 's the face-powder I 's interested in with my partner here."

Mr. Jones puffed at his cigar and bowed in acknowledgment.

"Still, the business is idealistic, it is. But there ain't no reason in the world why ideals should be losing propositions! No, siree! And if a woman of lighter shade comes up I give her a diet of two-times-a-day fish and a little more vegetables three times a day. And I give her the right kind of face-powder, a little lighter. For it 's the face powder I 's interested in with my partner here. And the right kind of face-powder. And if a woman whiter than that comes she gets fish only once a day and the use of a different kind of face-powder. And I knows face-powder because I 's been interested in face-powder all my life. There are eight hundred and forty-nine different kinds of face-powder to choose from. And I selects the right kind after studying the grain of the face and the hands. I 's a di'tishion and a sci'ntist, a chemist."

"And then you think that will straighten out a woman's hair?" I asked.

"I ain't interfering with another end of my business; that is hair-culture. No, siree! But do you knows the

DR J CHADWICK JONES
BEAUTY SPECIALIST
PERMANENT ARROW-HAIR
CLAIRVOYANT
CHURCH
MANNA CAFE
SERVICE ALA CARTE
HOT CHITLINGS 25
WITH BATTER 30
HAM HOCKS
PIGS KNUCKLES 25
WITH BATTER 35
40
PORK CHOPS 35
SOUTHERN FRIED
CHICKEN 60
GRITS AND GRAVY 10
SWEET POTATOES 10
HOMINY 15
OLD. STYLE
CORN PONE 25
YES WE HAVE
WATERMELON

Bible? Do youse know the Bible? I asks." He waxed more enthusiastic as he continued. "Do you remember how Jacob got them striped sheep from his father-in-law Laban? He fooled him by putting the half-peeled branches from the trees in front of the water-well, where the ewes used to come to drink. And so most of the sheep were born flecked because the ewes looked at them. Well, do you remember it?"

I nodded.

"Well, that am exactly how I do the things. Nothing like the Bible for an honest man. Study the Bible for ideas. It 's all in there, in the good book. The good book. There ain't no gold enough to pay for it. I loves it. I do. I got in my house the most expensive Bible there is. Gold bound and everything. I have a woman eat fish and give her the proper shade of face-powder, and she 'll be looking into the mirror at herself a dozen times a day. Women is that fallacious, vain, and perspicacious. And watch her offspring. That is sci'ntific. Like Laban's lambs got striped, her offspring is gwine to be whiter. . . . It 's in the Bible, sir. If you believe in the Bible, you can't dispute this here fact, or you is a heathen. For I 's a sci'ntist and di'tishion and benefactor and a student."

I told him he was wonderful, whereupon a dozen more gentlemen and ladies, evidently already the clients of the firm of Smith & Jones, crowded our table. And my friend affirmed to them that I had said it was wonderful.

"And this gentleman knows, for he is a celebrated sci'ntist himself, and a student of the Bible."

Who will ever imitate the nice jollity and naïveté of the

man? The music played, and the couples danced, and as they passed by the women patted his cheek assuring him that he was wonderful. And they were getting such tender and sweet glances in return! Even his own wife, who was with him, in a fit of amorous tenderness could not hold her arms away from his neck or her lips away from his. And it was not drunkenness that had done it, not the wine in the bottle.

A little later I questioned the man as to the status of certain white and colored women who came and went. Too delicate to say in the presence of his wife and the other persons what he thought they were, yet unwilling to leave me in error, he closed his eyes for a little second, and then explained:

"Them is the kind of women who permit a man to assume with them marital relations without legal obligations."

What a perfect Gilbert & Sullivan line! What fine, delicate phrasing!

There are a hundred, a thousand, different charlatans of his kind in Harlem, who want to make the colored people happy by making them look like whites. Every other house on the avenue holds a practitioner of some sort. The colored people are easily separated from their money. They are naïve and confident. Not only all the sciences but also all the superstitions flourish in like manner. There are a horde of representatives of schools of medicine I have never heard of. Podopractors, manopractors, pedipractors—doctors all of them.

In the anteroom of the famous place of Barron Wilkins, which is practically a spiritual continuation of the old

Marshall place, so famed in days gone by, Marshall's place which was the origin of all cabaret life in New York City —in the anteroom of Barron Wilkins's a group of colored men discuss intensely sociology, housing conditions, medicine, psychology. Big, powerful Wilkins, whose pull with police and politicians is greater than that of any of the other four hundred thousand negroes in the city, sits and listens intently to the discussion. There is a tender, loving gaze in his eyes as he watches every one having his say. He seldom says anything, but how he reads down to the very soul of the man who is talking, analyzing the wisdom and sincerity of what is uttered! His entrance, while the conclave is sitting, is like that of some governor or other high political person. There is power vested in him. He comes in, six feet three in his stockings, proportionately broad and stout, with a loud call of "Good evening, gentlemen!" Every one rises to his feet. "Be seated." And uncovering his gray head, he nods as he occupies his chair.

Wilkins's place on 134th Street is a club. Only members are admitted. It opens on week-days at about eleven o'clock P. M., officially, but the place really never gets started before one o'clock at night. It is frequented by white men, with only a sprinkling of negroes, although it is known as a colored man's cabaret. *Bons viveurs* from all the strata of society, financiers, lawyers, and theatrical people, with their women or in search of them, are dancing to the negro jazz band, while expensive food and drinks are being served at the tables, and the thick smoke of cigars and perfumed cigarettes hovers low over the white-haired heads of the males and the wavy hair of the females.

Between the dances a professional singer or dancer is doing his or her stunt, and as the entertainers are always

negroes the art is generally a very special one, fit only for the sophisticates of Barron Wilkins's club. One must have his purse well garnished when visiting the place. A hundred-dollar bill will not go very far and is not intended to do much service in this luxuriously fitted-out cabaret. But what charm! What exoticism! One easily forgets that all Harlem is not like it! Harlem, the Harlem of the poor, overcrowded, underfed, with children crippled with rickets and scurvy.

Wilkins's has undergone several changes in the last years until it has chameleoned to its present form. It is no longer the happy-go-lucky place of the time when it was partly owned by Jack Johnson, he with the big laugh and flashing teeth. Somehow one feels that the loose ends have been pulled together by a more expert hand in affairs than Jack's. Jack's fingers were wide open; gold just flowed between them. In its present form Wilkins's is the rich man's black and white cabaret. Southern gentlemen coming to the city, who cannot very well get on without negro society, are the first to look it up; and they learn to know after an experience or two that they must be on their guard. No affront or insult to the colored race would be suffered by any one of Wilkins's associates.

Another well-known cabaret is the Nest, one of the owners of which is part Italian and part negro. It has the reputation of having the best dance band in town. Its clientele is more evenly divided between blacks and whites. The white attendance outnumbers the black only on a Saturday or Sunday night. It is also a very luxurious and expensively fitted-out place. It is Broadway's next.

There are any number of other cabarets, some with very sinister names, like the Bucket of Blood, where the "goings-on" seem to be put on to attract the rubberneck looking for extraordinary sensations. And there are any number of "genuine" places 'way below Lenox Avenue frequented by Harlem's population of below par, bootleggers, prostitutes, pickpockets, gangsters, and all that the Bowery once held of the white man. No one seems to bother much about them. Wine, whisky, and narcotics are sold freely. The police are in on everything. I once saw a Southern gentleman punch a negro who had offered a white powder to a white woman. The gentleman did not resent the traffic. He was himself an addict. He resented the commerce between a black man and a white woman. He resented the familiarity. Even the degenerating dope had not softened the Southerner's contempt for the negro. That accident explained why so many negroes leave the South yearly.

The advent of Marcus Garvey, who styled himself the Emperor of the African race a few years ago, has had very much to do with the factionalization of Harlem. The full-blooded negro was made to feel, through Garvey's propaganda, that he was better than his brother of lighter skin. The blacker the greater the pride. And a thousand and one disputes have been going on since Marcus Garvey's advent. Undoubtedly this negro Moses started out as a saint with high ideals, with great love in his heart. His desire to take his people out of this country and lead them back to Africa had a solid emotional background. It was unfortunate that he should have become involved in the financial intricacies which ultimately led him to jail. He was a picturesque and imposing figure with a sad and eloquent voice and magnetic gestures. Somewhat of a *poseur,* yet—genuine. There are any number of people to this day in Harlem who still believe he was honest and who cannot be convinced that he ever swung aside a single penny which they gave him. They bought shares in the different enterprises that he started; and the Black Star Line, so much scoffed at when its lone vessel was confiscated by the prohibition agents for carrying whisky, is still something of which they dream. "Garvey was jailed," they say, "because he is colored." They will tell you big interests were behind his persecution. He was a black genius of organization and therefore dangerous. Some even spoke of him as the Gandhi of the negroes—a Gandhi nipped in the bud.

Marcus Garvey's influence is still strong in Harlem. It has worked havoc in the relations between the West Indian negro and the native negro. This antagonism breaks out in all fields. It is of frequent occurrence that a West Indian ruins another negro in business. They boycott one another's stores, restaurants, and dancing-places. There is no peace between the West Indian negro and the rest of the population. They neither associate nor intermarry, and seldom if ever belong to the same society, lodge, or congregation. It also so happens that the West Indian negroes are of more astute commercial make-up than the other negroes. Most of them have become quite wealthy in a very short time. They are not as happy-go-lucky as the other negroes. They save and invest their moneys in sound ventures, and do not part with their gold for hair-culture salves and the like. They are seldom as profoundly stirred in their emotions as the others are. They take religion more casually. They don't dance as well. And one of my colored friends said, "They are the Jews of the colored race"; by which he evidently meant to say, the business men of the people. They are quite satisfied to stay black, are proud of their race. There is less white blood in them than in the native negro.

A most interesting little man is Mr. Roach, the owner of the Renaissance Dancing Hall. A wealthy man and influential in the community is this Mr. Roach. He confessed to me he had once had literary ambitions, and had drawn his inspiration by being a cook for Mr. Irving Bacheller. Later on he became a servant to a Miss Watkins whose writings he admired. But it availed him naught. He had great difficulty. Write as he would, imitating as closely as possible either of his two masters, his stuff did not sell. In despair he became a valet to Mr. Wilton Lackaye, the actor, whereupon he promptly had better luck by selling a moving-picture scenario for sixty-five dollars. This made him think about pictures. To-day he owns a picture theater, has invested in a colored production company, and is the proprietor of several buildings and dancing halls. Had any of his stories been accepted he would to-day be a publisher.

A little below the Renaissance, on Lenox Avenue, is the Lafayette Theater, once the home of the Ethiopian Players, of which Charles Gilpin, now of national fame, was once a prominent member. The Ethiopian Players have produced a number of negro actors who have won national fame. They have staged Shaksperian plays, plays by Shaw, Oscar Wilde, Ibsen, and plays by local authors, mostly on negro subjects.

There are a number of very remarkable dramatic art

readers who from time to time are called to read before the many cultural organizations of the district. At present, the Ethiopian Players having been disbanded, the Lafayette Theater is a vaudeville house, in which mixed acts are being staged. It is one of the most popular houses of the neighborhood, and plans are again on foot for the Lafayette Players to start in a new series of productions.

Among interesting Harlem figures are men like Dr. Dubois, the editor of "The Crisis," and James Weldon Johnson, the poet, whose commemoration of the fiftieth anniversary of the emancipation of the negro was published in the "New York Times" in 1913. It was one of the most widely discussed poems of the year. His poem, "The Young Warrior," set to music by H. T. Burleigh, almost became the national hymn of Italy during the World War. Mr. Johnson has published several books of poetry of his own, and is the editor of "The Book of American Negro Poetry," published by Harcourt, Brace & Co. Walter F. White, my companion during my Harlem days, is a novelist and one of the best known figures in Harlem. Welcomed everywhere, known everywhere, a fluent talker and fiery orator, as ready with tears in his eyes as he is with a smile on his lips, he knows Harlem and knows his people. He is, for this and many other reasons, one of the most valuable assets of the negro race. He has investigated almost every riot and lynching for the past ten years; and should one want a nightmare, without going to the trouble of eating Welsh rabbit, and meet with Walter White, he can have it.

Claude McKay, the author of "Harlem Shadows," though a Jamaica negro, is one of the most pampered poets of Harlem. Young, handsome, and fiery, with undeniable talent, he is loved by everybody, and even his escapades are being recounted with great gusto. McKay is now in Russia, the guest of the Soviet Republic. Another interesting figure was Mrs. Lillie C. Walker, who became both famous and wealthy from her hair-straightening process. Branches of her parlor are now in operation all over the country, and her bottled preparation is selling in almost every drug store. Mrs. Walker, who in her lifetime made several million dollars through her invention, and from shrewd real-estate investments, was also a speaker and a singer and one of the most race-conscious negroes in the country. When she died she left her estate to her daughter, who, a most handsome Amazon, as though hewn out of dark bronze, stands fully six feet in her stockings. She is living in great luxury in a palace she has had designed and built for herself by a negro architect, in Irvington, New York, surrounded by all the luxuries of life and by social secretaries. A well-traveled and cultured woman, she, too, is a very proud negro. Her father having been killed in a riot, she is anything but passive on the subject. Rising from her chair as she talked to me, she looked more like an African empress than the offspring of a former slave. Speaking about negroes whose relatives and parents have been killed either in riots or in lynchings, her frame trembled, her lips quivered, and her eyes filled. She looked like an avenging Nemesis. But white Irvington objects to her living there. She is as isolated as if she lived on an

island a thousand miles from a shore . . . except when her own people come to visit with her.

In general, what one feels very distinctly in Harlem is that it is composed practically of two elements: those whose ambition it is to "cross the line" or have their offspring cross the line, to live with the whites as whites; and another much better element who refuse to live with whites under false pretenses, who want to live as negroes, race-conscious, who hope by their achievements to compel the white people surrounding them to recognize them as their equals. And they insist that their best men have been full-blooded negroes. To them the great number of people now invading Harlem and New York is very agreeable. They have them all together. They can hold meetings with larger crowds. They can lecture to them. They can make them race-conscious and with their help agitate for such legislation as is favorable to the race.

At a meeting in a church, when their greatest woman orator, Mary Burrows, spoke, they raised a young fortune in ten- and twenty-dollar bills for propaganda work. She made it quite plain that the negro was no longer going to submit as he has done heretofore.

"America must awaken or she will find herself weighted down with a millstone on the neck that will drag her to the lowest depths," she thundered, speaking about anti-lynching bills.

People like her and the crowd of the Association for the Advancement of Colored People are laboring for the education of the negro by making his life more complete, by pointing out to him values in literature, by making him conscious of a poetry all his own, a theater all his own, encouraging sculpture and painting and higher education; building a new edifice on an old foundation, by pointing out the great arts that flourished in Africa in olden times and down to the time their ancestors were ravished from the coasts of Africa and brought as slaves here. Native music and dance are almost entirely of negro origin. A visit to musical comedies such as "Shuffle Along" and "Runnin' Wild," which have been tremendous hits on Broadway and in most of the principal cities of the country, proves their contention. These comedies have been written, staged, and executed from first to last by negroes, and have a quality all their own. The tunes and dances are both intoxicating and infectious. Not one risqué or obscene joke. And yet the woman dancers have been forced into tights by our censors, while the white dancers in revues and follies romp bare-limbed in other theaters. And when a man like H. O. Tanner, the painter, becomes famous, the negroes get angry because he is referred to as an American painter, and not as a negro, which he is.

At the moment of writing I am informed that negro realtors have bought two blocks of real estate formerly belonging to the Astor estate, on 116th Street below Lenox Avenue. That will relieve in part Harlem's congestion of population. What will soon happen can be readily foreseen. Within a short year the blocks between the newly acquired property and 125th Street will be vacated by the white population and become part of negrodom. One Hundred and Twenty-fifth Street, the Broadway of Harlem, has till now resisted all invasion, but its days are numbered. Every group section in this city has its own amusement center, its own Main Street; 125th Street is the natural Main Street of Harlem.

How prejudice against negroes has been melted in New York is perhaps best illustrated by the recent enormous success of the singer Roland Hayes. For years and years this great artist sought an opportunity to show his ability and his great art. It was refused to him only because of his color. Managers raised their brows. No white public would come to hear a negro singer, they said. In despair Hayes went to England, where in less than a year after his arrival he had been summoned to sing before the king. When he returned to New York on a visit to his parents in 1923, he found quite a different attitude. His success was overwhelming. I counted four white persons out of every five in the audience at some of his concerts. And although he sang very beautifully in several languages, he never reached such heights or depths as when singing the simple spirituals of his own race. Even those who had come to scoff remained to praise and admire, and looked at one another somewhat ashamed of themselves.

Daily hundreds of negroes arrive in New York from

every Southern State. It is pathetic to see the eagerness with which the other negroes, poor and overcrowded as they live, extend to them their hospitality. Yet hundreds find themselves on the street. The Harlem Forum, where many are taken care of out of charity, is overcrowded nightly with shivering, ragged, hungry creatures, who look as though they have just escaped from hell. There is no way to stop the invasion. There is no way to enlarge the houses in which negroes live. Space inclosed by walls is rigid. Segregation breeds immorality, criminality, disease, and increases mortality. One twelfth of the population of a city cannot harmlessly be restricted to live in one fortieth of its area, and be excluded from most decent means of earning its livelihood. Prostitution, bootlegging, and charlatanism are rampant on every corner. The saloons are wide open. So are gambling-dens and dope joints. I have been accosted by boys under twelve who offered to sell me gin, while the policeman on the corner twirled his club and looked aside. I have been winked at by women from windows and doorways of houses before which children played dice. Rents are high. Wages are small. Trade-unions are adverse. And yet . . . Harlem goes earlier to work than any other district. Street-cleaners, dish-washers, chauffeurs, elevator men, and home-sleeping servant-girls have to be early at work. And at night ten thousand men, exceedingly well dressed and looking more prosperous than the others, go to their employment; for that many are nightly employed in cabarets and dance-halls as musicians.

And yet . . . watch them in the street-cars, subways, and elevated trains. They laugh and giggle. The eyes sparkle and the white teeth flash; recounting last night's dance, last night's party, last night's meeting, last night's affair at the church. Never do they call one another by Christian names. It is always "mister," "missis." And when one of them recently gave me his visiting card it read:

Mr. Eleazar Godson
Chief Indoor Aviator
etc., etc.

I puzzled long before I discovered "Indoor Aviator" meant elevator man, and that "Of Hygienist Bureau" meant Street Cleaning Department.

If another such displacement of negroes from the south to the north should take place in 1924 as took place in 1923, when close to five hundred thousand abandoned their home States, the day is not far off when there shall be a negro population of a million in the city. Their political power is already a considerable one. Political machinery is at work to swing it this way and that, in exchange for winked-at privileged liberties and favors. Whether the negroes in New York can be permanently segregated in one particular quarter is very problematical.

And one of them bitterly remarked to me the other day: "They sing our songs, the whites do. They dance to the music we make. They dance our dances. And the bullets made no difference when they killed us in the war, whether we were white or black. And yet when it comes to renting us an apartment they turn up their noses. As soon as I get enough money I shall go to live in France where they don't discriminate against us."

## CHAPTER X

### IN THE BALKAN COUNTRIES

SUPPOSE you want to go from Africa, in Harlem, to the Balkan countries. One might very profitably do the trip on foot and thus hurriedly pass by many remarkable buildings, chief of which, if one would take the westward road, is the Cathedral of St. John the Divine, one of the most imposing buildings in the country. From the Amsterdam Avenue side, at night especially, it awes one with its massiveness and power. The circle of its squat dome against the sky makes it look much more like a giant center of a mosque than a Christian church. With the moon over it, the grayness of its façade of stone, back of the imposing wide steps, is a never-to-be-forgotten sight. The adjoining buildings, belonging to the cathedral, detached though they are, seem like fledglings of some giant bird ready to crawl under its wings, so airy is the whole structure in spite of its enormous size. Looked at from the back, from Columbus Avenue, the edifice loses none of its magnificence as it slopes down the hill.

A little further down are the college buildings with their portals ornate and Florentine, suggesting entrances to inner villas and palaces; they are built very much in the sugar-candy style so dear to Florentine architects of a few centuries ago. Passing street by street on foot, one catches glimpses of the Hudson River, silvery and shimmering. From a distance through the narrow streets one gets the feeling he is looking through one of these old-fashioned stereoscopes, so fixed is the sight because of the tall, styleless buildings that slope down from Amsterdam Avenue to Riverside Drive. There is a sweet smell of burning wood that comes from across the river early in the spring, when the bushes are being burned in Edgewater or Hackensack. And in the summer the houses, partly hidden by the green growth on top of the Palisades, are like toys in a fairy-land. At night the glimmer of the lights on the boats passing on the blue waters, the spread of an occasional white sail fluttering in the wind or lying flabby in the calm, the myriads of lights across the river advertising this and that, enhance the fairy illusion.

From this side of the town you would want to take the bus that goes along the river to Seventy-second Street, and then swings eastward to Broadway, going through part of the western town to Fifty-seventh Street. You will have more than a glimpse of the Fifty-ninth Street circle, with an entrance to Central Park on the eastern side, and on the western side a row of theatrical buildings, gorgeously illuminated with lamps of all colors in an attempt to compete with the lower part of Broadway and to hold that part of the population there for its commerce as well as for its pleasure.

The bus swings then into Fifty-seventh Street, passing by Carnegie Hall. And if it is not late and it is the right season you will see thousands of people waiting outside for the opening of the gates and doors, within which this or that celebrated musician is to play within the next half-hour or so. Young men and young women in their street-clothes, just from work, though tired, stand in line for hours, waiting for the moment when they can buy the cheaper tickets which will permit them to enjoy music from the upper galleries. For to the population of New York, the French, German, Russian, Jewish, and Balkan populations, music is much more of a necessity than a luxury. A good many of these working-men and working-girls, earning their meager salaries in factory or sweat-shop or by clerking in stores, spend more for concerts and serious dramatic presentations than they do for clothes, and many of them would forego half a dozen breakfasts in the morning so as to have the price of a ticket for a concert. By listening to music of composers of their own countries they compensate themselves for the loss of other joys and of more intimate pleasures they had in their own homes.

But the bus goes on. You are on Fifth Avenue before you have had time to look around and observe a little more. You are being rushed through Fifth Avenue without many stops except one at Forty-second Street to let the traffic pass from the west to the east or from the east to the west. Another stop at Fourteenth Street for the same purpose, and then, instead of going to the end of the bus-line at Washington Square and passing through the arch on the site of which was once the public gallows, stop at Eighth Street and walk eastward. You may see again a large crowd, at the doors of the Cooper Union Institute; in fact, very frequently a larger crowd than around Carnegie Hall. The crowd is composed not only of those who are eager to listen to some celebrated speaker or to some one who has just returned from Europe and brings tidings from home for the people of his nationality; it is also composed of a good many people who have nothing else to do and are eager, during a cold rainy night, to spend a few hours indoors. And as you pass around to get into St. Mark's Place you will also see a number of dejected-looking creatures, men and women, sitting on the benches in the little square which surrounds the statue of Peter Cooper.

There are several cafés on this part of St. Mark's Place. There is one to the right side, which is the professional waiters' café, to which the waiters come to be served in turn after they have finished serving other people. It is interesting to know that the waiters come here not for the coffee and cake or the tea or any of the other things they consume, but for the privilege of finding a scapegoat for all they have had to endure during the day or night. If you have made during the day a reproach to your waiter, and a good many have done likewise, you may be sure that he will take it out at the end of the day on the waiters serving him in this coffee-house of his. Go in for a few minutes, if you have nothing else to do, and you will see a man in street-clothes (so happy are they to get rid of their professional habits that they get into street-clothes as soon as they are through working) calling down a waiter, reproaching him for the manner in which he served him, returning the knives or the forks, or looking carefully at the napkin, the plate, or sniffing at the food that was brought to him, doing exactly what others had done to him during the day.

It is a little inversion of the scriptural dictum. "Do unto others what is done to you," seems to be the waiters' credo.

At your left hand is a dancing-hall, the Arlington. Most of the Polish weddings in the neighborhood are celebrated there. You might be just in time to see one, and see most of the guests come in their national costumes. And if you care to have a glimpse inside you will see them dance the mazurka as you have never seen it danced before. The women are in high boots and white skirts embroidered with yellow and green, and sleeveless cassocks of red and blue, with white silken head-gear hanging from the forehead to the back of the shoulders. The men wear their beribboned small hats and are also in high riding-boots. They stamp the floor, laughing wildly, while the women take their dance very seriously. It is not always advisable to remain very long in such a place, for weddings do not always end happily. There might suddenly appear a slighted young man or a slighted young woman, and the festivities may end at the police station—if not worse.

Go down a little further, to 31 St. Mark's Place; look close down. There is a curiously painted sign on which is written "The Tub," right over the basement. And right and left of the entrance artistically done signs announce that this is the conclave of democratic students of the arts and drama and sociology. The place opens early in the evening for a few hours, and all the tramps in the vicinity are served a hot dish, a cup of coffee, and a piece of bread, for a maximum sum of five cents for those who have the price, and food is given free as long as it lasts to those who don't. The man who runs the Tub is Ledoux, who under the name of Zero won national fame a few years ago, during the unemployment succeeding the war, by auctioning off able-bodied white and black men and women in Boston and New York, so as to avoid their starving. It is very probable that you will meet Ledoux if you stay a little while in the place and talk with those sitting on the benches at the long white-pine table. You will find, much to your surprise, extremely intelligent men discussing calmly or passionately questions of weight and importance. They plunge into abstract discussions of art to forget the misery facing them, for the Tub attracts only what is known as the "intellectual tramp."

The place closes at about ten o'clock at night, and reopens after midnight for a very short time to let in those who have not succeeded in finding shelter for the night elsewhere. They sleep on the bare floor, propping their heads on their elbows and covering themselves with their coats. They will get another cup of coffee in the morning, and, if there happens to be one among them skilful with the razor, they will be shaved and made presentable to find work during the day. Should one find work he will, as soon as he gets his pay, return such an amount of money as he thinks he has cost the Tub; so that the place may go on without seeking support from charitable organizations. Most of the tramps are strongly opposed to any dealings with institutionalized charity.

Around the corner of St. Mark's Place is an open area, with St. Mark's Church on it. The old church has recently been painted over and made to look very much like some medieval French church. It is surrounded by different groups of statuary, the work and the gift of George Gray Barnard. Within one of these thick walls is the grave of Peter Stuyvesant, former governor of New Amsterdam. All the territory down to the East River was once his Bouwerie. Old Stuyvesant, irascible and ill-tempered, was very strongly opposed to the Jews when they appeared in the city during his governorship. What irony of fate that his Bouwerie should now be the stronghold of the Jews and of people of so many tongues! Peter Stuyvesant disliked all other non-Dutchmen quite as much as he disliked the Jews. What irony of fate that the square around his church should be one in which political compaigns are carried on all through the year in a half-dozen languages, from soap-boxes and the rears of trucks!

Looking down Second Avenue from Stuyvesant Square, one is struck by the innumerable electric lights flashing from both sides. It is the East Side's Fifth Avenue, or, better still, the East Side's Broadway. There are several theaters, foreign-language theaters, numerous vaudeville houses and moving-picture homes. A little upward is the old Royal Coffee-house, with its piazza on the sidewalk, which makes one forget that he is elsewhere than in Budapest, Vienna, or Bucharest. Within the inclosure of the piazza are a number of small tables, around which sit the intellectuals of a half a dozen nationalities discussing, over their tea or coffee, or while they eat watermelon, the respective arts and literatures and musical news of the day. They have their set tables. Each one of them appears as regularly at his table as if he had to punch a time-clock.

First of all appear the actors, to have their evening meal and chat before performing on the stage. The German actors playing in the Irvington Theater, the Yiddish actors of the neighborhood, the Hungarian dramatists and mu-

sicians and painters, and the newspaper men of all these nationalities, as well as the Russians, have their tables and hours. And they all talk loudly in a Babel of tongues. And though each of them is wearing European or American clothes, the shape of the cut of their beards and the cast of their heads and features emphasize each one's nationality.

For here indeed congregate the brains of foreign New York. On the walls are posters and announcements of balls, concerts, and performances in a dozen languages.

Across the street is the Russian Bear. Until not very long ago this place was one of the last of the residential places that had held out in spite of the foreign invasion moving from the east westward. But it, too, has succumbed. The middle walls between rooms have been pierced through to make a large, narrow hall, at the end of which a mezzanine platform has been built. The walls have been painted with that Byzantine touch so dear to the Russians. In the center of the hall stands the Balalaika orchestra, playing those curious instruments strongly resembling the ukulele and producing a sound midway between a guitar and a banjo. The musicians play Russian music for the visitors, and on occasion there is a singer or two, dressed in Gipsy costume, singing the Russian Gipsy songs of which no real Muscovite can ever hear the last.

What one feels most is the non-professionalism of the whole place. Neither the owner nor the musicians nor the waiters seem to be caterers to the public by profession. And upon inquiry one finds out that they are not. They are mostly noblemen and noblewomen of the old Russian régime, who after finding refuge in this country are now trying to make both ends meet. And since they knew so well how to be served by others, they have found it comparatively easy to adapt themselves to the menial work they are doing. It is interesting to see how servile and docile these former noblemen and noblewomen can be. They smile quite broadly and bow very low at a liberal tip. As they rarely speak English, one has to order his food in the Russian language, which is written on the bill of fare in Latin characters; and if you have not succeeded after the first trial, just put your finger on the name of the food you have chosen. The strangely sounding name, which makes you anticipate some strangely composed dish, may disappoint you. Quite ordinary boiled beef and cabbage may appear at the table when you thought of something more exotic than that. But the tea is excellent. And the *kvass,* a beverage made of stale corn-bread, is still better. There are many, many very handsome women smoking cigarettes very gracefully and sipping tea with as great an abandon as if it were champagne. The atmosphere is a very pleasant and intimate one. Leon Trotzky and John Reed used to be frequent visitors at the Bear.

On Ninth Street between Second and Third Avenues is the Slovene Church, the Greek Orthodox Church, where the priest in long beard and velvet *calpac,* a silk hat without the rim, on his head, preaches his sermon in the old Slovene language. A little further along Second Street is the old Marble Cemetery, which stretches almost half a block. Some of the earliest notables of New York are buried there. It is still kept by caretakers, and through the iron fence one can see the floral tributes brought by descendants of the old New Yorkers on the graves of their ancestors.

In the blaze of light along Second Avenue are numerous restaurants and coffee-houses, with their inscriptions, "Rumanian Coffee-house" and "Rumanian Restaurant." Here one is in the heart of the Rumanian district. It has this in particular: it is not like the main street of any other town in Rumania. It strongly resembles in its atmosphere and assortment the principal street of Bucharest, the avenue in which the king's palace stands—beautiful gowns in the large windows of the shops and jewelry stores, beauty-parlors, pastry-shops, and coffee-houses, all so gaudy and loud. Most of these places are, as in Rumania, not kept by Rumanians, but are chiefly in the hands of Jews of all origins, Greek, Hungarian, and German. For in Bucharest also, the capital of Rumania, all business is practically in the hands of the same nationalities as have them in their hands here. They are merely catering to Rumanian tastes. One can realize more than ever why Bucharest is called Little Paris or the Paris of the Balkans. If you happen to be in doubt as to what language to use on going into any of these restaurants, every one of which seems to be presided over by a pupil of Lucullus, talk French and you will certainly be understood.

As if to remind one of the fact that we are in New York is the iron gate between two tall houses, leading through an alley into a back yard, where is an older branch of the Marble Cemetery. You can obtain permission to enter by applying to the caretaker in charge. It is between Second and Third Streets. Almost leaning on it are a moving-picture house and one of the Jewish theaters of the neighborhood. And while the throngs of extremely well dressed people are walking back and forth, making their daily promenades, just as if they were in the old country, music produced by all sorts of instruments is heard from a dozen different places, and singing, also. It mingles with the raucous tones of some radio loud-speaker or of the dozen and one stores selling phonographs and player-pianos. And if you can resist the blaze of light from the People's Theater, announcing some new musical comedy or the presentation of a Rumanian play by Rumanian players next door to the Winter Garden, do so, and go into Houston Street. There is an old church adjoining these theaters. It used to be the pride of the neighborhood. The illuminated cross on the top looks at night as if it were floating in the air. Walk eastward toward the river, and between Second and First Avenues there is a restaurant to which all Rumanians flock. Within it the owner is playing the cymbalom, that curious old instrument so dear to the Rumanian Gipsies. He is as good on it as anybody has ever been; indeed, he is the Kreisler of the cymbalom. No matter what hour of the night you might drop in there, you will have to struggle to find a chair to sit upon. For although the noise of the waiters and the guests is deafening, the neighborhood comes there more to listen to the man's playing than to eat. And his playing has been heard of in other quarters than the Rumanian one. Most of the journalists on American papers come down when they can spare the time and can afford it. Eugene O'Neill, the playwright, drops in from time to time. John Dos Passos, Heifetz, the violinist, and Toscha Seidel and Mischa Elman, and others of the musical and literary professions.

But those who want to dine in a more quiet fashion, and still crave the pleasure of eating food prepared in their own style, go to Broome Street, to the Rumanian Casino, where the owner's attention to every guest is one of the chief delights. You will be struck especially with the number of restaurants and the smell of exotic foods in that district, for all Rumanians are good eaters and drinkers. They are of lighter temperament than any of the other people in the Balkans, more given to laughter and song and dance, the men as well as the women. They do not carry the *Weltschmerz* on their shoulders like their neighbors two blocks away, the Russians and Bulgarians and Serbs. Although you will hardly find one illiterate among them, their chief concern is not about books and philosophies when they meet of an evening. They spend their money more easily than any other people and are indeed, because of that, here as well as at home, the butt of ridicule and the object of exploitation by all the other peoples.

The Carnegie Library on Rivington Street has one of the finest assortments of Rumanian books. Indeed, it is almost a complete library of Rumanian literature. Originally it was collected by Mr. Sebastian Liberty. Adjoining the library is the Rivington Street Settlement-house, the first settlement on the East Side. It is from this center that have gone out, after their experiences in the neighborhood, people like William English Walling and J. G. Phelps Stokes, and Anna Strunsky, and Rose Pastor Stokes, and Joseph Freeman, and a number of others. Jack London has lectured several times in that neighborhood. I remember meeting him on his return from the Russo-Japanese War. To make his visits from door to door easier, he became the agent of a photographer selling lapel picture-buttons, which were then so much in vogue. We lay down side by side one night on a bare floor in the house

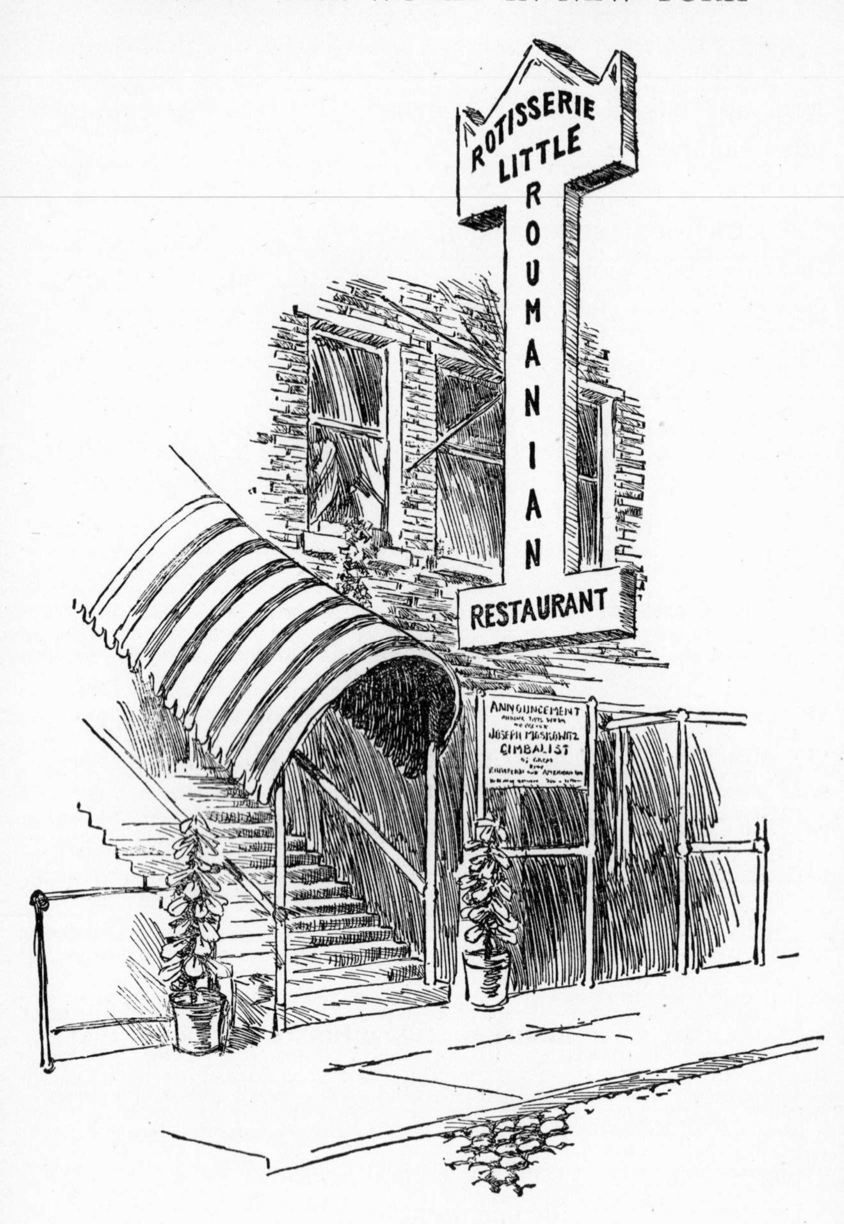
ROTISSERIE
LITTLE
ROUMANIAN
RESTAURANT
ANNOUNCEMENT
JOSEPH MOSKOWITZ
CIMBALIST

of a friend whose only bed was occupied by himself and wife, and talked to the wee hours of the morning. Many other notables have lectured in the settlement. And there are quite a few notables who have emerged from there. The settlement is still going on, only in a different direction, catering much more to those who have already Americanized themselves than to those who are to be Americanized. Further below, under the elevated railroad, dark in the day and bleak at night, are hundreds of stores selling imported cheeses and dried fish and smoked meats from Rumania. Food shops adjoin quilt factories, dressmaking shops, second-hand furniture stores, antique brass shops. They lean one against the other in a bewildering sort of fashion, thrown pell-mell with no care for the sort of wares that are within.

Orchard Street with its sordid push-cart business, with stores littered with everything on God's earth, with the cry and yell of the itinerant merchant, with phonographs sold from push-carts and player-pianos sold in the middle of the street, heckling, bargaining, cursing, swearing, is always swarming with people. The moment the push-carts are brought forth early in the morning till the time the acetylene lights, smoking black over their white flames, are completely burned out, the street is black with people. How any one can wear luxurious silk intimate garments that have been bought of a push-cart, how any one can bedeck herself with jewelry bought there, is more than I can understand.

Above all this sordidness of the street are the homes of the people. One would be surprised, on entering any home of the middle class, to see the luxury and comfort to be found there, the outside is so ugly and repellant, and the inside has been made so agreeable. Proud and strong physically, the Rumanian men and women, the Jews as well as the Gentiles, furnish a smaller percentage of applicants for charity than any other nationality in the city. Outwardly, especially in their business, they are not as ready to adopt American methods as the other people are. Yet on the other hand, with that peculiar ability which is theirs, they learn the language of the country much more rapidly than the others, while still keeping an eye on the culture that they have brought from home.

There are several cultural institutions and clubs, to which well-known Rumanian writers are invited from Europe to come and lecture. And at these *Sezatores* very much in the old fashion, sittings in which some one tells a tale, there is a thread that ties to home. One would be surprised to know that the Jews who left Rumania because of political persecutions should still have so much love for their country, should still be so anxious to keep in touch with its literature, its art, its politics. But then a good deal of the Rumanian literature was produced by Jews, and the same thing could be said of all the other arts in Rumania. The Rumanian Jews here point with pride to what they have produced and given to this country. Professor Solomon Schechter, deceased a few years ago, was the head of the theological seminary and one of the most celebrated biblical scholars of the world. They have at present several professors at Columbia University, the Rumanian poet Leon Ferraru, and Felix Vexler; and there are a good many other professors at Johns Hopkins University and other universities of the country. How isolated the Rumanian Jews are from the Jews of other nations can be seen by the fact that they have their own synagogue, their own burial-ground, their own charitable institutions, their own homes for old people, not to speak of their own newspapers. As if to emphasize the fact that this is a Rumanian quarter, one can on Forsyth Street see the numerous Greek coffee-houses where the Greeks living in the Rumanian quarter congregate. And over a former saloon on Forsyth Street is an old Turkish coffee-house, where the Turkish dancers are doing their stunt just as if that part of the town were the well-known Cetatzrina, the Turkish quarter in Braïla on the Danube.

And the Bulgars, who at home sell that cooling drink brewed from bran and millet, are doing the same thing here, selling *braga* to those who still have a taste for it after many years away from home.

In former years the Rumanian quarter did not extend as far up town as it does now. The uptown region was inhabited by the Hungarians, with the Bulgars below them. Indeed, during the period of the war when the Hungarians invaded Rumania, the Rumanian quarter shrank in the same proportion as Rumania had after the invasion of the enemy. But the Peace of Versailles and the interpretation of it by Rumania after the war, whereby the Rumanians retook the old territory which had once belonged to them, affected the Rumanian quarter here as well. The Rumanian population, which had meanwhile grown, expanded further into Hungarian territory. Restaurants and coffee-houses, as well as other businesses which had been till then known as the Hungarian this and that, suddenly became, by virtue of the occupation of new territory by the Rumanians in their own country, Rumanian restaurants and coffee-houses and this and that. Many of these inhabitants became, by virtue of the change at home, Rumanian subjects, instead of Hungarian subjects as they had been. And like the withdrawal, so has the expansion not been without conflict. They invaded with a vengeance, they expanded with a fury, knowing full well their enemies were beaten into submission. All through the war this had been taking place in all the other quarters of the town. The Bulgars had invaded the Serbian territory and were expelled afterward. And the Germans had gone as near to the heart of the French district as they had gone to Paris, only to be pushed back later. Even the occupation of the Ruhr by the French has had its counterpart in this city. The French went as far into the German territory as they possibly could, and many a German bakery became a French *boulangerie* overnight.

In the side streets of the Rumanian quarter live the Rumanian Gipsies. The men fare forth early in the evening, repairing to the different Rumanian restaurants to play their music, while the women go out to ply their trade of fortune-telling and basket-selling. And they, too, expanded into what was formerly Hungarian territory after the Peace of Versailles. Those of the Rumanians who have lived here a long time have indeed spread all over the city. There is a distinctively Rumanian quarter over on Seventh Avenue and Twenty-third Street. Most of the people living in that district are Transylvanian Rumanians, who were formerly subjects of Hungary. It is because of their supposed martyrdom and because they have remained faithful to their own nationality through all the vicissitudes of a thousand years that they consider themselves superior to the other Rumanians. It is they who are the heart and soul of the intellectual movement among the Rumanians all over the country. They are not as easy-going or light-hearted as their brothers from across the Carpathians. Of peasant origin, they are a more calculating and slow-going clan than the Rumanians of the old kingdom.

There is another Rumanian district up in the Bronx, at Washington Avenue and 175th Street. It is composed of Rumanian Jews, and Pindo-Rumanians, Macedonian Rumanians. Such Rumanians have for centuries and centuries lived in the lower Balkans among the Bulgarians and Serbs, Albanians, Greeks and Turks. During the last war their nationality was claimed by ethnologists in each one of these nations. But their language, with all the mixture that has been superposed on top of it, is Rumanian, or, better said, it is the old Latin dialect which the soldiers of Trajan brought to the banks of the Danube after vanquishing Decebal, the king of the Dacs.

There are any number of small Rumanian settlements here and there. The younger element, acclimatized, take part in the politics of the country, and political careers in America are a very strong attraction to them. They have at present a number of assemblymen and aldermen. The liberal professions are thronged. They have a large quota of lawyers, physicians, dentists, teachers, and college professors. There are in New York two daily papers printed in Rumanian, as well as several literary magazines. There are some thirty thousand people of Rumanian origin living in New York. According to the census there are over a hundred thousand of them all over the country, with large centers in Chicago and Detroit, Cleveland and Minneapolis, and Pittsburg, working in steel-mills and mines. Among the well-known figures of Rumanian origin are David Belasco, the Schildkrauts, father and son, Jacob Adler, the painter, Paléologue and Papini, musicians like Max Rosen and Alma Gluck, and a number of writers and newspaper men.

Further down toward the East River, between Avenue B and Avenue C, on Third, Fourth, Fifth, and Sixth Streets, live three other peoples of Balkan extraction and propensities. On Third and Fourth Streets live the Bulgars. There were a good many more than there are to-day, but, as many of them came here without their families, they were compelled to return to their homes after the outbreak of the war. And even those who remained here for a little while afterward dispersed to other districts, or perhaps other cities, because of the enmity between them and the Serbs, who lived across the street a little further east and north. Those animosities have many times reached the knife-point, with the people, during the war, mostly siding with the Serbs, whose nationals fought on the side of the Allies. But the Bulgars did not lack in support; for the population of the region is still partly German, the Germans not having been completely ousted from their erstwhile stronghold on the lower East Side.

Another people living in the neighborhood are the Montenegrins, who are to be distinguished from the Bulgarians or the Serbs by their tremendous size and width of shoulders, as well as by that peculiar lopsided gait so peculiar to mountaineers. The Montenegrins had still more difficulties than either of the other two nations during the war. As will be remembered, the little kingdom of Montenegro was the first one that went over to the side of the Central Powers, after much less than a battle with the enemy. They were friendly with neither the Serbs nor the Bulgars, and were hated cordially by the peoples on both sides.

There used to be restaurants which fed the two nationalities together, one of them not being enough to support the business. And as their national foods are alike, it was quite feasible. Little racial differences were buried at the common table in similar tastes—broiled lamb, cooked whole wheat, and *yoghurt*. One used to see "Montenegrin-Bulgarian Restaurant" or "Montenegrin-Serbian Restaurant" in the window-panes. But to-day, on passing one of the streets, one can see how half of the hyphenated sign has been scratched off.

There is in that part of the city a heterodox mixture. There are also Poles and Hungarians and Slavs and Croatians and Macedonians, laggers in the great migration further northward. It is curious that the migration of the people in New York should repeat, even though on a small scale, the order and method of migration into

Europe of the Indo-European races. For all through the Balkan countries one can see the descendants of those who lagged behind during the great Indo-European and Indo-Slavic migrations westward and eastward. And strange as it may seem, though they are living close together, with

their children going to the same school, and most of them belonging to the same denomination, namely the Greek Orthodox Church, there is no social relation between them even among the youngsters. There is no intermarriage, each one in the eyes of the other being of an even lower social and racial degree than the negroes. The little bullet heads of the Macedonians or Montenegrins would never be convinced that there is any race equal to their own, either in intelligence or in bravery. Even to this day every house of a Macedonian is adorned with a picture of Alexander of Macedon, and with pictures of other heroes of ancient days.

I shall never forget how I incurred the enmity of my friend Redout on Fourth Street, in whose restaurant I had eaten almost twice a day for months, because he had seen me walk side by side with a Montenegrin. Not that he disliked that particular Montenegrin or because he was a special enemy of his. But it was enough for any of his friends to walk side by side with a Montenegrin to lose caste with a Macedonian. I had been invited to the wedding of Redout's daughter, and had been promised a national costume for that occasion. Every one was supposed to come in national costume. But a few days before the wedding I was very brusquely told that the arrangement would not be carried out, that they would not dishonor a national Macedonian costume by permitting it to be worn by any one who had walked side by side with a Montenegrin.

Neither the Bulgars nor the Serbs nor the Macedonians nor the Montenegrins are permanently here. Some have been so minded when they first arrived, but have later changed their minds, waiting only until they have enough money, with perhaps a little over traveling-expenses, to return to their plains and their mountains. There are very few families of lower Balkan people here. Where there is one family, like the Stoumboffs on Third Street, the house is always too small to contain those who come to visit, to feast their eyes, as they say, on a woman's form, and rejoice their hearts with the sound of a woman's voice.

No better census could be taken of either of these nationalities than at one of the rare weddings. Practically every one belonging to the nation whose daughter or son is being wedded will be present, and they will each one vie with the other as to who will make costlier gifts to the bride and groom. And like the old traditional greeting of the Jews on the Day of Atonement, "That we meet next year in Jerusalem," so is the wish expressed by every guest that they meet next year in Cettinje or Sophia, or wherever their home may be.

Mr. Pupin, the Serb inventor and professor at Columbia, whose book attracted so much attention when it appeared, will never know what pride and jealousy he has stirred up among the people of his own country and its enemies. In his isolated Americanism he does not realize what he means to his people.

All of these houses on Third, Fourth, Fifth, and Sixth Streets, in which the Balkan people live, are of the oldest in this part of the city, with no fire-escapes and no conveniences of any kind, with walls almost falling by themselves and dark hallways and dark bedrooms. And the little light that would come in is obstructed by the rear houses—sun-leeches.

The restaurants are all on the basement floors, and the simple fare is served mostly in earthen dishes decorated with crude colored flowers of these people's own make and importation. Here and there a wooden spoon of the kind that is boiled in oil for hardening its fiber makes its appearance on a table. It is seldom that any of these people can speak more than a few words of the English language. They are mostly small tradesmen of the kind that masquerade as Persians. Like the Armenians and other Orientals, they peddle at night among the tables of the restaurants with rugs and laces and things of that kind. Some of them are occupied doing small carpentry work; others work in the adjoining sweat-shops and factories, which occupy both sides of Delancey Street from the corner of Forsyth Street down to the bridge. Gradually the strongest of them are being fed by the adjoining labor agencies to the steel-mills and coal-mines of Pennsylvania, especially when there happens to be a strike. Ignorant of the language of the country, desolate and sad, lonely, isolated, they are easy prey for strike-breaking agencies. They neither have newspapers in their own language nor are they of sufficient numbers to make it worth while for any one institution to keep them informed of things happening in the country. They are largely left to themselves, and such information as they can pick up from neighbors misinforms more than informs. I have seen many a one plodding over the Croatian newspaper "Narodny List," or the Jugo-Slavic, trying to understand what was in it, in the belief that these were American newspapers.

What a relief to come out suddenly from these hopeless streets, which reek with the stench of all the kitchens and sewers and the garbage piled up high on the sidewalk and the suffocating odors floating from the barges on the East River that carry away the dirt and waste of the city! What a relief when suddenly coming into Tompkins Square, with the wide acres that were once dangerous salt marshes, and the big, inviting houses all about the square. Children of the neighborhood play together in the sand or within the wire-inclosed fences, rough-housing one another, jumping over one another, but rubbing shoulders nevertheless, and learning to appreciate each other's qualities between two vigorous punches and a dozen curses. Immigrants without children are not an asset to America. . . . There should be a law about that . . . concerning landlords especially. There should be a law inflicting severe punishment on those who refuse to let their houses to people with children.

To the west, on Tenth Street, rises the big old annex of St. Mark's in the Bouwerie, in which the Leonardo da Vinci School is housed. Across from it is the Boys' Club. Further down are the Tompkins Square Settlement and the several day nurseries where tots with queerly shaped heads are crying in one and the same language for the arrival of their mothers. For really, if there is any hope at all for these people, it is in the squares and in the parks—playing in the sand or hoisting themselves on the bars of the gymnastic apparatus. The square is now being more and more taken possession of by the Poles, who are beginning to crowd the neighborhood, ousting the Italians, forcing them to move further northward. At night when the blond-haired Poles promenade on the alleys, arm in arm with their high-cheekboned beaus, Tompkins Square is Warsaw, Crakow, or Lemberg.

But I have already traveled away from the Balkans. There never will be peace there. There never will be peace here among them until their blood shall have disappeared among the other peoples of the neighborhood. Italians who have still remained in what was once their stronghold are intermarrying with them. In this respect the Italians, by intermarrying with almost every nation in the city, are doing the greatest service to America—absorbing small tribal bloods.

# CHAPTER XI

## SPAIN

MANY, many years ago, I hurried through the Balkans to Spain. Because of the urgency of my being at Madrid on a certain day, I had no leisure to stop anywhere en route. I saw the countries between Rumania and Spain only through the windows of the railroad-car and during very brief stops at railroad-stations. There was a very brief stop in Bucharest, the capital of Rumania. I had a glimpse of the illuminated roof of the city lying several miles away from the railroad-station; an eyeful of the people who crowded the station, peasants in their national garb, and women dressed in the latest style of gowns just imported from Paris and crowned with the most extravagant millinery from the modistes of Vienna. And then there were miles and miles of low brick houses. People going back and forth to their labors in the fields or in the factories. Horse-carts. Oxen yoked to low-wheeled trucks. Swift dream-like vistas of stations and people rushed from us until we reached the frontier, where customs inspectors came to give us the once over before letting us pass the border. The locomotive shrieked, the wheels of the cars ground the steel of the rails, bells rang, people called to one another.

And yet I could have told instantly that we had passed

into another country, though only an arbitrary line divided the two. And after many hours we halted on the border of still another country. We entered Austria. We rolled on and on, passing railroad-stations much trimmer and cleaner in appearance than the ones we had left behind, and people with more of their own characteristics and less of the Parisian and the Viennese flutter. There was a short stop at Vienna. The things I most clearly remember are the excellent fat beer and the *Leberwurst* we had in the dining-room of the railway station. I also remember the brand of beautiful waitresses. It was entirely new to me then. So cool and so clean-faced! The eyes so sparkling! The carriage of the head so passionate! And yet I remained with the impression that they were cooler and colder than any women I had seen. The men waiters were extremely polite and thanked one a dozen times for the smallest tip given them.

Another ride of many hours and we had passed through Germany, hardly seeing it. For although it was early in the spring a blizzard preceded and followed our train. We were unable to outride it. We entered France several days later and rushed through, post-haste, until we got to Paris, where, although I had many hours to wait before the last plunge to Madrid, I remained at the railroad-station, unwilling to be distracted from the plan I had made, knowing full well that were I to go out to see the city Madrid would have to wait. There was so much attraction for the visitor at the Gare St.-Lazare that I was afraid not to be able to resist the temptation if I so much as went out a hundred feet into the street.

I was complimenting myself on my fortitude when the train moved again. I arrived when due in Madrid.

I recalled all this as I traveled the other day from the Balkan section in New York to the Spanish section. I walked through the Rumanian section, a corner of the Austro-Polish section, the Austrian, touched the German section, edged the French one, and then arrived into Spain. Which only means that I went from Fourth Street to Eighth Street on foot, then walked along Second Avenue to Twenty-third Street, and followed Twenty-third Street to Seventh Avenue, the edge of the Spanish district. It extends from there southward to Abingdon Square and encompasses all that lies between Seventh and Eighth Avenues.

A visitor in Spain is struck by the fact that he can see very little of Spanish home life, except what he sees at public exhibitions, theaters (which are very few), bull-fights, and the market-places. And at that you can very seldom get near enough, as near as you can get to other people, when meeting them under similar circumstances. Whether it is the dignity of the old Arab blood that still flows in the Spaniards, or whether it is of more recent origin—a sort of grandeur from the days when they were, if not the masters of Europe and the world, at least in line to be so—I do not know. But as the Arab can withdraw within his tent, the Spaniard withdraws within his cloak. The women hide their faces, and the men have a peculiar somberness in their eyes that shades them as a veil, a veil which, though invisible, can seldom be pierced. Except the face of the Indian I know of no more enigmatic face

than the face of the Spanish man or woman. For though they have lived for so many centuries in Europe, the African influence is still there. You can see that in the architecture in Spain, in Granada and in Seville and Madrid and Barcelona. No matter how different the temperament of these different cities, they are at bottom the same. Architecture will tell. The Spaniards were more than neighbors and enemies with the Moors.

And so in New York, although there are some twenty thousand Spanish inhabitants, and although there are considerably more than twice as many of Spanish origin from the Central Americas continually in the city, one seldom sees them, one seldom notices their activity. Except at rare presentations of some Spanish company at a theater, one seldom hears of their theatrical activities; and in spite of their great ability and propensity for dancing one seldom sees any of that done in public. There are no Spanish dancing-halls in New York. There are no Spanish cabarets.

It seems to me that the Spanish are more reticent in this country than they are even at home. For the Spaniard still feels, because of Columbus's discovery, that this territory has been ravished from him. He still smarts under the blow of the Anglo-Saxon superiority which has taken from him most of his possessions in the Americas. He still turns up his nose at the upstarts who have robbed him of what was his. There is no forgetting with him. The days when Spanish gold was the currency of America are still in his mind. The emblem of a country is on its coin.

The Spanish stores and restaurants and societies are all behind curtains. Walk through Fourteenth or Sixteenth or any of the streets in the central Spanish quarter, and you will see how unobtrusive they are, how insolently modest in a country where modesty is a crime. A little sign in a window, black letters on a white background, a little tablet on a wall. When you go in you meet people who seem to accept your visit as a great honor conferred upon them, which they return with great dignity. And they are discreet and quiet and self-possessed. Everything within doors is absolutely Spanish. They take it for granted when you enter a Spanish restaurant that you speak Spanish, and will talk to you in no other language even when they understand yours. They will serve you quietly, discreetly. There is no loud clang of the cash-register when you have paid. Though dignified, the method of paying is also as discreet as if you were merely returning the compliment of a gift instead of paying and giving profit for what you have consumed. There is much less smiling on the part of the patronesses or the waitresses than there is in the French quarters. Merely looking at you they think they have conferred a great favor upon you, which is exactly the thought of every Spanish *doña.*

I once lived a year in the same house with four Spanish families. At the end of the year, although I could recognize the step of every one in the house, and knew from the touch which of the family of Cienfuegos, all of them musicians, was playing the piano, and would have identified even the closing of a door two floors below me, I was never as much as nodded to by any of the neighbors, let alone invited to conversation.

Living in the Spanish quarter of the town is one of my most agreeable memories. As the streets are very broad, and the stoops project themselves outside over the sidewalks, it was very pleasant to listen at night to the low-sung serenades accompanied by expertly handled guitars, when the young men visited their *señoritas.*

On Fourteenth Street in the Casa Sevilla, where most of the better class of Spanish young men used to come for their evening meals, there were some mysterious goings-on in the upper rooms. It possibly was nothing extraordinary! But they were so mysterious! The dining-room was entirely decorated in Spanish style. The odor and the taste of the food, as well as the brownish long faces of the visitors, completed the illusion of being in Spain instead of in New York. The owner of the place was an exceedingly stout *señora* of about fifty, who still affected her national garb behind her counter. Having had dinner with one of my friends one day there, we were served with some of the poorest wine I have ever drunk. Feeling rather communicative, the owner came over to our table and wished us good evening. I complained to her about the quality of the wine.

"It is what we get here for the guests," she replied. And then after a pause she added, "For my friends and myself I have a much better wine than that."

Whereupon I called out joyously, "Then in Heaven's name consider me one of your friends."

"Do you want to be one of my friends?" the *señora* repeated. "You shall drink of that wine instantly."

She withdrew behind the counter and emerged with a very ancient-looking bottle of Marsala wine and an additional glass for herself. It did not take us long to finish the bottle. My friend enthusiastically asked for another one, which was brought to the table, the lady partaking with us from this second bottle also. When I got up and asked for my bill, the two bottles of wine were not included on the check.

"See here," I said to the *señora,* "these two bottles of Marsala are not on my check. How much are they?"

Like a flash the *señora* stood up, her eyes flashing in anger. She was atremble, in tremendous fury.

"Oh!" she shouted at me, "you do not want to be my friend! This is why you offer to pay for the wine!"

I stuttered and blubbered all kinds of apologies, and

finally, humbling myself, I convinced her that I did not mean it in that way. We had to drink a third bottle of Marsala and kiss her hand.

Doughty, in his remarkable "Travels through Arabia Deserta," speaks of the wonderful hospitality of the Bedouins and the other Arabs. Once you have broken bread with them you are their guest. While you are in their house or their tent they will defend you with their lives even against their own brothers. But they will not hesitate to shoot you dead thirty paces away from their beyt. It is this wonderful sense of hospitality which makes the Spaniard offer you everything that is in his house when you cross the threshold; but watch out when you accept too much!

The whole district, down to Abingdon Square, on Hudson Street, with trellised balconies on the low, red-brick houses, and the Russian Tavern just across the street from it, is more of the Old World than can possibly be imagined, only a few blocks from Broadway and the busy thoroughfares of New York. The streets are a mosaic of trucks and carts coming and going to the wharves on the Hudson River. Flags of ships, masts, chimney-stacks, look at you from every street-end westward. At night the windows of the houses are not as brightly lit as in other streets. Kerosene-lamps are still in use, for not all the houses have been piped for gas.

Not only are Spaniards living in this district, which extends virtually from Abingdon Square to Twenty-third Street, but there are the Portuguese in great number. Guadeloupians, Cubans, Syrians; and there is a strong

Irish contingent who lived here long before any of these nationalities occupied the district. Catholic New York is living in that part of the town. Five different kinds of English are used here.

A little further down Hudson Street is St. Luke's Chapel. Built a century ago, with yellow-painted bricks, it looks more like a small village church on a Main Street than a wealthy church in a metropolis. Its additional wings, and even the parish-houses adjoining it for the different activities that are being added as the community enlarges are only afterthoughts. And then suddenly one runs into mysterious Jane and Horatio Streets, half warehouses and half residential, with a strong smell of dates and figs and other dried fruits that lie in the warehouses of the neighborhood. In the spring of the year the odor of fermenting St. John's bread is irresistible. When the dates and figs heat and the odor mixes with the scent of Gilead coffee, one gets sick for the Orient.

As if to keep up the architecture of the Spaniards, a trucking-house built its establishment on Gansevoort Street in the style associated with Granada and Seville. The architect must have thought of that when he designed the building. An artist really. There is the Old World church-like school of San Bernard on Gansevoort Street where Thirteenth Street crazily crosses Fourth Street. Its projecting images of Ignatius, its architecture, though it was built quite recently, are entirely out of keeping with what surrounds it. This is another proof of the haphazard conglomeration of what was once, as there is evidence in other buildings, a very restricted residential neighborhood, when Twenty-first Street was Love Lane, and when the Post Road ran through from Abingdon Road, and the whole neighborhood to Seventy-first Street, where was the Kissing Bridge, was one of lanes and pleasant woods.

The houses on Fourteenth Street between Seventh and Eighth Avenues are built on very narrow strips of frontage land. And each one, even though of the same height as the next one, is built in an individual style. There are houses of red bricks with black-painted windows and doors, and deep set-in sills over the round archway. And between a red and a gray house there suddenly looms up a yellow-painted stucco building, with narrow oblong windows and red-painted lucarnes between them. There is the Casa María, of rough yellow stucco, with beautifully lined windows and vaulted doors that are barred with wrought-iron. The basement entrance is as mysterious as the descent into one of the underground piazzas around the Alhambra.

A little further is the projected front of wrought-iron of the Guadalupe Church, as unlike anything on the opposite sidewalk, which is still Anglo-Saxon, as if the two were in absolutely different countries, with the middle of the street as the frontier.

There is the building on the corner of Seventh Avenue, with its ten floors of studded phosphorescence and blue squares between the large windows. On the ground floor is a Spanish bank, probably one of the most important in the city. It also sells perfumery and has a book-store as a side-line. All kinds of books in Spanish are to be had in that store. The most courteous clerk in the world is trying to help one; and so insistently does he explain every book, telling one the story within the book as well as the biography of the writer, that one cannot leave without buying from him. Never before has clerk in a book-store known as much about books as the clerks in that store. It is from them that I first learned all about Reuben Dario, the great Central American poet, whose works have astounded and astonished the Spanish world. It is from the clerks of that store that I learned of the existence of a number of other poets, Spanish all of them, who live in this country. It was, indeed, a great surprise to me to know how much of modern Spanish literature and poetry has been produced by the half-caste of Indian and Spanish blood. Many a passage was read to me aloud. Although I did not understand everything, the rhythm and the sound were as fascinating as an alternating mixture between a Spanish dance and an Indian prayer.

On the opposite corner is the Metropolitan Temple, to my mind the most beautiful symmetrical structure in the city of New York. As one hungers before spring returns for the sight of green fields, or as a man who has been brought up near the sea hungers for the sight of salt water, for the smell and the weight of it in his nostrils, so have I hungered many a time while wandering through the city for the sight of the lines of that building. Indeed, I have loved it so much that I have never yet gone within, in fear lest the inner structure should disturb the joy I have from looking at the façade. Let the traveler be pardoned for being so superficial and caring nothing more than for the outward beauty of a thing. It is the best that we all can see.

How much this district is of the Old World can be seen as soon as one passes Fifteenth Street and the huge barrack-like building of Street & Smith. The most decrepit wooden shacks lean between huge buildings, for which not the slightest care has ever been taken that they should also be beautiful; wooden shack after wooden shack, housing stores of old clothing, in no way disguised to appear as new, for there is great poverty in that part of the town, toward the shore. Only the poorest live in that neighborhood, with here and there a sudden redeeming of the whole district by some old house that has been renovated and repainted to make it look as much like a Greenwich Village house as was humanly possible. Were one, however, to take a photograph of some of the wooden shacks, with people living in them, on Seventeenth Street a little off Seventh Avenue, no one who tried to locate the topography of such a hovel would ever guess that it was in the heart of the city of New York. They look very much like similar things I have seen in the negro districts of the South, or like the broken-down cabins of the side streets of Tía Juana, just across the Californian border-line into Mexico. There are any number of such ugly shacks all through the neighborhood. Any number of junk-shops spread their ugliness away over the sidewalk. Every sense is assaulted and corroded. Children in rags shiver through the streets. Most of the dependents of charity are housed in that neighborhood.

But suddenly on Twenty-second Street and northward one is in Spain again. The streets are broader, lighter. It is a Spanish town. And across it, on Twenty-third Street, beyond Ninth Avenue, the row of houses on the northern side with the stout colonnades in front, set back from the street, each house fenced in with iron railings, with front gardens and large staircases, each house painted

NRA. SRA DE GVADALVPE

in a different hue, tears one away from the whole swirl and whirl of the city. One stops to listen for the sounds of guitar music. One remains fixed in one place. A *señorita* with a black lace hair-cover pinned on the comb of her hair and a red-flowered shawl on the pale-blue background wrapped about her bare shoulders appears from behind a door; her red-heeled slippers accentuate the manner of her walking, the movement of her hips under her wide skirts. Spanish women cannot walk; they dance. Neither can they speak well; they sing.

But one so seldom sees them. Harem-like, they are living within doors shielded from the gaze of men, peering only through half-closed shutters. This is due probably to the love of semi-darkness of all people bred where the sun is high and uncomfortable. Yet if you do want to see them, if you insist on seeing them, wait for a balmy summer night when the sultriness in the air from the river near-by and the strongly smelling acacia-trees after they have bloomed drive our Spanish friends out to their piazzas. There will be music-making somewhere. Through the transparency of the gauze in the half-open windows you will catch glimpses of young ladies snapping castanets, and you will hear the running rhythm of the heel-beat against the rattle of the castanets and the swing of the melody. Spanish women give fair warning of their feelings when they dance. One must learn to interpret that before going to Spain; it is more valuable than knowing their tongue.

Do not inquire too closely who the *señor* is; so poetic, so soulful. It might happen he is the barber from around the corner, the clerk from the bank, the waiter or the rather stout, sleek importer, who comes to court more out of habit than desire. A Spaniard goes a-courting as long as he is able to stand on his feet. They are never out of love—or hate. It is Spain's most valuable industry and asset.

Of all the foreign-language newspapers in the city "La Prensa," the Spanish daily, seems the best edited one. It alone tries to interpret the rest of the American world to its Spanish readers, with a sort of detachment no other newspaper possesses. And though one hears recriminations against the language used in the foreign newspapers of each nationality from its cultured element, who accuse them of ruining the language by introducing Anglo-Saxonisms, I have yet to hear such reproach made against "La Prensa."

A few years ago, when all America seemed to be at the feet of Señor Blasco Ibanez, there was a great revival of interest in everything Spanish in this city. It threatened for a while to usurp the place hitherto held by the Russians. For a short while publishers vied with one another in bringing out translations of many of the Spanish authors. Broadway, responding promptly to such interest, produced several Spanish plays with great success. It made the Spaniards of New York raise their heads with pride. It redeemed them from the position to which they had sunk after the Spanish-American War. But that interest seems to have waned again. The only benefit I can see from it is that the Spaniards, never late to return a compliment, got interested in American literature. Within the last few years more than thirty American authors have been translated into Spanish, with Jack London's works holding first place. The old *vachero* stories, the Spanish tales, were also revived and very much read.

A strong sprinkling of Mexicans is living among the Spaniards in the down-town district. A still greater contingent of them, with Brazilians and Cubans and other Spanish Americans, are living in Fifty-ninth, Sixtieth, and Sixty-first Streets, within a stone's-throw of Columbus Circle. In the good old days most of the political plots were hatched in the coffee-houses in that neighborhood.

The statue was a sort of meeting-place after midnight. And even to-day one can presage a political change from the mysterious whisperings and sudden departures of certain gentlemen, who seem to hold commutation-tickets between Chile, or Mexico City, or Havana, and New York. Filibustering, intriguing, and revolutionizing have regularly been hatched there. When one inquires as to the occupation of many of these well-dressed and strongly perfumed dusky gentlemen, one is answered with the raising of an eyebrow. At best one gets the answer that so-and-so is in the *servicia diplomática.* I know several hundred who are thus employed. And there were several very mysterious disappearances during the night President Obregón's Government was recognized by the United States. And there were other departures when de la Huerta took the field against Obregón. There is talk of oil and revolution from early morn to late at night. Oil, oil, oil. It drips from everywhere. As if Mexico were America's oil-can. Maybe it is so. People handle matters rather carelessly on this continent.

A good deal of double-crossing is being done in this so-called political game. A good many sudden displacements are effected. I was warned by a very good friend of mine against a trip to Mexico because of the coming de la Huerta uprising, fully twenty days before it had actually taken place.

There is another contingent of Spanish people around Ninety-third, Ninety-fourth, and Ninety-fifth Streets and Broadway, mostly Cubans of the better class who have come here to stay while their sons study at Columbia.

And there is of course a still other Spanish district on the lower East Side, hemmed in between the Greek and the Syrian districts. But those are the families of stevedores, with a mixture of Filipinos among them. And when a Spaniard wants to speak of anything that is unspeakable, when he wants to denote his contempt for anybody, he calls him a Filipino.

Her birthplace is Santiago, Cuba. Her pitch-black hair is coarse and thick and frames a round face of the warmth and firmness of ivory.

And there is great art in the way the *señorita* uses her eyes when she looks at a man. She needs no help from the muscles of her face when she wants to express something without the use of words. Her eyes are enough. She is part Indian.

Do you know Viva? No? So much the better for you, for your peace of mind, for the soundness of your sleep. The man who knows Viva is drunk with the wine of her voice, the cold glow and luster of her eyes, and the music of her step.

I won't tell you exactly where she is to be seen. Tramp, late at night, Twenty-third Street, all its length from the East River to the Hudson. Eliminate all the noises of the city as you go. Sift them as they assault your ears. Strain them as a prospector strains the gold through the sieve. And if you discover a guitar-twang or a vibrant low note that swells as it goes deeper, stop. Stop—or, better still, go on. Don't look up to see the silhouette on the transparent curtain. Hasten away.

Criton, Nicholas Criton, the Greek poet, was believed to be the successful suitor. We used to sit for hours and hours pretending to drink coffee and watching the lucky one receive the *señorita's* glances. His eyes were like those of a faithful dog, hungry for the master's attention.

And he was a lucky dog. Luckier than we were, each one of us, sitting separately at little tables and making vain efforts to appear unconcerned.

We hated one another. What did it matter that there were three million other women in New York City? Were we in New York at all? I think not. We were in Cuba. Once Ben Benn, the painter, had brought Viva a newspaper-clipping about Cuba and had received an extra glance from her. Forthwith each one of us brought her some clipping daily. Frequently the food remained untouched. We forgot to eat. We were in Cuba! And we were there for her, for Viva!

She spoke a few words now and then to each of us. She smiled occasionally . . . with her eyes only. . . . She sings a little every night in her room over the restaurant when the day's work is done. But only when she is alone. And everybody who comes to the Cienfuegos during the day promenades up and down the street as long as the guitar-twang and the contralto voice are heard. Love-songs, or dirges—who knows? Perfumed melodies, mysteriously passionate, the words by Ruben Dario or José Silvio. . . .

And then one day something happened. A big, blond young fellow entered the restaurant of the Cienfuegos. He was a stranger. He ordered some food and looked around leisurely as he ate. He evidently liked the food and the place, because he returned the days following.

He usually spoke a few words to Viva, as he paid before he left. A word of praise for the food, for the excellent coffee. And Viva, Señorita Viva, seemed to be much pleased. He was so tall and fair. The intruder, the blond-haired, blue-eyed fellow, continued his visits regularly, and Viva now looked in his direction more than the direction of Criton.

Criton hoped and hoped and waited and waited. Then one day, unable to live without her glance, he went to sit near the blond fellow.

It was the first time I had ever seen Viva smile—with her lips.

Criton and the blond fellow became friends. The Dutchman was also a poet. The Greek poet moved to the same boarding-house the stranger lived in. They invariably come together for their meals. Late at night they walk arm in arm before Señorita Viva's window and share the twang of her guitar and the sound of her voice.

Criton and his friend are satisfied to share one glance from the same woman they love.

And so we hate Criton.

## CHAPTER XII

### FRANCE

WHEN one says France one generally means Paris, though to the initiated many the two things are far from synonymous. Paris is as different from the rest of France as if it were not its capital but the capital of some other country; not only because Paris is a cosmopolitan city, not only because it is a city toward which stretch the necks of people from all over the world, but because it represents the spirit of the whole world as much as it does the spirit of France. Paris is Paris. No comparisons are possible. Parisians are Parisians, and neither Frenchmen nor Europeans. Parisians seldom, if ever, travel unless driven by absolute necessity from their city. They are a part so closely bound to the city that they cannot detach themselves from it. They are certain to be disappointed wherever they go, whatever they see.

The dislike of displacement, however, can be held against all Frenchmen. Frenchmen are held back from travel by strong love of traditions and dependence on them. Except the Chinese, no other people is as given to ancestor-worship as the French. They are *routiniers*. What has been done for centuries is the only right thing to be done. Frenchmen live in houses, not because they are convenient, but because their great-grandfathers lived in them. Long after the soil of a farm has become exhausted the farmers continue to work it in the same old manner as their great-grandfathers, because it has been done so for generations, It is the one characteristic trait of the whole French nation, though in many other things they are so different. The Savoyard, the Basque, the Breton, the Norman, and Toulousian are men of vastly different bloods and races, speaking dialects so different as almost to be different languages—and many of them like the Breton and Provençal are, indeed, different languages—although they are conglomerated under the common name of "Frenchmen."

And so, if you travel from the Spanish district in New York—from Twenty-third Street between Ninth and Tenth Avenues, where is that beautiful row of columned houses on the north side, rising like great pillars in the mist that settles from the river early in the morning—you will have the sensation of traveling, as you go toward Fortieth Street, through the lower part of France. From Andorra to Montauban and Limoges and Lyons, and then to Paris. For on the way the low houses and the disorder of heights and building-materials, and the names on the signs, with a sprinkling of Greek Macedonians and the beginning of another Italian quarter and a duplication of a Greek quarter elsewhere, right about Thirty-seventh Street, is very much like an imitation of Paris's outlying districts. This is merely a general impression; the French quarters in New York are really the Parisian quarters in New York, although of the forty thousand French inhabitants there are hardly more than five or six thousand

Parisians here, but this matters not, for proportionately they are in the same ratio as they are in Paris. And yet they are the dominating element. The Parisian quarters are near our Broadway, our white-light district, which not only outdoes in light and noise the Boulevard des Italiens, but absolutely outdistances in lighting brilliancy and noise of streets anything Paris can ever hope to achieve.

There are many Frenchmen living further south, and those who have been here for a longer period live as far down as the Village. Around Eighth and Ninth Streets there are old French families, and there are many more on Thirteenth Street and Fifteenth Street west of Fifth Avenue. Those are families who have been in this city for over a hundred years, and the houses they live in are the same to which they had originally come and which they to-day own. These houses have a certain French fragrance of style, and with that typical traditionalism of the French they have not heeded the changes about them. The houses are as picturesque as they ever were, with trellised balconies and vines creeping over the long windows and the low doors.

As their center of the old French district, at the Brevoort Hotel, and at the Lafayette Hotel on University Place, the older Frenchmen still gather for their *apéritif* or mid-afternoon absinthe, even when such things are no longer obtainable. One could easily have forgotten the very existence of New York in either of these cafés before prohibition came, seeing the men and women around the small tables playing their *bézigue* while sipping the greenish drink from tall glasses and smoking their cigarettes from long cigarette-holders. To this day the Brevoort and the Lafayette are the rendezvous of the older French colonists in this city, although the Village artists and pseudo-artists have also made of them their general rendezvous.

Not long ago in talking with M. Délut, at a dinner in honor of Chaliapin, the great Russian singer, I remarked that he was talking a very fluent English with a very strong French accent. We chanced a little later to talk French together, whereupon I discovered he used a good many Anglicisms in his language, although his accent was purely Parisian.

"You must have lived a long time in this city, M. Délut," I said.

"Indeed," he answered. "Forty-five years."

It did not seem to me that the round-faced, jovial man was much older than that, indeed even that much, and so I said:

"Then you must have come here as a child?"

"No, my father came here as a child," he answered. "I was born in this city."

And it turned out that M. Délut had never been in France. His family had come here during the revolutionary troubles of 1848, as a good many other families did. There are indeed several thousand old French families that came here during that period. Evidences of that can be found in almost any district, as well as in the many French names in the liberal professions. And still most of them cling, even to the third and fourth generation, to French habits and French customs, which have been transmitted from parent to parent.

There are at least a dozen old signs of "Boulangerie Française" and "Boucherie Française" through the Village, and many more French signs further up town, where the *boulangeries* and the *boucheries* are very much like the ones at home. But it is up toward Broadway, between Fortieth and Fiftieth Streets, and along Sixth and Eighth Avenues, that the French quarter, as it was, exists. There are any number of the good old *cafés chantants* of European origin, where a *diseuse* or a *chanteuse* in abbreviated skirts and old-fashioned *décolleté,* looking more like a circus-rider than a singer, is holding forth from a small platform at the end of the hall, while the good bourgeois who have come from long distances to their accustomed

tables, which they have held at certain days of the week year after year, discuss their family affairs in a French curiously corrupted with the few English words that they know.

There are dozens of *pensions de famille* with stout and marceled rubicund ladies surveying the work of the quiet-spoken waitresses from Cantal. For Cantal furnished almost all the waiters of France. There one could have his *panade* or his *choux de Bruxelles* served in exactly the same manner as it is prepared in the sixty thousand restaurants of Paris. If one should search very well on Forty-fifth Street there is a place where *lapin au vin* is the great specialty of the house, where the pot, as in Anatole France's "Rôtisserie," has never been taken off the fire for the last thirty years.

There is not a single branch of industry in this city, especially in those industries where great skill and neatness are demanded, that does not employ one or more Frenchmen. The big bronze foundries, where statues and the like are molded, employ French molders. The art jewelers pride themselves when they have Frenchmen, and if all the modistes and dressmakers announcing themselves with the prefix "Madame" were French, the French population would be six times its size in New York City.

There were several small French theaters in New York City before the war, in feeble competition with the German theater at Irving Place. The German theater was by far the better, having a better repertoire and much better actors than the French theaters of those days. But at the beginning of the war Copeau with his theater Le Vieux

Colombier came over here, and they were given the old Garrick Theater by Otto Kahn, which was remodeled to suit them, after the plans and drawings of Jouvet, who was both an excellent actor and an architect. Never before had New York seen such ensemble acting, never before such perfection, such simplicity, or heard such diction. The theatrical world will remember for ever and ever the staging of "The Brothers Karamazov" on that little stage. The stairway that led from the central room to the upper room, where *Jon* commits suicide, was the most perfect and impressive thing ever seen in any theater. But they were a bit too austere and insisted on playing classics, the Copeau Players. And the French colony here encouraged them only meagerly. After two seasons in the city Copeau and his players returned to their theater in Paris, very much disgusted with the lack of support of the French population here.

How much more can be done in this way was immediately proved by that unique artiste, Yvette Guilbert, the *diseuse.* Season after season she filled the Maxine Elliott Theater, although she was the only one on the stage from beginning to end, reciting French poetry, mimicking and singing as only she can sing the old French *chansons.* It is not only the French colony who come, week after week and month after month, but people from all our nationalities. It was, indeed, a great treat for any one interested in the stage and for any one who wanted to learn French.

From time to time a French troupe does come over from Paris to play, but like most other Latin people the French are very bad propagandists, and very seldom has the best come over here, in spite of the occasional and frequent farewell visits of the late Mme. Sarah Bernhardt.

The Parisian district of New York begins at Thirty-ninth Street and Sixth Avenue, right at the Metropolitan Opera-house. In spite of the fact that the Metropolitan is an Italian institution, although it is the national opera-house of the United States, even in the days when German opera was the almost steady fare there, French was the official language of the opera-house. From William J. Guard, the press representative, the politest gentleman in New York (from whose garb one can recognize whether the performance that night is a gala performance or not, for his silk hat and cutaway tell the tale), to the head of the institution, French is the official language. And then, as if Sixth Avenue and Broadway were the Boulevard des Italiens, the streets running westward to the river, up to Fifty-fourth Street, like the faubourg extending westward from the celebrated Parisian boulevard, are Parisian quarters. And like the faubourg those streets change in character with the distance from Broadway. The restaurants and the *pensions* rarefy themselves toward Eighth Avenue. The prices on the bills of fare go down and downward as you go further west. And suddenly the streets, the hum and the drum of Broadway diminished, begin to be the quiet streets in which the families of Parisians are housed. For except a few families that have been here for generations and that have already been absorbed to a certain extent, most of the Parisian population of the city is a commercial one, and includes, also, a good number of artisans who have come here to better their condition but who are largely a temporary population. The Parisian soon begins to long back for his faubourgs and the little nooks and corners of the Bois de Vincennes.

Parisian youngsters do not mix readily with the youngsters of other nationalities, not because of their superiority complex, but because of great difference in interests. The Parisian young boy is not half as much interested in baseball, football, and prize-fights as the American boy is or as the son of the new immigrant of any other nationality might become. Not considering our civilization superior to theirs, the Parisians are not eager to imitate our customs or adapt themselves to them. Jazz may have won a hold on the *boulevardiers* of Paris because of its exotic quality, but it has not taken hold of the simpler folk, who stick to the minuet and the pavane and the polka and the waltz. A visit to any celebration of the youngsters of the Church of St. Vincent de Paul on Twenty-third Street would be enough to convince one of that. The St. Vincent de Paul has a branch of its church called Notre Dame de la Miséricorde on Washington Square, where the same thing may be observed at any of their celebrations. Not even proximity to the Village, with its pseudo-Latin-Quarter atmosphere, could accomplish that. And if any one should doubt it he might visit the French Evangelical Church on West Sixteenth Street. A good many of the old residents are members of the congregation; indeed, some of the oldest French settlers here occupy the pews. But they are as French as if they had only come yesterday. The fact is, many of this congregation have never even seen France.

How separated from the rest of the community the

Parisians live could also be seen in their daily and weekly papers, the "Courier des Etats-Unis" and the "Gazette Franco-Américaine," or in their magazine "La France," which, though fully intended to create a *rapprochement* between the two nations, is very far from attempting such a move, even if it were at all necessary. These papers are interested chiefly, like all good Frenchmen, in the things that directly concern thém. The Frenchman, the Parisian especially, is notórious for his inability to learn other languages or to concern himself with interests of people other than his own.

The enforcement of prohibition, such as it is, has hit the French population very hard in New York City. I am not speaking of the commercial end of it, though a good many, probably one-quarter, of the commercial houses in this country were importers of wines, liqueurs, and champagnes. Such houses really had to adjust themselves by making arrangements to import other goods or else be completely wiped out. But I am now speaking of the Frenchmen accustomed to have their wine at the table. To them wine has always been part of their nutrition. The absence of it has hit many of them so hard that they have found it impossible to remain in this country in spite of all their home-brews and substitutes. Accordingly they have returned home. Because of that the old Gallic gaiety and light-heartedness has been abated. One no longer hears, on passing a French street, as much gay and light laughter, as much gay and light song as one used to hear. The many little family cafés to which the working-man used to take his whole family on a Saturday afternoon or a Sunday, for lunch or for dinner, to break up the monotony of his wife's housekeeping routine, are no longer. They have been wiped out of existence; where they still exist, the old gaiety is gone. Unable to drink the good wine in perfect openness, between long discourses and story-tellings and politenesses and laughter, the Frenchman has abandoned his cafés. These places are frequented by such people as drink their wine as if it were medicine, in sudden big gulps and by stealth. Drinking wine to a Frenchman, apart from being a necessity, has also been a sort of ritual. I know of a number of Parisians who have moved out to the country, where they potter away the long evenings of the summer near the vines they have set, and the evenings of the fall watching the little juice they can press out of them. How wine-drinking is with the Frenchman a social affair can be seen from the number of guests at such out-of-town homes on a Saturday or a Sunday.

The French district in New York has never been in any way a fixed center; the French have not been numerous enough to form a quarter of their own, and their occupations have been more varied than those of any other of our foreign populations here. The two thousand or more French theatrical people in this city, season after season, live mostly in the hotels in the neighborhood of Broadway.

The commercial element, when not actually housed permanently here, lives further down toward Washington Square, while the working class live here and there and everywhere, getting together only at church affairs, labor meetings, or on such occasions where something specifically French is given. The Metropolitan Opera-house becomes a social center when a French opera is performed. Half of the audience at a performance of "Louise," by Carpentier, is Parisian.

In connection with this opera I remember a very amusing story. I was sitting with William Guard, the press representative, and another friend of mine, in one of the boxes, and watching the performance. In the box next to mine were two ladies, both evidently from the newly rich class. Though they took great pains to handle the lorgnette it was quite evident they had not yet completely mastered the manner of doing it. In the second act of "Louise" is the celebrated dressmaking shop scene. In the dressmaking shop where *Louise* works, together with twenty other young ladies, the girls sing a good deal while they work, many of them dancing snatches while the street musicians are playing below the windows. There are diversions caused by the apprentice girl, an extremely disturbing *gamine,* who is intriguing between the girls. The whole scene is one in which a good deal of the spirit of the French *midinette,* lively and care-free yet sentimental, is displayed.

After the ovation to the singer, at the end of the act, one of the ladies turned around and asked her neighbor, seemingly her guest, what she thought of it. The lady pursed her lips, raised her eyebrows, and with a gesture in which she showed her disapproval of the waste of time and inefficient manner in a French dressmaking shop, she said:

"No wonder French dresses are so expensive."

Speaking about the Metropolitan Opera-house I must tell another amusing story, which will probably show that there are more than two reasons why most people come to the opera. They were playing "L'Amore de Tre Re." In the second act the old man kills the faithless wife of his son. After strangling her he carries her off stage on his shoulder. There were two seats vacant at my right throughout the first act. But at the beginning of the second two ladies speaking German came to occupy them. The music had hardly begun for the second act when the two ladies began to snooze peacefully. They had been asleep for only a moment when one of them woke up and asked the other one: "Hat man ihr schon getötet? Have they killed her yet?"

The older one opened her eyes, peered at the stage, and said: "Noch nicht. Not yet."

A little later they had both closed their eyes again, only to open them after a moment and ask whether the murder had been committed. As it had not been, and there was still some time until the deed should be done, they again closed their eyes.

I took pity on them a moment before the murder scene was to be enacted, and, tapping my neighbor on the shoulder, I said to her: "Jetzt geht's los. Now it is going to happen." They watched the scene, bending over forward as far as possible so that not a single gesture or the slightest movement should escape them. They were so tense that I could not even hear them breathing. When the deed was done they both sighed deeply and reclined on their seats. Then the lady I had tapped on the shoulder turned toward me, and, bowing deeply, she said: "Danke schön. I thank you." They left at the end of the second act.

It is almost a practice with me, whenever I want to meet a French friend I have not seen for a long time, to wait until some specific French affair takes place. I am quite certain to meet whom I desire any time Jacques Thibaud, that most eloquent of all violinists, is playing, especially so when the Chausson "Poème" is included in the program.

I know whom I will meet when Cortot, the pianist, plays. Indeed, there is *tout Paris* when Yvette Guilbert is giving one of her performances.

Except for the few homes of Frenchmen in lower New York, there is no architectural distinction of any kind typically French in the French upper New York district. It is not like the other districts, where the inhabitants have created something that resembles as nearly as possible their own habitat. The Parisians came to live in a district which had already imitated their former home as closely as possible. I am speaking of the theatrical district. They have not added anything to it architecturally.

In spite of that, their existence is strongly felt there, not only because of the numerous cafés and restaurants, but because there is something peculiarly theirs floating about them. One could distinguish a Frenchwoman walking up or down the street anywhere on earth, not because of her inimitable grace but because of an inimitable quality which, quite apart from being beautiful or not, is hers. The manner in which a Parisian woman can wear the most common thing, and, by giving it a twist, a turn, creasing it here and there with her finger-nail, make it look like a gown a hundred times more expensive than it really is, is too proverbial to need further discourse. There is a Parisian toss of the head and movement of the hand. And there is the Parisian "Voilà" no one can imitate; not even a Frenchman from another part of France. All over the city the influence of the Parisian is strongly felt; and they have taken no pains for it. If it is true that every intelligent man has two countries, his own and France, it is also true that every man has two languages, his own and French. And those Parisians who have come to live here have brought with them that spirit which has forever been admired by the rest of the world.

I remember my friend Barnabatte, who had worked for years as a cook in one of the large French restaurants here. He had saved up a good deal of money, for both he and his wife were working, and they were very thrifty people. I used to meet Barnabatte frequently at the houses of other friends of mine, especially at the homes of Planas and Banville, two French engineers who have greatly contributed to the development of the automobile. Barnabatte was a happy soul, gaily cutting into every conversation with his loud Gascon laughter and his thick Gascon accent. No matter what one said, Barnabatte was against it; and his wife always seconded him with her eternal, "Mais oui. Mais oui."

We may occasionally have disliked him for his eternal interruptions, but we sorely missed him after he ceased to come to any of these gatherings at the beginning of the war. And there were those who thought that though he was exempt from military service he might have returned and offered to do such service as he was capable of. Having more time than the others, I was delegated to make inquiries. Accordingly, after we had missed him for about eight weeks I went up to his house to see him. I found his wife alone in the living-room.

"Where is Edouard?" I inquired.

She put her finger on her lips to hush my voice.

"Good heavens! Is he ill?" I inquired. "Where is he? I must see him."

She drew me to the opposite end of the room, and in whispers she told me, "He is in the other room with his teacher."

"Teacher?"

"He will presently be out," she assured me.

And at that very moment the door from the other room opened and a gray-bearded gentleman in a long Prince Albert coat, which had once been black and was now green, was taking his leave. M. Barnabatte stood at the door.

"Bonjour, monsieur," the gray-bearded gentleman said.

"Bonjour," Barnabatte answered, in a very unusual tone of voice.

It was not my Barnabatte at all. There would have been a good deal more zeal near the "j" in "bonjour" if he had pronounced it in his own way.

"Bonjour, camarade," he greeted me, with that slight "h" before the "r" which is the privilege of every Parisian.

"What is all that?" I asked Barnabatte, on seeing the disk phonograph on the table with a number of books. "And why have we not seen you?"

"Oh, I have no time," he excused himself. "I am studying to become chef."

"Studying to become chef?" I questioned.

"Mais oui! Mais oui!" Barnabatte assured me. "One can never become chef, no matter how good he is at his trade, with a Gascon accent."

He is chef to-day, having worked more than a year to eradicate his southern French accent. But he has also lost his good, thick, pleasant voice, and acquired a falsetto, this being the only means to disguise his origin.

There is a café somewhere northwest of Forty-second Street. For some reason or other to a certain group that café is known as the River of Doubt.

Its clientele varies with the hour. Up to noon it is the rendezvous of all the Parisians of New York. At the noon-hour it becomes the eat-and-run place of the office-girls in the neighborhood. After two it is the rendezvous of aspiring and superannuated theatrical folk; hopes and dreams meet regrets and old successes.

At four the center-table is occupied by the eminent music critics dropping in from Æolian Hall for a cup of strong black coffee; and Debussy, Strauss, Wagner, and the rest are blown with the smoke from pipes, cigarettes, and thick Havanas. And from then on to an hour after midnight all the Americas, the rest of the world, and all professions from the loftiest to the lowliest pass in review. Plans for plays, symphonic themes, great novels, plots of revolution and murder are hatched under that roof.

Alex and myself were discussing Merejkowski at one of

the little brown tables edging the brown wall decorated with leopard-skins when Riviers, the French poet, entered with a very Anglo-Saxon-looking young woman.

"My teacher of English," Riviers introduced her, and the two sat down at the table back of us.

My discussion with Alex came to an end soon. We agreed on almost everything. It is what has always worried me when I am with Alex. I can't find out whether I agree with him, or he with me, or that we both agree.

"You have hands *très, très,* oh, yes, now I find—you have hands very beautiful," I heard Riviers saying to the teacher, and my eye caught the fact that he had taken one of the girl's hands in his.

"No, you should have said, 'Your hands are very beautiful,'" explained the teacher.

"Your hands are very beautiful," repeated the poet; "thanks, thanks!"

"What color are my eyes?" asked the teacher.

"Your *yeux, non*—eyes, eyes, are beautiful. Very bleu."

"No, no. Your eyes are a beautiful blue."

*"Bien,* blue, blue, blue!" repeated Riviers, trying to memorize.

"Your beautiful hands very *chaud,* fire, burn; you know —you know—"

"Ah! You want to say, 'Your beautiful warm hands burn like fire.' Say it."

"That 's it, that it, *c'est ça,"* jubileed Riviers, and patted the hand he held in his.

"Your hand is ice-cold," the teacher said. "You understand?"

"Understand, understand—my hand cold because your beautiful hand is very warm."

"Bravo, bravo!" the teacher complimented. "You learn so rapidly."

"You have very extraordinary *tête,* you know—"

"Head, you mean. Yes, but say it so, 'You have an extraordinarily beautiful head.' "

"Yes, yes," and the young poet repeated the words of his teacher with great enthusiasm.

"I will write *une poème*—"

"A poem, a poem," corrected the young lady.

"Yes, I will write a poem to this beautiful head."

"Oh, you learn a new language very rapidly; you have a gift for languages."

"You very fine. Always must I think of you. In six months, maybe in one year, when I go away, I think of you just the same. And I *songe*—you know what you sleep and think—"

"Dream, dream, you mean."

"Yes, thanks; I dream we are very good friends."

"That was too long a sentence for you, Mr. Riviers."

"I love your *voix,* you know, you know—"

"Say, 'I love your voice.' "

"I love it; I love your voice," the poet repeated rapturously.

An hour later they were still there. His vocabulary had augmented marvelously. He spoke rapidly, and the lady corrected fugitively, more as a matter of form or habit. It was a torrent of love-words. Her face was as flushed as his, and her blue eyes darkened to violet. People passed by and looked at them as they held hands, their heads almost touching. But they did not see. They were alone amid the hundreds of people. Riviers' cigarette had burned by itself, untouched after the first whiff; the two cups of coffee were cold.

Two hours later they were still there. The young woman was talking to him, and as he did not understand her good English she talked one mixed with French and Italian and Latin and used all available means to make him understand what she wanted.

"You see, you see, you no understand because I no talk the Engleesh well," Riviers complained.

"You do, you do, Riviers. You do, my dear. You talk English wonderfully. I understand everything."

"No, no. You very intelligent and you talk French very well."

"No, I don't."

"Yes, you do. I understand everything."

*"Ma fiancée,"* he introduced her to me several days later.

"Well, well; now you will learn English rapidly, Riviers," I laughed.

*"Mais non, non;* she speak the French *parfaitement."*

"I really don't know more than a few words," protested the English teacher.

"You do; you do; I know you do."

"You see his English has improved wonderfully in the last few days; don't you think so?" the girl exclaimed as she bowed herself away to a distant table.

# CHAPTER XIII

## GERMANY

IT is well, before one decides to visit a country, to know something not only of its geographical position but also of its history. Otherwise a good many things one should see either completely escape him or are so misunderstood as to add to the world's already formidable stock of misinformation.

The war has caused a good deal of it. Forgetting that almost a sixth of the population of this country is of German extraction, we have gone on ranting, school-boy fashion. The friends of the Germans exaggerated their cultural value, and their enemies disparaged it, until either nothing on God's earth of any value was ever done by a German, or everything that was ever created by civilization from the day of its beginning to the end of the war was done only by Germans.

Now that our patriotic ardor has cooled off, there are a few things that might be told. How many a son who has been in Pershing's army is unable to look into his father's eyes, when he remembers the battles in which he has taken part against his father's people. The older German people were expected to rise to the same degree of patriotism as the people of the other populations in this city. Even if they did not, one must concede to them far greater spiritual difficulties in the situation they were plunged into by the war. A good many of them had to be like the sinner, holier than anybody else, compelled as they were to wave the flag three times as frequently and ten times as loudly as the others. There is many a wife who finds living with her husband well nigh impossible since his return from across the water. She had brothers and uncles abroad who have gone to their graves following the course they thought was right. The wonder of it is that there were not during the war many more conscientious objectors on the ground of fear of fratricide and parricide. One must not forget the stigma put on the Germans when the names and addresses of all the so-called "enemy aliens" were published in the papers and are to this day obtainable in the public libraries of the city; it is the ugliest thing that has resulted from the war hysteria. It is easier to forget victory than defeat. Forgetting defeat frequently amounts to knavishness, while forgetting victory always earns admiration for the victors. "Vae victis" is written in heavy red letters in the history of the world.

There are a few facts in the development of the city of New York which it may do no harm to know better. The Germans were here virtually from the very beginning of the city. Wolfgang Roma, a German, was the first one to lay the foundation of what is to-day the port of New York. Nicholas Meyer, a German-born gentleman, in 1676, at a time when any office-holder in New York was little more than a pirate on the seas of public money, was one of the most public-spirited mayors of the city. Christiansen Klef, one of our first pioneers, although a theologian himself, fought bitterly for religious freedom against all odds, odds that the German founders of the Lutheran Church in New York could not have overcome, if they had not been as steadfast as they were in their belief in religious freedom.

Jacob Leisler, a native of Frankfort-on-the-Main, who was elected temporary governor by the people of New York, called the first congress of the American colonies. A fearless defender of the people's rights against the oppressions of the Government, he was brought to trial for treason and hanged in 1691, the first martyr of the long struggle of the American people for liberty. Johann Peter Zenger, the owner of the New York "Weekly Journal," which he founded in 1733, saw numbers of his paper publicly burned by the hangman for his criticism of the acts of the Government. Thrown into prison for his fight for liberty, he was the man at whose trial the freedom of the press was definitely established in America. Peter Minuit, the first director-general of the New Netherlands in 1621, was a German. He it was who closed the bargain with the Indians by which he purchased Manhattan for twenty-four dollars, instead of fighting and shedding blood for the strip of land. The Astors emigrated here from Germany; Rockefeller is of German ancestry; so, also, are Wanamaker and Siegel. The man who built the Brooklyn Bridge, then probably the most brilliant feat of engineering on this side of the ocean, was Roebling, a German. After designing the bridge he fell ill and could only watch the construction of it through a telescope from a considerable distance.

And then came 1848, when after an unsuccessful revolution in Germany the best minds, the most active ones, were compelled to flee their country. Many of them came here. One need but mention names like Carl Schurz, Siegel, Ottendorfer, Kapp, Solger, and Dr. Jacobi, not to list a hundred others of lesser importance but of equal quality in every direction, to recall to mind the best men this city has had.

With the forty-eighters and after them came the great immigration from Germany. In the German festival of May 8, 1848, when Frederick Havemeyer was mayor and the German flag was flown from City Hall, fully sixty thousand Germans participated. The Schiller festival in 1859 lasted five days. And when Lincoln's call for volunteers was heard, the German *Turnverein* poured volunteers into the ranks of the army. Their elders who had battled for the freedom of the people in 1848 in their own land were the ones who, if they could not themselves go because of age, stirred the younger ones to go. Look at the names of the Civil War veterans.

Now, as to their cultural value. It is doubtful whether we should have had such musical organizations as we have in the city if it were not for the German love for music. The Philharmonic Society was founded in 1842 by Germans. As early as 1880 there were sixty *Gesangsvereine* in the city of New York alone. In 1856 Karl Bergmann produced "Fidelio," by Beethoven, with choruses trained here. In 1870 the Germans had their own *Stadttheater,* which for those days, and even for this day, equaled the best anywhere in the world. Leopold Damrosch and Anton Seidl produced Wagner as early as 1888. Most of the

great orchestral and operatic conductors in this city have been Germans—Alfred Hertz, Leopold Damrosch, and his sons, Walter and Frank Damrosch. Francis Xavier Ahrens, the former leader of the People's Symphony Orchestra, has by himself done more to popularize orchestral music than all the other musicians of this country combined. P. A. Schnecker has written more church music of the finest sort than any other man living to-day. What Grau and Conried and Hammerstein did for opera in New York and for music in general, only those closely connected could tell.

Wherever the German lives he must have his *Gesangsvereine,* his *Liedertafeln* and his *Turnvereine.* When they commemorated Wagner at the Hippodrome on December 27, 1913, more than a thousand voices, three hundred of them female, took part in the chorus. Mme. Schumann-Heink was the soloist. George Gemunder, undoubtedly the best violin-maker of the last century, whose violins will in time be appreciated with those of the celebrated Italian masters, lived in this city from 1850 on.

One could go on and on, and never finish the list, of what New York Germans have contributed toward the aggrandizement of the city. The Guggenheims, Belmonts, Strauses, Oelrichses, Eberhard Faber, the pencil manufacturer, the Frohmans, the Schiffs. They have contributed as much as any single nation, if not more, to the construction of the elevateds and subways, to merchandising on a large scale, to banking, and that most beneficial of all institutions, the life-insurance companies.

At the time when they had Das Deutsche Theater on Downing Street, with the highest artistic ambition, the American stage was virtually non-existent but for a few erudities and importations from abroad. The German papers, the first of which, "Deutscher Freund," was founded in 1820, the "Staats-Zeitung," the "Volkszeitung," and the "Herold," have been examples of what newspapers should be.

Our first flower-raisers—beginning with Jacob Sperry, who had his garden on the Bowery not very long ago, before the Italians took over the profession—were all Germans. The Hessian, Schwerkopf, introduced strawberries into this country. He was also one of the first horticulturists. And how careful and beautiful German workmanship can be is exhibited by the piano-manufacturing houses of Steinway, Knabe, Weber, Somer, Kranich & Bach, and others too numerous to mention. One must not forget that up to 1880 virtually all the musicians of the city were Germans. The same thing could be said of druggists and physicians. To this day they are largely represented in the city, with men like Dr. Herman Knopf of Columbia University, one of the greatest authorities on the eye and ear in the world, and the famous Dr. Jacobi, who departed only recently.

The kindergarten system in New York was established by a German woman, Mme. Maria Kraus, and is still largely continued on the lines she laid down. As early as 1843 Columbia University established a chair for the German language and literature, and there was a great effort to make it compulsory in our public schools. Years later Jacob H. Schiff endowed Cornell University with a hundred thousand dollars for a chair of German literature.

There are, including the Austrians, over a million German-speaking people in New York. Their quarter begins somewhere on First Street, between Avenue A and Avenue B, skirts Tompkins Square on the east side, and extends northward, touching the Hungarian quarter at Fourteenth Street. It spreads further east to Avenue B and C, and sometimes to the very edge of the East River, up to Fifty-first Street at Beekman Place. From there, jumping over a few streets, which are left to the Swedish population of the city, it spreads northward and westward, sometimes even crossing Fifth Avenue, then turning back toward Lexington and Madison, and holding its course westward to Eighty-sixth Street and Third Avenue. The tendency of the German population is strongly to the north and timidly to the west, imitating the spread of the German Empire in Europe. And, as at home, the German population here touches on the west side a corner of the French quarter, further north the Scandinavian, and on its east side the Czecho-Slovak and Polish districts, not to speak of the Hungarian district, which is almost continually on its eastern flank.

Unlike other nationalities, the Germans, except in the Harlem district, which was taken over by the negroes, have never completely abandoned a region in which they have lived by moving westward or northward. Wherever the Germans settled, early in the history of the city, down on the East Side toward Clinton and Norfolk Streets, at the time Clinton Hall was the Astor Opera-house, they have clung to that district and held on to it, spreading only as they multiplied, without ever completely giving ground. In witness of that are numerous German churches which

still exist in the districts now largely occupied by Jews and other peoples. On Sunday morning hereditary members of the congregation come to sit in the same pews where their grandfathers sat, whether they live fifteen blocks away or fifty, in the German Catholic Church on Second Street or the Lutheran Church on St. Mark's

Place. Other nationalities, in moving away, have given over their churches, or whatever other social halls had been in their possession, selling them at a profit to the new arrivals who have taken their places, but not so the Germans. Even their *Liedertafel* places and *Turnvereine* and *Gesangsvereine* are still where they originally were, in spite of the fact that their members now live miles away. Neither are the original German owners of houses willing to part with the old buildings their forefathers first erected, or to remodel them so as to make them more in keeping with the buildings going up about them. One can still see rows of houses on Thirteenth Street and Nineteenth Street, set back from the sidewalk, with little flower-gardens in front of them and vines creeping over the windows, while large apartment-houses have gone up on both sides and in the back, robbing the houses of the light that had been intended for their windows. There is no doubt that these houses would be eagerly snapped up by buyers at considerable prices if the owners were willing to sell. But most of them are not, and prefer holding on to their properties as of old . . . as homes for themselves.

One of the examples of this German tenacity can be seen on Fourth Street, between Second and Third Avenues, around the Beethoven Hall. Many, many years ago, when the houses were far apart, that district was German. Being near the Bowery, where all the amusement places were, in that district were several *Weinstuben* and a few German delicatessen stores. The generation which patronized these places is long since dead. The German colony has spread further north and northwest, but the *Wein-*

*stuben* still exist in spite of prohibition. The delicatessen stores are still there. And Germans, probably the sons of the original patrons, or the grandsons, come from wherever they are for their little glass of cider and *Gemütlichkeit* to which they are accustomed, at the same table, sitting on the same chair, and looking at the same inane lithographs with the same quaint inscriptions under them. How these delicatessen stores live and exist is beyond any one's understanding. But they do. Frau Hausmann, who bought pumpernickel and *Kläse-käse* for her mother fifty years ago, is buying them now for her daughter or granddaughter, from the son or grandson of the man who used to serve her when she was in knee frocks.

On Fifth Street, between Avenue A and Avenue B, is my friend Werner, the violin-maker. He is a very old man now, probably eighty years old. He came to this country around the fifties with his father. He is undoubtedly one of the finest violin makers and repairers in this city. Kneisel, Kreisler, Ysaye, Elman, and other great violinists and cellists bring their violins to him for repair and conditioning before they leave for abroad or after their return. And yet Werner's shop is no larger than it was when his father opened it when they first arrived here from Germany. I dare say it will not be larger fifty years from now, when his son will be as old as his father is now. Father and son have been working now for two generations together. Calmly, slowly, diligently, with the usual five interruptions a day for their meals, which are brought from the back of the store where the family is housed, and with the glasses of beer that succeed one another at regular intervals, father and son are at their bench until five in the afternoon, when old Werner, undoing his leather apron, calls out, *"Feieramt;* finished," and the day's work is done. Should father happen to forget to call the day's end at the exact minute, the son will continue working. Then, still silently, each one lights his pipe. There is a *Lehnstuhl* dragged out to the door, if the weather is warm, or placed in the middle of the shop if it is cold; and the cronies from the neighborhood, their long beards stained with tobacco-juice and smoke, gather in the place to discuss in rare and quiet monosyllables the events of the day. Because of some physical defect, Werner, Jr., did not serve in the army; and his father, who has always been saddened because of his son's short leg, has repeatedly told me how God has been good to him. Old Werner, although he came here as a little boy, can hardly talk English. It is of him that people have said, "He considers the Americans stupid because they have not learned German in the sixty or more years that he has been here."

Further up west on St. Mark's Place, between Second and First Avenues, is the Lutheran Church. Those who have the time and inclination to hear beautiful choir singing and magnificent organ accompaniment and directing would do well to stay around the church after seven o'clock some evening. I lived only a few doors away from the church some years ago, and I found it impossible to do anything during those hours but listen to the strong and beautiful singing of the Lutheran hymns as it floated through the open windows. I moved away from that district because of the silly organ-playing at the same hour from a moving-picture house on the corner. It maddened me, and as I could not drown out the noise it was best for me to go.

All along on Avenue A and Avenue B are hundreds of old *Weinstuben* and saloons and coffee-houses, which vegetate now. Further along, toward Tompkins Square, was the old Heimath place, and next to it the Rathskeller. At the Heimath, a spacious basement, gathered nightly around the twenty or more pine tables all the homeless German unemployed. Until twelve o'clock at night everybody was served with a glass of wine and a large hunk of bread for five cents. Exactly at midnight the proprietor, a big, stout man, would yell out at the top of his voice as he extinguished the lamp, "Schlafen!" As if by some witchcraft all the voices were hushed immediately, and those who did not leave instantly went to sleep where they were. The proprietor closed the front door and went to sleep in his own room, which was in the back.

At the Rathskeller things were quite different, though on the same order. Here all the young pseudo-intellectuals gathered to discuss Heine and Goethe and Schiller and music. The Germans have never been much interested in the other arts. Literature and music have always been their forte. And many of them beguiled away their night's sleep while discussing things of greater importance than mere physical rest. I have many a time heard wonderful poetry recited by poets who have since become famous here and abroad.

Both of these places were closed during the war, although several transformations were essayed to keep them alive.

Westward on Second Avenue is the German Eye, Ear, and Nose Hospital, which is one of the most celebrated in the city and has done a great deal for the inhabitants of the neighborhood. The poorer class have flocked to its dispensary, the hospital also helping to implant a respect and love for everything German. The Bulgarians, Serbians, Albanians, Rumanians, and all the Balkan people living in the neighborhood have much more confidence in a German doctor or a German druggist than they have in a doctor of their own nationalities. For centuries Germans have occupied similar capacities in their own countries. Indeed, in parts of Rumania a druggist is called a German whether he is German or not. And the word *"Artzt"* is as common among the Albanians for "doctor" as if it were a word of their own language. There is an old story that tells how, when the old druggist in a Rumanian village died, the peasants took a German fiddler who happened to be there and compelled him to become their druggist and doctor in spite of his protests. Was he not a German? Therefore he was a doctor and a druggist.

Not far from the hospital is the Ottendorfer Library,

where the books seem to be regarded more sacredly than anywhere else. Old ladies, brought to the door by their young daughters or granddaughters, are reading the old German illustrated weeklies that come there. It is the most complete German library in town, owning many old volumes long out of print, which would be the pride and envy of every collector.

Stories of German-American life have been many, but the best of them were written by G. Stürenburg and have been gathered into a book after they had appeared through several years in the "Staats-Zeitung."

On Fourteenth Street is the old Luchow's Beer Parlor and Restaurant. In former years it was the center, and the most fashionable of all the German places. It is still frequented by the more cultivated element, because of old associations, the excellence of its food, and the band that plays for luncheon and dinner. How easy it is to forget there the noise and hubbub of the city! How easy it is to forget one is not in München, with the foaming big schooners brought by smiling and adept waiters, while the music plays dances and songs that have long since been forgotten elsewhere. It is, I am afraid, the only place in the city where jazz is taboo and Straus is still king.

Further down, on Nineteenth Street, is the Graaf House, the owner of which used to furnish for ten dollars apiece barons and counts to ornament the dinner-table of such as desired their company. In Graaf's eyes a baron or a count, to be genuine, had only to have his pedigree with him to prove his right to the title. He also had to look the part. He had to know how to wear his monocle and his white vest over his starched shirt-front. A good many of Graaf's counts, he will tell you, who have been introduced by social climbing mothers at a dinner-table, have married their wealthy daughters. Mr. Graaf finances such affairs to the end. I am told that he has also financed many French and Italian counts in search of wealthy heiresses. But the business has gone down considerably of late, since the Russian Revolution caused so many Russian princes and counts and nobles to flee to America. Really these Russians have much more style and dash, and know how to do the thing in much better form, than the German barons and counts did it. Accordingly a good many of the old German counts have become waiters or valets to the newly rich, whom they instruct in good behavior.

And so the district meanders along, with German bands playing around corners, and German stores selling old zithers, and pastry-shops adjoining one another, up to Fifty-first Street, where is the *Kellnersheim,* the home of the old waiters. Then it swerves eastward toward Beekman Place, where suddenly there is a crisscrossing of narrow alleys paved with cobblestones, and houses facing this way and that, set back into the lots, some of them projecting too far over sidewalks, with large brownstone stoops and bay-windows twisting this way and the other. People will show you the place where Nathan Hale was hanged, and others will show you where Horace Traubel, Walt Whitman's celebrated biographer, lived with his friend Karsner for several years previous to his death.

Speaking of Traubel, who was a dear friend of mine for many years, I must tell what happened at his funeral.

Traubel was of mixed parentage, his father having been a Jew. When he was brought here for his funeral his wife decided to have it take place from the Community Church on Thirty-fourth Street. Many of his friends protested, telling Anne Montgomerie they were certain Horace Traubel would not have wished it so. She overrode all the objections.

The funeral was to take place at three o'clock. The hearse had no sooner drawn up in front of the church when some one came rushing out, calling, "Fire! Fire!" A moment later there was the clang and rush of the fire-engines.

The fire did a good deal of damage to the church, while one of Traubel's friends, master of the situation because of the bewilderment of the relatives, jumped up beside the hearse-driver, and the whole procession rode to the People's House on Fifteenth Street, from which the funeral actually took place.

One can see Blackwell's Island from Beekman Place, and beyond it the loud signs and lights from the Brooklyn side of the river, and sailing-boats and steamers and yachts going up and down the river. It is the most intimate corner of the city. It has remained as segregated and different from the rest of its environment as an island in the midst of the sea. It still is one of the quaintest places in the city. But it has changed in character of late because it has been discovered by the wealthy up-towners, who have, after buying up several of the old houses, built their costlier residences where formerly were one- and two-family houses. I am tempted to hope that the summer odors from the slaughter-house not far off will drive them away in the summer, and thus perhaps help restore the place to its former slow, individual, village life.

There is a beautiful *Gesangsverein* in the neighborhood, where most of the Bavarians in the city come to sing their evenings away. They came for many years, and have returned again, after two years' absence during the war, to the old place, only to find that it has lost a good deal of its former charm because of the intrusion of the wealthier class.

There used to be a beer-garden in the neighborhood, which I am told had been there since 1680 or 1690, from the time when the Kissing Bridge near-by was one of the city's institutions. It has been swept away in the recent remodeling of the quarter. Big ugly houses occupy the spot where the *Halle* once stood. The gates and the doorways and the windows of the old building lay in a small alley against the wall for years, with nobody to claim them and nobody to take care of them. And the people respected the theoretical property rights of some one who had forgotten all about these things. As long as the population was strictly German no one touched them. But a southeastern European group came to settle in the neighborhood. Shortly afterward all the unclaimed things disappeared. The wrought-iron gates and finely chiseled doorway found their way to some junk-dealer's cart for the few pennies that he paid. The Germans object to everybody else as "foreigners."

Helferich's violin repair shop on East Eighty-sixth Street, between Second and Third Avenues, was known as the "old man's hospital" to the ten thousand or more professional violinists, fiddlers, cellists, and contrabassists of New York, scraping their way through life on gut strings.

When a stringed instrument became "cranky," when the "walls" bulged or the "belly" cracked, when the "neck" had to be shaved down or the bow repaired, the invalid was brought to the old man. And if—(but he very rarely found any too sick to remedy) the instrument was thrown on the scrap-heap.

One left his violin or cello with Helferich, said, "Do what you can with it," and went for his glass of wine or cider or white beer in one of the *Apfelweinstuben* near-by, or for a real dinner in the *Heimath,* some twenty feet below the street, where the tables were of white pine, where the buxom waitresses had long eyelashes, and a *primas* from Budapest with waxed mustache and oiled hair played the latest and the oldest *czardas.*

And if the visitor had ever been in "Pest" or Vienna, it did not require much generalship to invade a congenial table in the *Heimath* and make of a trip to the "hospital" a real holiday. You see, the men were from Vienna, the women hailed from Budapest. One could drink, be merry, and forget many things in such a company.

I suspect that Helferich's renown was due quite as much to the location of his shop as to his workmanship. But as to that, *basta!*

In his young days Helferich had been known as a great violinist. Yellowed old programs and newspaper clippings with frequent mention of his name hung framed in the shop and attested to Helferich's great playing at courts and palaces. But in an accident he lost two fingers of his left hand, and his playing career was ruined.

So he learned to repair the instrument he played so well, and came to New York. And in his shop he hung the fiddle he had used, the one given him in Vienna by the Austrian emperor. He hung it in a glass case on the wall over the door which connected the shop with the living apartment in the rear.

In due time he married and had two sons. The older one, after finishing at the public school, was kept at home to learn the trade and help his father. The younger one was destined for higher things.

As Helferich's fame spread, he accumulated a good deal of money. He never drank except when others paid. He never smoked other cigars than those given him by his customers. But these kept his heart continually warm and cheerful and the shop in thick clouds of smoke. And when he was tired or dreamy, old Helferich would turn his chair so as to face the rear wall and sit looking at the precious Steiner that the old emperor had given him.

If a customer arrived when the old man was thus absorbed, Joseph, his son—"the young man," as he was called —walked on tiptoes from his bench to receive him, and the ensuing conversation was carried on in low whispers:

"Ssh—ssh—the old man has the blues."

Then one day came a telegram to old Helferich calling him away to Cincinnati to the bedside of a dying sister. He took his wife along with him.

"Take care of the shop, Joseph," were his parting words to his son, with a nod toward the fiddle.

"Don't worry, father," the young man replied.

At the door the old man turned again to give advice. "Und if a fire there is, *Gott behüte,* save the Steiner first, Joseph. You are responsible for the violin."

"Don't worry, father."

But the following morning the violin had disappeared from the glass case on the wall. Joseph was struck dumb. His father's Steiner, the gift of the emperor, was stolen! He would commit suicide. He would disappear. He could not face the old man again.

When he quieted down a little later Joseph had an idea and sat down to work. He worked the whole day and the whole night and the day and night following. Before the sun had risen on the third morning another violin, looking very much like the Steiner, appeared in the place of the stolen one.

That very night Helferich returned from Cincinnati.

"Mein sister is not sick at all. She neffer sent no telegram. *Verdammt, verdammt!*"

The following night old Helferich turned his chair to look at the fiddle. At midnight he was still looking at it.

On his deathbed a few days later he asked for pen and paper and wrote in his best hand in presence of witnesses:

> To my wife and son Albert I give everything I possess, and to my son Joseph I leave the Steiner on the wall.
>
> FRANZ HELFERICH.

And to this day Joseph Helferich has a puzzled look in his face.

"Do you think he knew?" he asked me the other night in the *Weinstube* next to the shop.

And suddenly you are at the Fifty-ninth Street Bridge over the East River and across to Astoria, where the younger generation of Germans, as well as the younger generations of other nationalities in the city, flee the Ghettos that give them a hyphen. They desire to be known only as Americans instead of German-Americans or French-Americans or Jewish-Americans.

The German district stretches as far as Eighty-sixth Street and Lexington Avenue. From there on it begins to dwindle as it goes upward.

The beer-saloons in the German quarters in New York have played a greater rôle than the saloons anywhere else. They were not places where one drank oneself to insensibility. On the contrary, probably because of the great beer-drinking capacity of the Germans, drunkenness was a more or less rare thing in them.

In the back of these saloons have been organized a good many organizations which later on became an important factor in the life of the community. Many *Liedertafeln* were in the backs of saloons. A celebrated *Männerchor* met for many years back of a saloon in Harlem before that district was taken away from the Germans by the negro population of the city. The socialist movement, which was originally a German movement in New York, was begun in back saloons. Indeed, it was so German that I remember once at a meeting, when one of the speakers got up and began to talk English, the rest of the visitors were so much astonished that they howled their dis-

approval. It would have fared badly with the speaker had not the chairman turned the tide by announcing that it was indeed a very good sign when the English-speaking population began to join the movement.

Johann Most, the celebrated anarchist, held most of his meetings with his people back of a saloon in Harlem, and he even edited his paper, "Die Freiheit," from there. I remember him well. He was one of the most interesting figures I have ever met. His knowledge of things historical was so tremendous and his memory so good that he could discourse upon the history of the world at any period and from every possible angle with the greatest ease and authority. In spite of a rather unpleasant appearance because of the deformity of his face and the thickness of his tongue, he was a most fiery orator. He did more leavening of minds than converting to his theories.

There being no prospect of any considerable German immigration in the near future, with the second generation of the forty-eighters who brought German culture to this country dying out, the German population is slowly merging with the rest of the population. There is still great reluctance about intermarriage because the Germans consider so many races inferior to them, the inferiority of this and that and the other race to the German one having been insidiously taught for generations. And yet the eventual absorption is bound to happen.

My neighbor Talhouse, familiarly called Henry, is a first-generation American. His father, a forty-eighter, left Germany practically with a rope on his neck, and, footing it to the nearest shore, embarked for America, where he changed his name from Hochhaus to Talhouse. It is said of the old man that he rose two hours earlier than he had to every morning so as to hate Germany and the whole of Europe two hours more every day. This hatred for Europe was inherited by his son Henry, whose Americanism was merely hatred for the Old World.

In his delicatessen store Henry has propounded the most drastic action against "them foreigners" and has even risked his bread by rechristening *Leberwurst* into liver sausage and refusing to serve sauerkraut unless it was served under an American name.

At one time during the war a cardboard sign over the counter announced, "No foreigners are served here." It was the most effective custom-getter, that sign, until his competitor, Hans Shiller, on the advice of his customers, hung out a similar legend.

Well, Henry—fat, blond, blue-eyed, small-eared, low-browed, bow-legged—hated foreigners more than he loved Americans, and said so. But his store was always clean, his stuff fresh, and his prices reasonable. His opinions were his opinions. And if he liked to utter them freely, well, they did not weigh on the scales and did not increase the price of ham or pumpernickel.

Elizabeth Talhouse was not allowed to play with foreign children. Whenever she was seen coming home from school with other children, the father put the question, "Are they foreigners?"

"I don't know, father."

"You don't know, hey! You don't know?"

Slap, slap.

Henry Talhouse would not have his daughter associate with other than Americans. And so Elizabeth, blond and pretty, grew into maidenhood and was sent to college.

While in college she met and fell in love with John Smith, the son of Fire-eye Eagle, a Cherokee Indian chieftain. John was tall, brown, and handsome and spoke very little but very wisely. Except the noble dignity of his carriage, there was no other outward difference between himself and the handsomest young college man. When Elizabeth came home from her college, Henry Talhouse exhibited her to his customers. "Und she goes to college mit only Americans. She vas trained not to have notting to do mit furriners. Und ven she marries she vill marry a American, und her children will be third-generation Americans! Understand that! *Third!*"

Back of the store, the partitioned-off home of the Talhouses, Elizabeth confided to her mother:

"He is handsome and big and strong, mother. I love him so!" And she hugged and kissed her mother.

"Und what does he say, Lisby? Does he lof you?"

"Mummerl, mummerl; of course he does. He told me so."

"Und will he come to see you here?"

"I will write him to come. But we must not say anything to papa when he comes. It will be such a surprise to him. Such a surprise."

It was on a Sunday afternoon that a tall, brown man knocked at the store door of Talhouse. Henry looked through the pane in the partition and announced to his wife and daughter, "One of dem furriners who don't know that delicatessen stores are closed on Sundays."

But the man knocked again. "Lisby, you go and tell him. Und tell him that delicatessen stores open from five to six on Sundays in America."

Henry Talhouse, startled, looked into the store, and what he saw made him forget his English.

"Who is this man, Lisby?" he yelled. "And what, what business comes he here, I ask!"

"But, father, quiet down. It was all a surprise for you. This is John Smith, the man I am going to marry."

"What? *Donnerwetter!* Marry this man? This man. A furriner!"

"But, father, listen."

"Listen! My daughter, marry a furriner . . . Heraus, heraus!"

"But, father, listen. He is a Cherokee; listen, a Cherokee."

"A Sherokee marry my daughter! My daughter will marry an American."

"Who is not an American?" quietly asked John Smith, as he approached the irate delicatessen dealer.

"You Sherokees . . ."

So John Smith, Fire-eye Eagle's son, shed his acquired civilization and did a war-dance in good old Indian fashion then and there.

Henry was looking on in mortal fear from behind the pane of the barricaded door. The police had to quell the riot in front of the store.

But now, two years since, Henry is proudly exhibiting the picture of a little half-breed.

"The third generation. The real American. That comes from bringing up children mit the right idear."

## CHAPTER XIV

### HUNGARY

FROM almost any street of the German quarter you can enter the Hungarian one. For it runs parallel with it from Tenth Street north. The Hungarian district takes a bit of Second Avenue as its main street, from Ninth Street to Eighteenth and Nineteenth Streets, and then, extending eastward, it sinks below the lower avenues, A and B, and with few interruptions runs along in the same way to Sixtieth Street. There the Magyar district takes a short jump of about ten or twelve blocks where the Czecho-Slovaks live. Skirting their territory, the Hungarian quarter continues from it to Eighty-sixth street, always running parallel with the German district.

New York is the second largest Hungarian community in the world, Budapest, the capital of Hungary, being the first. There are between a hundred and forty and a hundred and fifty thousand Hungarians in New York, and most of them live in the district alluded to. You can easily follow their traces by the signs in the windows. Do not expect the word "Hungarian" to appear very frequently. The Hungarian seldom refers to himself as such; he prefers the word "Magyar." And though the world has occasionally spoken with horror of Attila and Arpad as Huns, no Hungarian has ever looked upon Attila or Arpad with other eyes than those of admiration. And even the epithet thrown at the man who brought them to Europe a thousand years ago from Asia, "the Scourge of God," is not displeasing to Magyar ears. A Magyar respects force, respects violence, respects anything that results from force and vio-

lence. Indeed, one is no sooner in the presence of a group of Magyars, at home in one of the cafés in their own district, than one feels the air thick with passion, violent and active. The Magyars are great lovers and good haters. They are a race of hard workers and hard livers.

Long before the women of other nationalities had thought of independence, the Hungarian woman had it.

No one who has visited Budapest could have failed to notice the freedom of carriage and of action of the Magyar woman. A thousand years is only as yesterday in the psychology of a people. The Magyars invaded Europe with their women, who rode side by side with the men and fought side by side with them, hacking their way through most of the countries they passed. The horde of Magyars was not composed of men only. And their women knew no tents. The heat of the ridden horse between saddle and back served to cook the strips of meat underneath. Women fighting side by side with men under such conditions are the sort who have equal rights with their men, even if more recent political conditions have not given them votes. A Hungarian household is ruled by the woman. The Hungarian woman is an excellent business woman. There are very few Hungarian women artists, painters, writers, or musicians, but a good many of the cares elsewhere incumbent upon men are lifted from Hungarian husbands' shoulders and taken over by their wives. In New York, in the restaurants and cafés and pastry-shops and in the embroidery business, in which a good many Hungarians are engaged, or in any other business that they happen to be in, the Hungarian woman is the actively engaged member of the firm. The husband is frequently the ornament, the official owner. The Hungarian woman recognizes rights of her man aside from family life. The wife attends to business while the husband, with waxed mustache and sleek oiled hair, is taking a stroll or going visiting with several of his friends at a café. There is no servility. The women are capable masters because they are good servants.

Many of the European countries adjacent to Hungary consider Hungary a breeding-place for servant-girls. Indeed, in my own country, Rumania, although there has been a long-standing enmity between the two peoples, I venture to say that eighty per cent of the servant-girls are Hungarian women. They are being brought down in batches, hundreds, by employment agencies. The children in most households learn to speak a little Hungarian; for the servant-girls never stay long enough anywhere to learn the language of the country. As soon as they have accumulated a little money from their wages they return home to spend it in their own way, mostly as dowry for a husband.

A good many of these customs still prevail in the Hungarian district here among the more recently arrived immigrants, and will prevail subconsciously among them for generations yet to come. The institution of dowry giving is not one likely to die very soon among them. And yet nowhere is there as intense passion as among the Hungarians. I have often wondered whether the music alone is Gipsy; I have often wondered how much of Gipsy blood has been infused in the Magyar by the children of the Ganges! There is a certain nearness of race, also, the Magyars being Asiatics as the Gipsies are. Indeed, there is even great kinship of language. The "deep Calo," the secret language of the Gipsy, contains a good many words like the Magyar idiom.

The houses of the Hungarian district in New York are more or less of the modern tenement type. Outwardly, in structure, those houses do not differ from any other houses anywhere. It is within that the homes are different from the homes of the people of other nationalities, although the rooms are littered with most of the good-for-nothing furniture manufactured somewhere and sold on the lower East Side on the instalment plan. Ah, those poor chairs and tables, rickety and weak, slapped together in any way, varnished and polished to look as if they were of some use, and which are semblances of what they pretend to be as long only as they stay in the parlor as ornamental pieces! Superposed upon this ready-made comfort is the Hungarian woman's own love for color and arrangement of such kind as she has seen in her own home, across the Carpathian Mountains, or on the borders of the Tisza River.

But it is in the kitchens of these houses, spick and span, with walls hung full of copper kettles and copper pots and colored dishes, flowered and deep, with here and there a piece of earthenware brought from home or sent by some loving relative to the exiled ones, that one can notice the differences of national character. Love of good food, spicy and tasty, is one of the characteristics of the Hungarians. At home the kitchen, which is generally also the largest part, is the most important room. It is because of love of food and drink that the kitchen is such an important institution in a Hungarian home.

There is scarcely a single industry or a single art in which the Hungarians of the city are not engaged, yet very few of their women work in factories or shops. There are hardly more than one tenth of the Hungarian population of second generation in this city. I doubt if there are that many. And yet they have already acclimatized themselves to a certain degree and have taken root in all the professions and industries. There are any number of carpenters and bricklayers and iron-workers, music teachers (a profession in which they excel), with a considerable number of waiters and a preponderant proportion of busi-

ness people of all sorts. The embroidery business is almost exclusively in their hands. There are more than four hundred Hungarian restaurants spread over the city, for the savor of their food is now beginning to be appreciated everywhere.

But given conditions as they are, it is not in their places of business or in their homes that one can see the Hungarians at their national best. There is a restaurant and wine-house at Eighty-first Street and Avenue A. A Gipsy music band plays there during the dinner-hour and late into the night. The walls are decorated by a man who was until not long ago known as a sign-painter or something of the sort. But after he had decorated the walls with scenes from his native land, artistic New York flocked evening after evening to look at them. Some of the panels on the wall have the simplicity and beauty of El Greco's. It is interesting to observe that the proprietor did not appreciate the beauty of the paintings. They seemed to him too crude. They were not the conventional things he had been accustomed to see in the lithographs that had formerly been hung in the place. It was only after Alexander Popini, the artist, had offered to buy the panels at three times the price the proprietor had agreed to pay that the artist got his money. Hung with vines over a latticework ceiling, the white pine tables covered with red peasantish spreads, with a band of Gipsy musicians at the end of the hall and a few dancers always in national Hungarian costume, the place was a great attraction for those who were homesick for their own land. Rigo, the celebrated Gipsy violinist, used to play there nightly. But the sensational Gipsy's performances have greatly contributed toward the deterioration of the place. Broadway, having discovered it, insisted on being there nightly after theater hours. Seizing upon the popularity that had been gained, the proprietor increased his prices until the native element completely abandoned it.

It was Alice's third visit to New York in one year. And every time she had come from Jamestown she had been disappointed that I did not take her to hear Costica, the Hungarian Gipsy violinist.

She had heard of Costica's great adventure, how a princess, a real princess owning castles and palaces, had abandoned titled husband and children and eloped with a plain Gipsy fiddler from one of the cafés on a Parisian boulevard.

The affair had been an international scandal. Several sensational novels with the affair as a *motif* had colored it and had given to the two principals a sort of heroic glamour which they enjoyed, for they were both theatrical.

New York being the center of the world's vortex, all, ultimately, are swerved here. And thus it happened that, at the death of the princess, Costica, who had drunk and gambled away the palaces and châteaux at Monte Carlo and Cairo, Costica, the Gipsy, raked enough money together to come to New York to trade on his fame.

He bluffed through several concerts in New York. In truth, one is forced to say that he was a very poor fiddler, and people did not display satisfaction. The dear besilked and beribboned children of fortune sat in their boxes and wondered and admired . . . the princess who had had the courage. And in the galleries the less beribboned children of toil felt in the same way.

Having bluffed through a few concerts, Costica drank and gambled away his money again, and soon the best he could get was a job as the fiddler at a restaurant famous for its food and its Tokay.

News, sensational news, travels through unknown channels. In a month all the young girls from shops and schools, and the less young ones living within a radius of a thousand miles, knew that Costica played at such and such a place. And those who had a chance to come to New York to see him did so and are still doing so. The Hungarian restaurant has never had so many out-of-town guests. They come in droves; excursions are arranged for the purpose.

But to return to Alice. It was the third time she had asked me to take her to hear Costica. So, unable to refuse a third and last time, I promised. Needless to say, Alice was busy that day from early in the morning to the dinner-hour. She fussed enough with her *toilette* to make one think she was preparing for the ambassador's ball. The restaurant not being far from my home, we walked the four blocks.

"You know," said Alice, "I am so excited, so upset. Fancy, I shall hear Costica! I shall see him! Dear me, I shall never forget it! You know, mother read the novel about him. I was only ten years old then, but I stole the book from the shelf and read it. . . . Oh! I am so excited!"

I did not want to disillusion her. I hoped the illusion could be kept up, for her sake.

We had reserved our table. Costica was at a table next to ours. I greeted him as we entered but did not tell Alice who the man was. You see, Costica was eating his dinner, and in an inartistic way, using his fingers where a fork could have done perfect duty.

I gave Alice the seat overlooking the whole place. She thought the restaurant had atmosphere, European atmosphere. I did not tell her that all the guests were out-of-towners, like herself, Anglo-Saxons, who had come to see Costica as they go to see the pyramids—one of the sights of the world, a Baedeker curiosity.

"It 's so exciting!"

The soup was taken away cold.

"When does he begin to play?"

"Soon."

The meat was taken away untouched.

"Why don't you eat, Alice?"

"I 'm not a bit hungry."

"Red, white?"

"Dear me, dear me, what 's all the noise?"

"It 's Costica getting ready to play."

Every one listened to him for a few minutes in silence. Afterward three hundred men and women began to whisper remarks. And those whispers completely drowned the sound of Costica's violin.

I watched Alice. Her eyes had grown to twice their ordinary size. Yet in a few moments the muscles of her face relaxed, a little too much, I thought, and a cynical line dragged down the corners of her lips.

"I don't see why a princess should have left her husband, children, palaces, and castles for that man," she finally said.

I did not answer.

"You hear? Did you hear what I said?"

"I did, Alice."

"And—"

"I was wondering why a Gipsy should abandon a perfectly beautiful free nomad life for a princess, and that."

There is another place on Eighty-second Street which was opened for the native element after the first one had become a Broadway resort. While visitors at the newer place are not frowned upon, they are not catered to as eagerly as in the other place. The new one is plainly one for Hungarian workers and their families. And there, when the mood seizes them, the assembled audience sings along with the musicians the Hungarian folk-songs. And if a *czardas* is played, couples rise from the tables, and, putting arms upon shoulders, facing one another, they perform their national dance until they fall exhausted to the floor. I have seen the *czardas* performed at this restaurant by thirty or more couples until absolute exhaustion came. And while they were resting, a woman of about forty-five, formerly a very celebrated singer in Budapest, with a warm voice which was already cracked, sang such songs that the Magyars wept and screamed and writhed in pain. It is the Hungarian's idea of a good time, to let down the bars and free his starved passions. How ridiculous the European clothing they wear, when they are so stirred. How eager they seize upon anything in the place that has color, even to the table-spread, to drape it around themselves.

There is Cato, beautiful Cato, who was brought here by

her parents when a child. Her soul wandered aimlessly because of her parents' desire to make her an American girl. But she found herself after she had seen the *czardas* danced and heard the Hungarian songs from which her parents had kept her in their desire to have her an American. And so passionately and beautifully does she now dance the *czardas* that at Gipsy Land every one sits breathless when she dances. It was difficult for Cato to speak English while in such a mood, although she generally spoke English much more fluently than Hungarian. For though she had never seen it, the music and the dance of her native land made her long for it.

It is the great tragedy of the first generations of all immigrants in this country, whether born here or brought here as young children, that there is always something between them and life. Their parents never cease to speak of their homeland. And there is this new land of the youngsters in which they are strangers, in which they feel it is only the language of the country they are using and that the spirit of it is far from there. It is this longing which when expressed becomes great art. Most of the modern art in America has been produced by first-generation immigrants.

Another great center of the Hungarians is the Hungarian Workers' Home, the pride and the strength of the organized industrials of the Magyars living in the city. The Hungarian Workers' Home on Eighty-first Street is not only the official center of union locals. It has, also, a valuable cultural and educational background. It has a dramatic organization which gives plays by Ibsen, Björnson, Shaw, and Shakspere, wonderfully directed and beautifully acted. It is from the Hungarian Workers' Home that word about the Hungarian playwright Molnar was first breathed. Since then the American stage has had occasion to see many of the plays of the Oscar Wilde of the Magyars. Works like "Liliom," "The Swan," "Lunzi," are gems in the world's dramatic literature. And Molnar is not alone among the great dramatists of Hungary. There is Lajos Biro, and Vajda, whose play, "Fata Morgana," created such a sensation only last winter. At the Hungarian Workers' Home there are weekly concerts of considerable importance, and exhibitions of paintings, and lectures on arts and literature, as well as courses in English. There is no similar institution in the whole city, and it is one of the most frequented places of the district.

Among Hungarian artists living here are men like Hugo Gellert, whose strong pencil has caught with great charm the life of the laborer of the city; Willy Pogany, one of the most famous of portraitists and illustrators, is one of the most sought-after painters. His work for the stage has made him famous the world over. But best of all are his illustrations to "Gulliver's Travels," which surpass anything done before. Essentially, as a painter and a colorist, Willy Pogany harks back to Hungarian traditions. One could unmistakably recognize his nationality by looking at any one of his paintings. They have the flavor of Tokay wine and Gipsy song.

There has been something of a constellation of young Hungarian violinists who have made their appearance in New York and over the country within the last few years, chief of whom are Munkácsy, the son of the great Hungarian painter, Dulci Kerekiarto, and a number of others. Hungarian music needs no introduction here. The Liszt Hungarian Rhapsodies and the Brahms Hungarian Dances, really Hungarian Gipsy music, have already given a taste of what Hungarian music is like.

Since the war there has been a great exodus of Hungarians back to their homeland; for a good many, having saved considerable amounts during the war, were anxious to go home and see their people. Many of them have remained there, caught between the different strifes that have rent their homeland. A good many of them were desirous to wait out until things should become quiet, impossible as it is for them, because of the immigration quota, to bring their relatives and friends here with them. Intellectuals who were living here before have also returned home. Many of them have played a considerable rôle in the readjustment process of Hungary, a readjustment of which a good many things are better left unsaid. The bloody pogroms against Jews in the principal cities of Magyarland rivaled quite successfully the pogroms of old

Russia. It has always been a mystery to me why we have heard in American papers so little of what happened there! I have never understood the reason for that silence.

There are a great number of Jews of Hungarian origin living in this city, and most of them live in the Hungarian

district among their Christian brethren. The Hungarian Jews, though there are among them some who are strictly orthodox, are much more liberal than the Jews of other nations. There have been mixed marriages in Hungary for the last hundred years. Even the type of the Hungarian Jews is totally different from the type of any other Jews.

Neither do they speak Yiddish, the language spoken by almost all the Jews except the Spanish ones. The Hungarian Jews here have their separate synagogues, not because their rites of worship are very different from the others, but because of their clannishness, and because of their feeling of superiority, by reason of the fact that they had political equality in Hungary long before the Jews of other countries were so privileged.

Among the principal Hungarian churches are the Roman Catholic Church of St. Stephen of Hungary, on Fourteenth Street, and the Fourteenth Street Presbyterian Church. The First Magyar Presbyterian Church on Sixteenth Street is led by the Rev. Michael Kozma. Many Hungarians attend these Presbyterian churches because of their similarity in doctrine to the Protestant churches of Hungary, and the Presbyterian Magyar Mission operates a settlement-house on East 116th Street. There is also the Hungarian Reformed Church on Sixty-ninth Street and the First Hungarian Baptist Church, led by the Rev. W. Dulitz, who also has charge of a mission in Brooklyn.

There are three Hungarian daily newspapers in the city. The "Amerikai Magyar Nepszava" is edited by Geza D. Berko, who also edits the "Berko Kepes Ujsazga" ("Illustrated News"). There is also the "Szabadsag" ("Liberty"), and the socialist "Elore," edited by Charles Varga, which for the last two years has been gotten out coöperatively by its employees, who also manage the shop where the paper is printed. There is also the "Amerikai Magyarsag," a semi-weekly edited by Lorand Simay; and the "Sportvilag" is devoted to sports. Martin Himler is editor of the weekly "Hungarian Miners' Journal" and Ernest I. Mandel of the weekly "Munkaslap," another labor paper. All of these are very ably edited and anxious to convey in the Hungarian language the spirit and the soul of what is happening in this country. Plays and books are reviewed and commented upon, and a good many things are translated from the American into the Hungarian, especially now when they are so much pleased with the fact that some of their great writers and painters have won recognition here.

I went the other day to hear "L'Amore de Tre Re." Not liking the music of the first act, I looked around me. When my eyes had accustomed themselves to the semi-darkness I discovered an old Hungarian friend in the next box. With him was a beautiful woman. During the first intermission we were introduced. "Mme. Solmers," my friend said, "an old friend of mine." Then they went out to stroll in the foyer.

I sat waiting for the second act to begin—the second and best of the three of that opera—but my mind was away. Solmers; where and when had I heard that name? I was sure I had heard it in connection with some great tragedy, but could not recall when and what.

The music began, the curtain was parted, and lofty love-scenes followed the aimless coming and going, singing and posing of the principals. During the great scene of passion I heard the short, crisp laugh of Mme. Solmers. Our eyes met. It was as though we said, "That fifteen-minute kiss is a boring business." But while the thing went on, Didur, immense in kingly robes, but blind, appeared on the stage. Muzio, after having seen her lover escape, sang beautifully and acted splendidly but did get into the hands of the ferocious old man, who then proceeded to choke her in full view of the audience. It was a most realistic piece of work. Suddenly I heard a cry, and my friend was half carrying, half leading Mme. Solmers out into the hall.

I did not see them during the third act. After the performance I found my friend, wild-eyed and despondent, sitting down to a cup of wine at Gipsy Land.

"Yanosh," I asked, "what happened to your friend?"

"Oh! I am the most stupid, the most tactless ass under the sky," he answered after offering me the chair opposite him. "You know who she is, don't you?"

"I do remember the name, but not the connection."

"Awful," Yanosh cried. "Don't you know she is the wife of the Hungarian actor, Solmers, who died insane some years ago?"

"I remember now."

"But what you don't know is how he became insane. They were playing—she and her husband—a most realistic tragedy in the theater of Budapest. In that tragedy a woman married a painter, an artist of high rank, and proceeded by her extravagance to ruin him, driving him to commercialize his art. At the end he is nothing but an unknown quantity, a memory, an example of what artists should not do. An article in a magazine written by an eminent critic tells it all pitilessly. The artist reads it. Tears stream down his face. He looks up to his wife, expecting

MAGYAR MUNKOIS OTTHON
HUNGARIAN
WORKERS HOME
RESTAURANT
SERVICE A LA CARTE

a consoling word from her, but her face is hard and cold. The article dishonors her; she can no longer face her friends. And, what is more, every word is true. He had deteriorated. 'But,' argues the man, 'you know why I have done it, don't you?' and he points at the luxurious things about him and to his wife; 'why and for *whom?*'

" 'Oh,' answers the woman angrily, 'nonsense! If you had been something real you would have gone on the real way regardless of me and done your work.' The painter leaps from his chair like a tiger. His hand clutches the woman's throat, and he murders her.

"Well, the Solmerses were playing that. Solmers was a capable actor. He had married his wife at the beginning of her career and taught her everything he knew. She had genius; she had talent. The morning after the première the Budapest papers were wild about her and dismissed him with a few kind words, 'A very capable actor,' and all that, you know. They quarreled—professional jealousy. He accused her of monopolizing the stage; she answered back, and it wound up with her saying that if he had been a great actor he would have shown it before all his hair had fallen out. He was just beginning to get bald.

"That night they played. There was liquor on his breath, but he played better than usual. The last act he did marvelously. Tears actually streamed down his face, and he found such new accents in his voice that she was thrilled, and regretted all she had said to him. But when the moment came for that tigerish leap, she gave a horrible yell. She knew herself in the power of a maniac, who was going to strangle her in view of the whole audience.

"The stage-manager became suspicious of the too-realistic acting. He lowered the curtain. He had a hard job to loosen Solmers's hands from the throat of his wife. She still bears the marks on her throat.

" 'A most realistic performance,' said the critics the following day.

"Solmers never came to himself after that. He died in a strait-jacket. Now, tell me whether I am not the most tactless man under God's blue sky to take her to hear and see that second act? How stupid! How stupid!"

And my friend was thinking of his own tragedy while telling the other.

## CHAPTER XV

### CZECHOSLOVAKIA

UP to the beginning of the war, if any one had asked where Czechoslovakia was in Europe, even the best student of geography would have looked at his questioner doubting his sanity. To-day Czechoslovakia is an independent country, though it originally was only an American invention. Masaryk met President Wilson, and the invention received the finishing touches before going upon the market. There are Czechs and there are Slovaks. But the Czechs and the Slovaks have never lived in close friendship. Only for a brief space while Masaryk and Wilson were planning the liberation of Bohemia from the yoke of Austria did the Slovaks and the Czechs make believe they got on very well, and then merely to carry on their propaganda of liberation in common. It was only the feeling against the common enemy that bound them. Once that enemy was vanquished, the old natural enmity between them again rose to the surface, and the Slovaks are bringing against their friends the Czechs accusations of similar nature to those they used to bring against the Austrians and the Germans. The Czechs, they cry and thunder, are oppressing them, interfering with their religious liberty, and so on.

The Czechs are natural politicians. Of a higher culture,

individually and in mass, than either the Poles or the Slovaks, their perpetual enemies and occasional friends, they have always outwitted them in the long run. There are fewer illiterates among the Czechs than in any other nation in Europe, the French not excepted. What is equally important is that there are fewer illiterates among the women. Because of their national misfortunes all Czechs have a natural inclination toward the study of history and politics. The average Czech knows more of these two subjects than the average university professor of those branches, either here or abroad. It is this knowledge of history which has won them their independence. It is this knowledge of history which has given them a superiority over the Poles and the Slovaks. It is this knowledge of history, coupled with great organizing talent, that will eventually make the Czechs one of the most powerful nations in Europe. Progressive and cautious, hardy, and daring without being adventurous, they have their most powerful weapons within them. They can think of the future in terms of the past and study the past with an eye to the future. It is a rare educational treat to hear an every-day Czech working-man discourse on European political history.

The first Czech arrivals in this country were in 1847, when a group of deserters from Mainz in Germany found their way to New York and settled on the lower part of the East Side, near the East River, below Fifth Street, which was then populated mostly by Poles and Ruthenians, who had preceded them in great numbers only a few years before. There is no doubt that the Czechs were received with open arms by the Poles and their brother Ruthenians, for a greater number of them, political refugees, followed the first group, in 1848 and 1850, on the heels of the '48 revolution, which had shaken the whole of Europe. Krikava, Juranek, Korbel, the younger Hubaceks and Mracek, the leaders of the refugees, were received as hospitably by the Poles as by their own people. They fraternized, the Czechs and the Poles, to a great degree. Austria and Russia were the hereditary enemies of both nations. They met in the same halls, had banquets and weddings in the same places, and theatricals and concerts in the Narodni Budova, the National Hall on East Fifth Street.

With their aptitude for organization the Czechs formed a society in 1850, to give advice and succor to fellow-countrymen, which did not exclude any of the Slavic peoples under the yoke of the Austrians, Germans, or Russians. Even the Jan Hus Church was frequented as much by the other nations as by the Czechs themselves. In 1861 they formed the Slovenska Lipa, a social and educational club which also included a language school and a circulating library. A short time afterward their first paper, the "New Yorkske Listy," appeared from the same group, with different organizations springing from it, like the Czech Slavic Sokol Benevolent Society, and the Union of Czech Women, and the Union of Catholic Women. There was hardly a Czech in the city who did not belong to several organizations which did their utmost to keep the national aspirations alive. Yet in spite of their fraternization with the other nations the Czechs never forgot that their interests, their national interests in Europe, were not wholly the same as those of their friends. The Czech is an extremely practical and methodical individual.

Like every other nation, the Czecho-Slovaks have special trades in which they excel and which they have more or less monopolized. For more than sixty years, since the Czechs first came to this country, cigar-making has been their special occupation. The Cigar Makers' Union was one of the first organized industries in this city. But although Czechs have been making cigars more than sixty years, very few if any have risen to the rank of great manufacturers among the workers. The Greeks and Armenians are now at the head of the industry. The Czechs have at different times opened coöperative shops, which they organized, especially during strikes against their employers, in order to compete with them. But the Czech is naturally not a business man. Cautious and quiet, without dreams of wealth, he prefers to better his condition as a working-man, bringing his sons up to be working-men like himself, rather than to live in a haphazard way in an unorganized industry and hope for his sons that they might be able to earn their living otherwise than by the sweat of their brows.

Another occupation virtually in the hands of the Czechs is pearl button making, which has always been a Czech industry even in Europe. The Prague pearl button makers are the most renowned in the industry. Piano making, especially the carpenter's work in piano making, is another industry in which the Czechs excel and in which a great number of them are occupied and have been occupied for generations. Czech trades remain in the family and are transmitted from father to son. Even to-day, among the new generations, one is quite certain to find that the young cigar maker is the grandson of a cigar maker, the young piano maker is the great-great-grandson of a piano maker, and so with the butcher, the dressmaker, the furrier, and the saloon-keeper. With all the friendship the Czechs have for Poles and Ruthenians, there are no Poles and no Ruthenians in the trades more or less exclusively Czech.

But fraternizing with the Poles ceased at once when the Grand Duke Alexis of Russia came to America in 1871. The Czechs of New York and Chicago sent delegations "to greet our brother Slav." This "act of perfidy" on the part of the Czechs so angered the Poles that they immediately seceded from them and left every organization which the Czechs had had a hand in organizing. For the Poles have always considered the Russian a greater enemy than the Austrian, not because they have suffered more under the Russians than under the Austrians, but because they always have considered themselves superior to the Russians and consequently chafed more under their yoke As a matter of fact the Pole considers himself superior to everybody. And so unpleasant did the Poles, who were in greater numbers, make it for the Czechs that the Czechs left the lower East Side and settled along the East River near Fiftieth Street, spreading northward until they have now reached Eightieth Street, always hugging the river.

Of all the surprises New York offers to the New Yorker, none is as great as the suddenness with which one passes from the center to the rim of the city. There is no gradual change from lofty buildings to hovels, from riches to poverty. There being only one generation from shirt-sleeves to shirt-sleeves, the city is also under the same influence. Twenty-four wonders may rise to-morrow on the place of a tumble-down shack, and a prosperous quarter may suddenly stub its toe and go the way all things of flesh and brick go.

Ivan Opffer and myself had just left Fifth Avenue and were descending Fiftieth Street. In a few minutes we were at the East River, where a steamer from the tropics and a hundred other craft were plying.

That portion of the river is the most God-forsaken section of our city. The population is a mixed one. It was exclusively Irish until a few years ago. Then the Italians came, and before either of the two nationalities was dislodged the Polacks attempted a stampede and only scattered a few Jewish families westward and southward of the city. It is now Czecho-Slovak.

And over that section of the city rules Big Pat, who knows where to look and what not to see. And the authority of his club is so much greater than that of the other policemen because it is seldom used. Some grown-ups skirt Big Pat when they have to pass him by, but the children of the neighborhood are not in the least afraid of him. The lighted cigarette of the barefoot urchin disappears mysteriously into his mouth by a trick the whole neighborhood possesses until the policeman is out of sight (Big Pat is a sworn enemy of the cigarette), but otherwise the youngsters look upon Big Pat as their representative and not their enemy.

While Opffer was sketching roof-tops and distant domes I looked around to find Big Pat, who is an old friend of mine.

I approached one of a group of children with pails and shovels in their hands and asked, "Where is Pat?"

There being only one Pat, the answer was, "Around there, by the candy factory."

"How 's Pat?"

"He is mad because of a Polack," was the answer.

"What is the matter?"

The youngsters looked at one another and shrugged their

shoulders with the movement which in that section means, "I know, but I won't tell."

I found Pat standing in a sort of niche in a brick wall watching, without being seen, a great stretch of the street opposite him. He motioned to me not to approach him but to keep on walking to the next corner.

I waited and waited. Something was sure to happen if Pat waved me away so anxiously. His thick mustache bristled with anger, and he had brought his cap well over his ears in preparation for quick action. I decided that the watched place was down near the river, against the wind, and that Pat was afraid to lose his cap on the run.

The group of children with pails and shovels, having circled the block, passed by me and returned to the foot of the street, where they soon became active at a heap of burned-out coals and picked whatever was not completely worthless for the stock at home.

While the children were busy picking the coals a huge, blond-mustached, overalled brute emerged from behind a wooden fence and began to steal up nearer to the coal-pile. Big Pat flattened himself completely against the wall. But when the overalled brute was half-way to the children the policeman crossed sidewalk and street in two noiseless jumps, was himself soon hidden by the bulging irregularities of the broken-down fence, and was gaining on the man who was coming upon the children.

Suddenly there was a loud cry, and the little urchins started to run. But it was too late. The man had his big hands on two of them, the bigger ones, and was holding them both with his left hand to have the right one free for punishment. He lifted his arm high, and the little shoulders of the boys curved in for protection.

But before that hand had been lowered another arm behind it had gone up and shot down, and there was a horrible yell in an unearthly tongue, a scuffle, and Pat and the man in overalls disappeared behind the fence, whence I soon heard short yelps and long whines and the thud of a fist against flesh and bone.

The whole thing lasted less than a minute. Big Pat was first to come to view again. He put his cap at the proper angle, pulled his coat, wiped his hands on a handkerchief, and walked slowly away as if nothing had happened.

A little later the other man came out; holding one hand to a bleeding nose and the other to a rumpled ear and howling like a beaten dog, he limped painfully to the open gate of the old factory, while the children pelted him with pieces of coal and stones.

"Don't talk to me now," said Pat, passing me by; "I am busy."

The following day Pat was talking in a friendly fashion to a badly mussed-up man.

"Rub in some liniment to-night, man, after washing the sore carefully," he advised.

"Thanks," the man said as he walked slowly away.

"Don't forget, Slitzky. *Wash* before you rub in the liniment," Pat called after him.

"Who is that fellow, and why have you beaten him up?" I asked.

"That 's the new watchman. I learned him yesterday a lesson. We had a talk, we did. No beating of kids in my district. I got children of me own. And, God knows, coal is high enough this year." It was Slitzky's first lesson in fair play and sportsmanship. He and Pat are great friends to-day.

Given freedom within a limited space for any national group to search for its habitat, it will always look for a spot which resembles as nearly as possible the place it came from. It is why so many rivers and mountains in Europe have names similar to rivers and mountains and hamlets in India. During the great Indo-Slavic migrations the invaders settled near such places as recalled to them their natural habitat. And, in doing so, they called the river, or the mountain, or the valley, by the same name as the river, the mountain, or the valley from whence they came. It is one of the reasons why the group-formation of nations in this city repeats the group-formation of nations in Europe. The fact that their neighbors have always been their enemies counts for little in such settlements. No other factors are taken into consideration.

No part of the city could as much resemble old Prague as Fiftieth Street and thereabouts up to Seventieth Street. There are tunnels, and streets to which one must ascend through stone stairs two stories high, crisscrossing one another, cobblestone pavements, old shanties heavy with time upon them. Trellised balconies, vaulted alleys, and vine-covered façades of old brick, with sudden elevations and vistas upon the river; old outlying New York which has remained behind in the upbuilding of the city, and still resembles Old-World cities.

Given a Czech national holiday, with the sun shining

over the people marching in their national costumes with their curiously embroidered flag at the head, with the yellow and black of the women's embroidered white dresses waving amply and freely in the wind, while the band marches before and behind them, such a procession is a never-to-be-forgotten sight on the upper East Side of New York. It is Prague on a national holiday. The national costumes are the dearest possessions of every Czech household. A Czech home in New York with the walls covered with bits of rugs, and with the celebrated Bohemian colored glassware on the mantelpiece, is as clearly distinguished from any other home as if it were on the shores of the Moldau River.

The numerous saloons in the Czecho-Slovak quarter have never given rise to any intemperance among the Czechs. The saloons were merely means for keeping up the numerous meeting-halls in their rears, the saloon-keeper being more often than not an enthusiastic follower, if not the leader, of this, that, or the other social or political organization. The Narodni Budova on Fifth Street was such a place. In 1882 a number of organizations which held their meetings there, for which the place had now become too small, bought it out and rebuilt it. The ground floor still remained the saloon, but in the rear the organizations erected a stage, on which they had almost weekly performances of plays produced and played by amateurs. On the second floor they had a library, and on the floor above that they had their meeting-halls. When the Czechs moved up town they took along with them all these organizations;

even their club-houses and churches followed them northward.

But no Czech is a real Czech unless he belongs to a *sokol,* which is a gymnastic organization similar to the old German *Turnvereine.* The care of the body is as highly developed among the Czechs as it was among the old Greeks. No church organization, no socialistic organization, no political organization, is complete without its

own *sokol.* And every *sokol* has also its singing and dramatic clubs. It should be mentioned that when in 1917 eighty-four members of the Blue Sokol marched to Fort Slocum to volunteer, not one was rejected on physical grounds, although there were many beyond military age.

I shall never forget one evening at the Seventy-first Street Sokol. I came in during the latter part of the evening while gymnastic exercises were in progress. To see the hundreds of perfectly formed bodies go through the callisthenics and more difficult exercises with the utmost mechanical precision was one of the most beautiful sights my eye had ever beheld. The bodies glistening, the muscles rippling smoothly under the perspiring skin of arms and legs, moving with the lightness of sprites to the rhythm of the music and the commands of the leader, they carried out the most intricate and difficult figures. And then came the women, who went through similar exercises while dressed in abbreviated national costumes. They did the movements even more beautifully than the men. What a surprise to me when the exercises were over and I mingled with the people! There were men and women of all ages ranging from twenty to sixty. Yet the muscles and joints of the older men and the women were fully as supple as those of the younger men. There was no desire to wrestle or to box, this not being considered by the Czechs as a physical advantage.

It is largely through these *sokols* that the independence of the country has been won. The *sokols* have been more than "gym" organizations. There soldiers were prepared, ready for all eventualities. The bodies and the spirits were kept healthy and strong. "Be ready," was the watchword of the Czechs for centuries. And they were ready when the hour struck.

The singing of these gymnasts was as beautiful and precise and as rhythmic as their physical exercises. I have seldom heard more beautiful group singing than that of the Czechs. Indeed, to hear them sing their folk-songs, one would never realize, because of the accent of joy and happiness in them, that they were the folk-songs of an oppressed people. Through all his tribulation, the Czech has not suffered from an inferiority complex, neither has he acquired the arrogance or the whining propensities of other people. The Czech waits. A good Czech knows how to wait. The independence of a country was fought for and won on the upper East Side of New York.

There is a beautiful free and unrestrained relation between men and women in the *sokols* of the Czechs, a charming gallantry which is beautiful without being patronizing. A Czech never raises woman on a high pedestal in order easier to enslave her later on. And in all the Czech organizations the women have always had as much say as the men. And this without any Lucy Stonish show or affectation. Being as strong as the men, they assumed the same duties and had the same privileges.

The Czech American Working-men's Sokol on Seventy-second Street between Avenue A and the East River fully rivals the Hungarian Working-men's Association near-by with its manifold cultural activities. It is a beautiful building, said to have cost over a quarter of a million dollars, and houses a *sokol,* a dramatic club, a language club, and a lecture-hall in which the ablest lecturers have delivered courses on many topics. The picnics and balls of the Czech American Working-men's Sokol are probably the most worth-while amusements of any of our foreign populations here.

But their great pride is the National Hall on East Seventy-third Street, which is the central body of all the Czech organizations, not only in this city but in the entire country. It is from this hall that volunteers against the Germans and Austrians were equipped and trained until by the time they reached the battle-field they were the most perfectly drilled soldiers in Europe. I remember meetings in the *sokols* during the war. Those who could not go gave everything they possessed to alleviate the sufferings of those who were left behind by those who did go. It was pointed out to me that poor working-men who had barely saved anything, fathers of three or four small children, were not only not detained by their wives but were urged by them to go, regardless of the hardships in store for the family when its only earning member had left, with very little chance that he would return.

I remember my friend Riggle, who had very pronounced anarchistic tendencies. I remember him at the beginning of the war thundering against all the Governments in the little Czech paper he published weekly; writing it and setting it up himself, although he was by trade a carpenter and worked at his trade daily. Ruddy-cheeked, deep-eyed Riggle, who had thundered against every capitalistic Government, began to soften more and more as he came to see a chance for his own country to become an independent state. I remember him suddenly explaining to me that one cannot be an internationalist unless one belongs to a nation, and that there could be no nation unless it had a government. "And after you have a government," he told me, "you fight against it."

Little by little Riggle's paper changed from an anarchistic one into one of the most rabid national sheets published during the war. And greatly to my surprise Riggle began to frequent the *sokol,* neglecting everything, even his family, so as to put his body into condition. I have seen him crying when he was at first refused a soldier's uniform. He returned to gymnastics and training and succeeded better at his second attempt. How proud he was of his body, when I visited him one evening! His wife and his two daughters stood aside and admired him as he went through all the exercises.

"Touch here," he asked them; "touch here"; offering his limbs. They had indeed become vigorous and supple.

There was not a tear in Jankzia's eyes six months later when the news came of Riggle's death on the battle-field. Indeed she called out to me, "You know Riggle 's died on the battle-field." It was such a joyful cry that I myself answered it with almost a jubilant greeting. But the two American daughters, born here. were not as enthusiastic as their mother.

"Poor dad!" they said. "Poor dad!"

But Mrs. Riggle exclaimed: "Poor! Why, he was the happiest man on earth!"

As an example of the Czechs' political activity in favor of their country could be cited the advent of their first newspaper, the "Lucerna" ("Lantern"). The Czechs all over the country called mass-meetings in 1870 to protest against Germany's attack on France. A New York meeting was held at Cooper Union on November 19. All the Czechs of the city crowded into the hall, with several overflow meetings outside it. As a result of that meeting, one of the speakers, Lev J. Palda, from Chicago, remained in New York to edit that paper, entirely written by hand, several copies of which were made by William Jandus of Cleveland and distributed and read at subsequent meetings. It was the only issue of its kind. Copies of that paper sell now for hundreds of dollars and are very rare.

"New Yorkske Listy" was edited by Jan Reindl, a music teacher of distinction, who was also a fine tenor enjoying great popularity. A short time afterward, under the management of John Capek, of the same family as the present Capek brothers of "R. U. R." fame, the "New Yorkske Listy" became a daily in 1877. It was later on absorbed by the "Delnicke Listy," the "Workmen's News," a radical paper from Chicago, with Palda as its editor.

Indeed, from their very first arrival, the Czechs have had one paper after another; the working-men, especially, have always had their own publications, which fought very effectively their cause and at the same time carried valuable articles of information and instruction. The files of these papers are almost encyclopedic in the variety of subjects treated.

One of the things the Poles and frequently the Slovaks have charged against the Czechs is that more than half of the Czechs who have come here have abandoned their inherited faith. It seems to me this is very far from counting against them. It only shows an inquiring and progressive mind. The Czech is never satisfied with any belief at all. Intensely emotional without being hysterical, he is forever inquiring and delving into his own soul. In this he is infinitely superior to his brother Slav, the Russian, who tortures his soul by moving in a narrow groove. The Czech mixes easily with other people, without ever losing his national ego. An experimentalist. A modernist. Czech art has always been the vanguard of new adventures in color, form, and sound.

Our Lady of Perpetual Help and St. John the Martyr's, the first on Sixty-first Street and the second on Eighty-second Street, both Catholic churches, are as well attended by the Irish as by the Czechs. The Jan Hus Presbyterian Church on Seventy-fourth Street is another Czech church attended by other nationalities as well. Half of the children of the Sunday-school of the Madison Avenue Presbyterian Church on Seventy-third Street are Czech. And although there are only twenty-five thousand Czechs in

New York, and five or six times as many Poles, the cultural influence exerted by them is far intenser and greater than that of their erstwhile friends.

The Webster Branch of the Public Library on Avenue A, which opened in 1906 with fifteen hundred Czech books, has now fifteen thousand in that language. It is the largest Czech library in the country. Additions to it are being made daily. For every Czech donates his books after he is through reading them. It is a pleasure to examine any of the Czech books. Apart from the fact that they are beautifully printed and beautifully bound, one is pleasantly surprised to see with what respect the readers have handled them. I have frequently looked at books that have been read by forty or fifty people during the first year of their appearance. The pages were still neat and clean. There was no evidence of disrespect toward them. No signs left by moistened thumbs. No dog's-eared pages. The books of a library are the best indication of the character of a nation.

The Webster Branch is not the only Czech library. Every *sokol,* every benevolent society, every lodge, has its own circulating library. Even the library of the "New Yorkske Listy," although used and used again by the staff and the readers who come in, is in the most beautifully preserved condition.

None of the younger generations born here are untaught in the Czech language. Continuing as they do mostly in the trades of their parents, they move in the same circles and are therefore continually in contact with the older members, who among themselves never speak any other language but Czech. One can see members of the younger generations at the *sokols* and the dancing-halls. I have heard American-born Czechs who have never seen their fatherland go up on the platform and speak as fluently as if they had never heard any other language spoken but

Czech. And yet they speak English quite as fluently. In all the investigations of child-labor in the city there was never found a single Czech factory in which Czech children below the legal age were at work. Most Czech children went through high school even before the law was made as strict as it now is. The Czechs have tremendous facility for learning languages. Indeed it is said of them that they have etymological minds. Any Czech can give you the derivation of almost any word you ask. It is this etymological mind which facilitates his learning foreign languages.

Among the Czechs who have become nationally known in this city are the painters, Fabry and Harrison Fisher, who is Czech on his father's side; Joseph Mazek; and Emanuel V. Nadheny, who has for years been on the staff of the "Herald." Rudolf Rujicka is one of the finest etchers in this country. Among sculptors they have men like J. Mario Korbel and Joseph M. Kratina, as well as Rose Krachikova.

But it is in music that they most excel. Rudolf Friml, the pianist and composer; Anica Fabry, the soprano; Anna Faka-Pangrac, the organist and composer; Alois Reiser, the violoncellist and orchestra director; and Josef Stransky, the director of the Philharmonic Orchestra, are but a few of the more celebrated ones. And the "New World Symphony," which is perhaps, more than any other musical composition of American essence, haunting and powerful, one of the symphonies that will live together with the great ones of Beethoven and Mozart and Tschaikovsky, was composed by Anton Dvorák, the Czech, during the eight years that he lived here. No one before him had seen the great musical values of the negro rhythm and negro spirituals for symphonic purposes.

Among the better-known Czech actresses are Blanche Yurka, Phyllis Phova, and Galena Kopernak.

A friend of mine was complaining to me of the lack of romance in New York.

"You see too much steel and cement in this great city of

ours," he said. "Too heavy, oppressive, unromantic. Too much hustle and bustle."

I was just going to answer something or other when a short man of about forty came out of the back door of a saloon and, walking unsteadily through the crowd, seized the friend by the lapel and asked him:

"Say, were you ever a boy? Were you ever a boy, I ask?"

"Sure enough," answered the friend, trying to free his coat from the not over-clean hands of the drunken man.

"Do you remember Monte, the bareback rider of the Sells-Floto Circus? Do you? Have you ever seen him? And if you have ever been a boy and seen him in his prime give me a dollar."

"My God," said my friend, finally freeing his coat, "the price of everything has gone up frightfully! There was a time when a man asked you for a dime. Now it 's a dollar."

"That was before prohibition. Drinks have gone up since then," the man answered gingerly.

"Here is romance," I whispered, but my friend would not hear it and disappeared in the subway station, leaving me alone with the little man.

"Were you ever a boy?" the man asked me.

"I was," I answered promptly. "Let 's have a glass of beer. Come."

We entered a saloon in the sixties near the East River.

"Atta boy—hip—hip—atta boy!"

At the third almost-beer he began to sob violently.

*"Wieder!"* called out the bartender. "Again! Ain't

you ever going to stop that? I 'll put you out if you ain't going to be reasonable. As sure as you live, I will."

"Have a heart!" begged my companion. Then he turned to me.

"Ridgi Monte! A finer bareback rider never lived; no, sir! What Ridgi could do with a horse no man ever done. And the kids and grown-ups that jest natcherly come to the circus all waited until Ridgi Monte's turn came. And the manager just kept on doubling the price every year. He was jest natcherly a good fellow. No, sir, not as much as touched a drink. A glass of beer once in a great while. A man has to keep sober. The stunts can't be done unless a man is sober. To jump through a circle of fire in the air and fall sitting on the bare back of a galloping horse. That 's no small matter. Oh, oh, oh! I have been known as the best rider in Bohemia!"

"Again?" yelled the bartender.

The porter, who when times were different had served as bouncer, approached our table ready to do the job. But some man in the place, with one foot on the brass rail, said: "Leave him alone, Tony. He ain't going to do it any more."

"Let 's have another one; what do you say?" And my companion continued his tale as he sipped from the newly brought tall glass.

"Then came the woman. A trapeze woman she was, a she-devil. And whom should she pick out of the whole circus but Ridgi Monte, the best-paid man of the whole outfit. And with a wife and a kid, too. Jewels, say, jewels! That she-devil was never satisfied with anything that cost less than five hundred. And when what there was in the bank was gone, she jest natcherly went out with other fellows.

"There was wife and kid, and the wife ain't knowing a thing of what was going on. She sees her husband, of course. Ain't bringin' her presents as he used to. No, sir! Givin' it all to the she-devil of a trapeze girl; a heathen Spanish devil without a heart and soul—but with burning black eyes and something about the swing of her shoulders as she walked and the way she had with her of smoking a cigarette and looking at a man through the smoke she blew in his face. . . .

"Oh, why did I not remain in Prague!

"What does a man do but take a drink to forget? A drink calls another. He comes home late, early in the morning—wife gets angry. He says something; she says something back. Then he can't sleep properly.

"Well, comes the following day, and when you have to make the *salto mortal* you ain't got the gumption to do it. Your stomach sinks. You ain't in condition. Then the she-devil laughs in your face and says something nasty in her own lingo. Between the wife's nagging and tears and that she-devil's deviltry, the best bareback rider of the world went to pieces.

"Then soaked, penniless, he goes up to see the woman. The circus was in Chicago then. She sits in a café with a few swells, and they jest natcherly drink and make love to her. She is wearing all the jewels he has given her.

"She won't even look at him when he talks to her. Then he gets mad, sees red, and hits some one with a bottle.

They sends him up for two years, and when he comes back he ain't got the equilibrium any more. He ain't no more capable of ridin' a horse bareback than if he ain't never done it.

"So, well, oh, oh, oh!" the man sobbed again, this time louder than before. The bartender and the bouncer lifted him from the chair and threw him into the street as one throws a bundle of rags.

I spoke to the bartender. "You must not be so severe with a man who has suffered so much. It 's no little thing to have been the greatest bareback rider of the world and to end up a beggar at forty."

"Bareback rider—who—what?" the bartender asked.

"Ridgi Monte, the man you just put out."

"He? Are you crazy? He is the barber's helper across the street. It 's a story of a bareback rider he heard a few days ago, and it has broken him up so he 's gone on a spree because of it and tells it to everybody. He 's told it a hundred times in the last few days. Every once in a while he gets that way over a story or a play he sees in the theater or in the movies. But he 's a good barber when he 's sober; I 'll say that much for him."

My companion of a while ago was standing on the street corner. His nose was bleeding, and there was an ugly gash over his eyebrow where his head had struck the hard pavement, but he had already stopped a passer-by, and I heard him repeat his question to the victim:

"Say! Were you ever a boy?"

# CHAPTER XVI

## SCATTERED NATIONS

### I

### POLAND

POLES came to New York virtually as early as the Jews. In 1659 the Dutch colonists of Manhattan hired a Polish schoolmaster for the education of the youth of the community. There are some half-million Poles in the United States, and if figures are true when given by the Poles themselves, I gather there are above a hundred thousand Poles in New York City alone. Yet they are not living, as most other nationalities live, in one particular part of the city, and developing their own center of activities. Whether this is due to their lack of clannishness or to the fact that they are more migratory than other peoples, because so many of them are unskilled laborers and are hired out from time to time to work in mines and in steel-mills out West, I don't know. But there is not a single place in New York where within walking-distance you could not find a number of Poles, little groups of two or three families, or perhaps ten, rarely more than fifty living anywhere apart from the others. You can see the signs on windows, "Russky-Polsky Restaurant" or "Polsky Restaurant," anywhere on the lower East Side from Houston

Street up. Polish book-stores, in the windows of which are those beautifully colored and illustrated and magnificently bound volumes of queer and unaccustomed formats, are almost anywhere on the avenues cutting the east and west streets from north and south. You can meet Poles everywhere. They are easily distinguished from any other Slavic race. There is a deeper blue of the eyes; and the longish face, in spite of the broad and high cheek-bones and the golden hair, is also of different cast than any other face. In the Italian quarter below Avenue A on Fifteenth Street the blond children are playing with the dark-faced sons of the South. In Jackson Park and on Tompkins Square the Polish children are playing with Hungarian and German children. Some of the older Polish inhabitants, perhaps three or four hundred in number, cluster over the area from Second Street to Seventeenth and Eighteenth Streets on what was formerly Stuyvesant's Bouwerie.

One knows whenever there is a Polish wedding in the neighborhood, for the noise and the quarrels and the dance and the stamping of feet and the sad singing disturb the night till the early hours of the morning. A certain kind of noise is called "Polish wedding" in the neighborhood.

There are Poles living among the Hungarians further up town in the lower East Side Hungarian district. There are Poles living among the Croatians and the Slovaks in the sixties and seventies. There are Poles living among the Germans and the Austrians above Eightieth Street. There are Poles in Harlem and Poles in the Bronx and Poles in Brooklyn, little groups of Poles all over the city.

And yet there is no Polish life of any magnitude among them. It is true that Haller's army, that band of heroes that played such a spectacular part in the war, was organized here. It is true that the Poles living here have shouted

louder than others, greatly helping to make the noise that drowned all other clamor for independence, and attracting the attention of other peoples toward them during the war. But it is also true that their patriotism did not go very far beyond that. No Poles have become impoverished buying Polish marks as the Germans have impoverished themselves because of their faith in their country, as the Czechs and Italians and Frenchmen have done. A good deal of the actual load of the Polish fight for independence was left to the few intellectuals, to the celebrated musician of their nationality, and to the American's habit of giving without much thinking.

The Poles of this city have not entered any of the activities that have given to the city its magnitude and size. Unskilled laborers of a comparatively low standard of living, with only a small earning-capacity and extremely large families, they have always been too busy with their own misery, scratching out a livelihood, to occupy themselves or to have leisure to think of any other thing but themselves; for among all the Poles in the city there are not a half a dozen whose names have to any degree reached national prominence.

And wherever they are they don't neighbor well in a social sense. They have inherited century-old quarrels and grievances with almost all nations. They sneer at the Jews. They detest the Russians. They are not at peace with the Germans or the Austrians. They consider the Czecho-Slovaks traitors. The only nation they have always been at peace with is the French.

And yet wherever these little groups are they add a certain piquancy, a certain color of their own, a pigment which saddens and gives pleasure at the same time. Their meetings and affairs are generally held in so tense an atmosphere that one can expect almost anything to happen. Even without understanding their language, I have frequently been moved to tears by the impassioned words of their orators. Their speakers possess to a high degree an arresting theatricality with gestures as cadenced as master poetry, a flow of language so perfect that it sounds more like the reading of some national epopee than an impassioned improvised speech.

Before the Poles won their independence the little coffee-houses down town were the senate chambers and the parliaments of the future country. Theories as to what was to be done with Austria and Russia, once they themselves were independent and powerful enough, were debated with the greatest earnestness; and there arose fist-fights over differences of attitude.

Apathetic to all political movement, more ignorant than their illustriously illiterate husbands, the women, in their own national colors of eyes and hair, distinguished from the women of other nationalities even if they did wear the haphazard clothing one picks up in the shops of lower New York, sat and listened to all that was said as if it were merely a gallant combat, with the winner always winning the ladies' hearts.

To-day the discussions are still going on, but in a much milder form. Really the Versailles Treaty played the Poles a shameful trick. They clamored for independence. They obtained it. And the world is now anxiously waiting to see what they are going to do with it. The first pogroms against the Jews may only have been a mistake of policy, but they are undoubtedly an indication. The boycott against Jewish traders, though not very harmful, is actively enforced in New York. And if all the articles in their newspapers were to be translated into English, it would easily be seen what un-American intolerance they are propagating.

But it is at Polish weddings that one can see Poles at their peasantesque best. A good many of them come arrayed in their national costumes. The polkas and mazurkas are danced with all the charm and fury with which such dances are executed at home. And while the dances are going on, the bride's mother and her relatives, standing in a corner, are weeping and crying and looking suspiciously at the parents or relatives of the groom.

There are so many castes among the Poles that social intercourse among them is only possible on a very small scale. For want of anything better, the castes in New York are established among them according to the rents they pay. I remember a case while I was doing some investigation work when I urged a Polish woman to call in a Polish neighbor, who lived two flights below in the rear of the apartment, to stay with her until her husband should return home. He had been arrested in some connection or other, and she had wept her eyes red. In her hysterical mood she clawed the doors and walls and hit herself with her clenched fists. Yet she remained dumb when I suggested that she call her Polish neighbor to stay with her while she was in such a state.

"What? She?" she finally called.

"Why, she is Polish," I answered, "and she is your friend most certainly."

"How can you think that, Pania?" she answered. "*Bozhemi.* She only pays sixteen dollars a month rent!"

## 2

### ARMENIA

In 1863 there were about ten Armenians in America, six of whom lived in New York City. In 1875 there were about seventy, all living in New York. There are some thirty thousand to-day. The Armenians themselves occasionally claim double that number, but next to the Russians they are the most advertised race in the United States. For every other Armenian one meets is the self-accredited publicity agent of his people, the self-accredited representative of some relief organization. The Turkish massacres in Armenia may have been as much exaggerated as only Armenians can exaggerate, but the fact of the matter is that had they been ten times what they were they could not have been more denounced, more advertised than they have been. For as every Oriental would tell you, and as every one who has come in contact with the Armenian knows, there is no shrewder business man than an Armenian anywhere on this earth. In the wake of the Armenian massacres in Turkey some of the largest businesses in Turkish and Syrian rugs were established in this city. Fifth Avenue, Madison Avenue, Fourth Avenue, Lexington Avenue, from Twenty-sixth Street up, and the streets adjacent to Third Avenue up to Fifty-second Street house some of the largest establishments and numerous extremely prosperous families. I doubt very much, from what I know, whether they have even relatively speaking contributed their quota to all the reliefs that have been gathered here in favor of their brethren in

Armenia. During the Tut-ankh-Amen flurry their antique shops were piled high with all the things Egyptian that had in some mysterious manner come to be theirs. There were things Egyptian which smelled of some New York antique factory.

But one has to be grateful to the Armenians for introducing into this country the Oriental rug, the quiet and peaceful rug, which, whether counterfeit or genuine, contributes more to rest the weary eye than any other single factor in this bubbling and sizzling city.

No sooner has an Armenian, a young man, stepped down from the boat and been admitted into the city than he steps into some business. By some manner or other the photo-engraving business, which had been in the hands of the Germans until the great photo-engraving strike that has almost become legendary in the industrial world, then passed to the Armenians. It is now largely in their hands. There is a continual struggle now by which the Armenians are trying to wrest from the control of the Greeks the restaurants in the business streets, a number of them having already been established in their own district, while a still greater number are spreading slowly all over the city. It is quite possible that the Armenians will win. Their special dishes are much tastier than the Greek dishes. From time to time Armenian theatrical troupes from Tiflis come to the city, and play in Madison Square Garden, where the Jewish Art Theater is housed, on off nights. I have seen several presentations of Shaksperian plays. And if mimicry is at all an indication these plays received marvelous performance.

Have you ever noticed, when humming a song or reciting a poem in a swiftly moving car, that no matter what the measure of the song or the poem, the rhythm of the wheels is the same as that of your song or your poem?

And this is why we meet people of our own kind, no matter where we are or where we go. And if the town be New York, where most people are seized with *Wanderlust,* the *Wanderlust* of the homeless toward home, one surely gravitates in the right direction.

A thousand newly arrived immigrants are let loose in the city at debarkation, and within an hour each one of them will find the path leading "home"; to Italy or Slovakia, to Greece or Armenia. And twenty years later he will still be there or on the way thereto, for a favorite song, an old friend, news from home, or a national dish.

So, once on the way thereto, I stopped in Armenia, which is along Lexington Avenue between Twenty-fifth Street and Twenty-fourth Street, east toward Third Avenue. The chief occupation of Armenians here seems to be selling rugs and food. Maybe the rugs are made in Armenia. But the food in Armenian restaurants is made here. And it is good food, and cheap, and has such fancy names that one expects to get broiled pheasants when only boiled beef is ordered. And the rugs on the walls look so fine in the semi-darkness that maybe they were not woven in Dobbs Ferry on the Hudson.

In one of these restaurants a blond (yes, blond) Armenian waitress serves all the tables.

Her voice is so sweet, when she calls out the names of the ordered dishes, that one begins almost to excuse the inexcusable Turk, even if one does not understand him. She is tall and thin. Her eyes are blue, and her voice is full and sweet.

I ordered the food. Miss Jenny Covan, of Brentano's foreign department, was sharing my table and my monologue. A little further from us a prosperous-looking Armenian was reading aloud to others an Armenian paper. We understood from his sad voice that there were new massacres in his homeland. Listening to the reading, his companions bared their heads as at a funeral procession.

Still they ate as they listened to the recitals of horrors and of death; only they ordered their food in hushed voices. Even the little light tread of the slippered feet of the blond waitress became softer as she flitted to and fro taking the orders and giving them in her turn.

"Ta-Skebab," she called to the kitchen.

"Ta-Skebab," she called again, softly. And then the telephone bell jingled. The proprietor of the place was called. He, too, had been listening to the reading of the paper.

After a short conversation he hooked back the receiver and began to push tables together regardless of noise and fitness of things. His funereal mood was gone.

The prosperous stout man looked at him furiously for a while. The others, too, turned around and looked at him as if they were ready to swallow him, starched collar, necktie, collar-button, shoes, and all. Oh, those big brown, almond-shaped Armenian eyes!

But—they vented their anger on the food, crushing the soft bones of the pork cutlets with their sharp teeth. After a little while the prosperous-looking man threw the paper away and called the proprietor to him. He upbraided him for his lack of feeling. I understood it immediately. He thumped on the paper.

"Here, here! Thousands are killed!"

Then it was the turn of the restaurateur to have his say, and he spoke English that so I, too, could understand.

"They kill Armenians! All right, they kill Armenians! What can I do? They call me up on 'phone. A wedding party is coming. All right. So I must prepare the tables. That 's all. Here they come—you see—"

A beautiful, slender, dark girl of about fifteen, locked arm in arm with a swarthy young chap of twenty and followed by a noisy dozen of women and men, was received at the door by the smiling proprietor. The men wore dark red fezzes, the women gaily colored dresses and happy silk shawls on their heads. In the belt of her skirt the bride had stuck a bunch of white roses. After a little preliminary noise and much laughter they all sat down to eat.

The waitress became animated again. The funereal mood had left her, also. Soon the bride's brother began to sing. One after another the men joined in the chorus of the song. Then the women fell in. The face of the prosperous-looking Armenian at the other end of the place lit up, and he began to beat the rhythm of the song with his fork on the plate. Then he, too, joined in the singing.

The others did likewise. All the tables were pushed together. Salaams and hand-shaking. An old Oriental song they sang. The Greeks claim it is theirs. The Bulgars say it is one of their *doinas*. The Serbs sing it at funerals, the Armenians at weddings, in New York, a stone's-throw from Madison Square.

"Ta-Skebag."

"Ta-Skebag."

"Pilaf."

By what other name more fanciful if not more appropriate than the one by which it is known could one call this big city of ours? Bagdad? Babel of Babels? City of gray steel? All the bazaars of Bagdad put together could be hidden away in a corner of one of our bazaars! All the languages with which the builders of the ancient tower were confused are heard in New York, off Canal Street, near the Bowery, a minute's walk from City Hall, in a little corner of Pearl Street where a few old gray stones of a still older Jewish graveyard attest the fact that the children of Moses had dared the sea long before, much before, it was crossed in floating, steam-propelled palaces.

Pearl Street! Why was it given such a name? There is nothing of the pearl about that street. The dark-gray warehouses on both sides and the elevated railway overhead give it more the appearance of a long, narrow box, a trap with two openings such as is used by crocodile-hunters on the Egyptian Nile.

The names of the business firms on the doors and windows of Pearl Street are painted in Greek letters, in Turkish, Arabian, Syrian, all making very decorative patterns for wall-paper.

If you can't read them, what 's in the windows is instructive enough: olive-oil, cheese in big, round, four-foot chunks, smoked meat, smoked fish, and a few bags of

*curubs,* which is nothing else but St. John's bread. Still more, I can wager that all these stores, wholesale and retail, are owned by a few Armenian gentlemen. For the Armenian can be Syrian, Turkish, Greek, Macedonian, Persian, or Arabian at will. He can speak and look the part if he so desires. In New York he can even be an American.

Wonderfully pliant. Linguistic and business ability of a high order.

Such are the Armenians. And there are millions of them. Though not all of them alive or, as yet, in New York. Some few hundred thousands were killed by the Turks. The Turks usually love the Armenian broiled—boiled—fried—any fashion. They are not particular. I know. I have seen it. And I am not the only one, by any means.

Now let me tell you the story of Yussuf Ben's tragic end in this country. It is a sad, sad story. But it is good to be sad once in a while. A friend, a physician, once told me that it is even healthy to be sick once in a while. Now the story.

At the beginning it sticks very close to the ordinary run of immigrant stories. Yussuf Ben came to New York a boy of twenty. He did not go at once to evening school to learn all about our Constitution and history. He made the rounds of our cafés and night restaurants peddling Turkish rugs manufactured near Dobbs Ferry on the Hudson; and Syrian laces, hand-made, on machines that are still turning them out in a shop on St. Mark's Place, near Second Avenue.

He looked well, Yussuf, in his outlandish clothes that had been tailored for him by a master tailor of Erzerum. Also, he had a red fez on his head and could not "speaky much Eengalish." But he knew how to ask twenty dollars for a piece of lace that cost him one dollar, and knew how to say, "Give the money," when some one offered ten dollars. The ladies, after theater hours on Broadway, declared he was "simply killing," that strange he was—Yussuf. And as long as he looked Turkish they were sure that the rugs he sold were what he pretended they were and that the lace was the finest the Orient could produce. And they marveled at the fine hand-made points they bought from him for next to nothing. There is nothing like a piece of really imported lace on a summer dress!

But a few months after Yussuf Ben's arrival his home-made shoes had to be thrown away and new ones bought. It was only natural that he should choose the most American-looking shoes, the kind with the nose turned up high like the prow of a racing-boat. And when he put them on a new step came into his feet, and in spite of the red fez and the home-made coat and trousers Yussuf was not half as Turkish as he had been on the previous day.

So the ladies began to suspect his wares. The rugs and the lace did not look half as "genuine," as imported, as yesterday. He returned home with fewer sales than before. Well! That 's how it is in business. One day is very good; the next day is a very poor one. But it averages up in a month.

Ignorant of the cause of his undoing, Yussuf intended to be more persuasive the following day. He looked into his English-Armenian dictionary and learned another dozen English words. Words of utility. "This good Toik rug. This best lace. Fine, cheap. See, leddy, nice."

"Hey, look at him! Listen to him," one of the "leddies" called to her friend. "He is not a Turk at all. He is a faker. He speaks American as well as you do. That rug on his shoulders—you can buy it for five dollars at a department-store. He may have bought it there himself."

That lady said a lot of other uncomplimentary things, sure that Yussuf understood all she said. The way she repeated "American" and "faker" was very uncomplimentary.

Yussuf only shook his head and said, "No unnerstan'; no unnerstan'," as he retreated from her table. But it was of no use. They would not buy from him that night.

Early in the morning Yussuf returned to his lodging, in a little room over a grocery store. There he consulted the English-Armenian dictionary again and added another dozen words to his vocabulary.

"What are you doing?" called out his room-mate.

"Learning America," he answered.

"You are crazy," the other replied, without giving any further explanation.

The following day Yussuf went out to visit the barber. His hair was too long. He intended to be neat. It pays when one goes around great cafés. The tonsorial artist cut Yussuf's hair American fashion, and even shaved his mustache—or as much of a mustache as Yussuf had grown at twenty. Of course he still wore the red fez. But a red fez on a clean-shaven face is worse than a silk-hat-and-overall combination.

And the rugs and the lace that Yussuf peddled simply shrieked their nativity from the shoulders of the Armenian boy. His increased vocabulary, clean-shaven face, and American shoes made his prospective buyers cry out, "Fake, fake!" Such of them as had already bought things from him decided to put the wares away in a corner and not to show them to their friends as picked-up bargains. That Turk was not a Turk at all, but a badly disguised American!

Still Yussuf did not understand. He only changed stores. He no longer bought his goods at the same place. And when things went from bad to worse, he thought he had discovered the cause.

He went down to Washington Street, to a wholesale importer, and loaded himself with the most genuine articles obtainable in the country. Then he bought a new shirt, a necktie, shaved again, learned another dozen English words, and went boldly about his business.

But it was all in vain! Even the genuine articles were declared fakes. He looked too American. His red fez looked counterfeit. People no longer spoke to him in broken English with many accompanying gestures to help him understand what they said. He did not look foreign. There was no sport in dealing with him. Moreover, he now answered in good enough American when they talked to him, and assured them that the rug he was selling was an "honest to goodness" Syrian imported, and that the lace was made in Erzerum. Still to no purpose. They did not believe him.

After Yussuf had walked from café to café, from restaurant to restaurant, for a full week without making a sale, he returned to the wholesaler. He could not sell the goods. Somebody must have thrown a spell over him.

"What shall I do now?" he asked Azri Mardouf.

The Washington Street wholesaler, who has lived twenty

years in New York but never gone further than Rector Street, looked at the boy, smiled, and said:

"Have you any money left?"

"Twenty dollars is all I have," answered Yussuf. "But I can talk American. I have learned new words every day for the three months I have been here."

Arzi Mardouf smiled again as he said,

"Go out, Yussuf Ben, buy yourself a hat such as they wear here, buy a pick and a shovel, and find work as a ditch-digger. They need ditch-diggers in this country. You know too much English to sell rugs, and you know too little to do other things."

There is a dish-washer in a restaurant on the Bowery who is called Joseph by the Austrian owner and Joe by the Irish waiter. It is Yussuf Ben. He earned more in one night before he threw away his old shoes than he earns now in a week of hard work.

Yet one cannot unlearn.

Among the most prominent people in the city of Armenian origin one cannot but bow his profoundest before Dr. Menas Gregory, the chief psychiatrist of Bellevue Hospital. Among specialists he is regarded not only as the highest authority but also as one invested with uncanny powers. Psychiatrists assert there never has been any one as able as is the nervous little man before whom everybody steps aside in that enormous building, the Bellevue Hospital.

Among the singers of the Metropolitan Opera Company, Mr. Palo Ananian and Mr. Armen Shah-Mouradian are among the most noted ones. Flora Zabelle, Mrs. Raymond Hitchcock, is of Armenian origin.

There is the Persian Armenian Educational Society, and the Ararat Club, for military and physical culture. There is the Armenian Colonial Association. And there are a number of papers in the Armenian language: "Cilicia," a religious weekly; "Gotchnag," an independent weekly; and "Yeghegetic," another religious publication. There is also the "New Armenian," in English, published every two weeks, of which Mr. Arshag Mahdesian is the editor. New York has both a Gregorian Catholic and a Protestant Armenian church.

## 3

## SCOTS

Statistics show that there are some fifty-four thousand people of Scotland in this city. According to the number of people of Scotch origin one meets here, there, and everywhere, there seem to be fully ten times that number. But they have been here so long, and having been in long association with the Anglo-Saxons and being near kin to the other Celtic races, they have been assimilated much easier with many other peoples. Except in their small organizations and societies exclusively for Scots, they do not live in special groups in the city. The new-comers are somehow engulfed here and there, living according to the professions they are in so as to be nearer their work-places, instead of seeking their own kin to live near-by.

One is very frequently surprised with Scotch parades of kilted men and kilted women. The bagpipe is heard frequently enough, but still somehow there is no Scotland in New York City, no single place of which one could say, "Here the Scots live."

Like the Jews, the Scots have always been with us. The first Highlanders to arrive in New York were the survivors of the ill-fated colony founded by William Paterson, the founder of the Bank of England. Twenty-five hundred Scots, with a capital of over a million dollars, set sail from Leith in two expeditions for the Isthmus of Darien, being nearly mobbed by crowds of men anxious to be taken along. But the colony was a failure. Most of the colonists died of fever, or were shot by the Spaniards, or starved trying to escape from the swampy jungle in which they were left.

Probably the first Scot in America to become famous was Captain Kidd, who was hanged for piracy on a technical charge, protesting to the last that he was innocent and the victim of foul play; the site of his house on Liberty Street was for years a fascinating spot for small boys in search of treasure. Philip Livingston, the first president of the St. Andrews Society of New York, was one of the several Scots to sign the Declaration of Independence. Alexander Hamilton was a Scotch Frenchman from the West Indies.

During the Civil War the Seventy-ninth New York, organized by Scots, was one of the most famous volunteer regiments. And J. J. McCook of this city was the youngest brother of the "fighting McCooks," all of whom, including Daniel McCook of Ohio, with his nine sons and his five cousins, were Northern officers.

And, in mentioning but a few, one must not omit Frederick MacMonnies, the gifted sculptor, who modeled the Nathan Hale statue in City Hall Park and the three decorative angels for St. Paul's Church, and who at the age of ten painted a creditable portrait of his father. James Gordon Bennett, who first brought out the "New York Herald" nearly ninety years ago in a Wall Street cellar, was a thorough Scot; and in our own day every one knows of Arthur Brisbane, the editorial writer, of Scottish ancestry.

There are many Irish settlements but not one distinctively so, not one that has a life different from the lives of other peoples. The independence of the Irish has been fought for and won as much in New York as elsewhere; and the Irish, even more than the early Dutch, are the most thoroughly absorbed of the nationalities of New York City.

There are some sixty thousand Swedish and some forty thousand Norwegians and seventeen thousand Danish and some fifteen thousand Finlanders and eleven thousand Hollanders, in all a hundred and thirty thousand Dutch and Scandinavians, living in this city. But my journey is at an end. They do not live anywhere in such groups that I should have been able to visit them. Or is it because there is something in me so alien to them that I could not discover them anywhere?

The Finlander is slow to anger. Near upper Fifth Avenue there is a coöperative apartment-house built by Finnish socialists. When the Socialist party was divided, some of these Finns joined the Left wing and some remained with the Right. They promptly resorted to the law-courts, seeking control of other properties they had hitherto held jointly, but the apartment-house remained, with its tenants on the best of personal terms.

This book is the result of fifteen years of observation and study, done during long peregrinations. I have tramped streets and sat in old coffee-houses and meeting-places. I have listened to foreign languages, some of which I understood, some of which I only guessed. I have followed strange funerals and danced at still stranger weddings. I have hovered about charitable institutions, mission-houses, wharves, police courts and churches and synagogues. I have during these fifteen years seen considerable changes in the aspects of the streets and watched the continual shifting of the nations from one place to another to adjust themselves to new conditions. I have seen changes of attitude toward people, transformations of dis-

tricts from residential into industrial places. It is possible that in finally putting down the things I have erred in many details. Things have changed since I first saw them and noted them down. New York is very much like a huge sieve into which everything is thrown as soon as it disembarks from ships and railroad-cars. There is a continual sifting and resifting, before the melting-pot begins its work. And then, even after this is done, nothing has been settled definitely. That, too, is thrown in another crucible and still another one. The Great War has somehow succeeded in giving cohesion to many elements, but it has fortunately not been long enough to do more than it has done. Time and trials, which are undoubtedly as much ahead of this country as they are of others, will do their work.

I have set things down as I have seen them. It is the privilege of the traveler to see things differently than they are seen by the natives themselves. Like the wind and the bee, the traveler carries the pollen from one place to the other.